JAN RUBES

JAN RUBES
A Man of Many Talents

by Ezra Schabas

THE DUNDURN GROUP
TORONTO

Copy-editor: Jennifer Gallant
Design: Alison Carr
Printer: Transcontinental

Library and Archives Canada Cataloguing in Publication

Schabas, Ezra, 1924-
 Jan Rubes: A man of many talents / Ezra Schabas.

ISBN 978-1-55002-685-6

 1. Rubes, Jan. 2. Basses (Singers)--Canada--Biography.
3. Actors--Canada--Biography. 4. Television producers and
directors--Canada--Biography. I. Title.

ML420.R895S29 2007   782.1'092   C2007-904683-5

1 2 3 4 5   11 10 09 08 07

We acknowledge the support of The Canada Council for the Arts and the Ontario Arts Council for our publishing program. We also acknowledge the financial support of the Government of Canada through the Book Publishing Industry Development Program and The Association for the Export of Canadian Books, and the Government of Ontario through the Ontario Book Publishers Tax Credit program, and the Ontario Media Development Corporation.

Printed and bound in Canada.
Printed on recycled paper.

www.dundurn.com

Dundurn Press	Gazelle Book Services Limited	Dundurn Press
3 Church Street, Suite 500	White Cross Mills	2250 Military Road
Toronto, Ontario, Canada	High Town, Lancaster, England	Tonawanda, NY
M5E 1M2	LA1 4XS	U.S.A. 14150

For Ann, as always.

TABLE OF CONTENTS

PREFACE

I first met Jan Rubes in 1952, three years after he had immigrated to Canada from Czechoslovakia. He was a presence then and still is. After studying his life and reviewing his many talents I am more than ever impressed with this remarkable man. As a singer, actor, director, concert giver, and educator for young and old, he has done much for Canada in the past fifty-nine years. He has sung in more than one thousand operatic performances, appeared in almost one hundred movies and TV films, and played and sung on radio, in the theatre, and for children countless times. No opera singer has toured this continent more than Rubes. I have explored the more important events in his life in order to clarify his image and reveal his achievements meaningfully. I have also tried to show the influence Jan had on his family, on his professional associates, and on his friends. Everyone I have talked to about Jan in the past twenty months has spoken with respect for his professionalism and generosity of spirit. And I couldn't resist delving into his admirable tennis playing. I played with him once and can attest to his superb game.

Susan Rubes, his wife of fifty-seven years, has played a key role in Jan's life. A gifted actress, an incomparable promoter of live theatre for the young, and an imaginative innovator on radio and TV, she quite independently merits a biography. Her work intersected with Jan's on many occasions. I have had numerous meetings with the Rubeses — in Collingwood, Toronto, and Sarasota. Jan's diaries have helped me enormously in keeping track of his busy life. The Rubes fonds, his files, his scrapbooks, and his videos of Rubes films have all been most useful. Jan carefully guarded everything, and I have reaped the rewards. Unfortunately, his memory is wavering, so I have been unable to include more of his present views of his work, although he talked and wrote much about it to the media in the past. Susan, however, remembers everything, and her input has been invaluable. The Rubes sons, Jonathan and Anthony, and their spouses, Judith and Brenda, have been of great help, as have relatives: Eva Rubes Weinberger (Jan's niece); her husband, Clem Weinberger (Susan's half-brother); Jan (Honza) Rubes (Jan's nephew); Henry Feith (Jan's cousin); and his wife, Barbara Feith. All of them have provided me with important and interesting information and insights.

I want to thank especially my wife, Dr. Ann Schabas. She has read every line in this volume and edited it mercilessly when required. I had moments of exasperation with some of her criticisms but, as always, I caved in. If this biography has strengths it is as much her doing as mine.

Many archivists have helped me. First I thank Brock Silversides, Director of Media Commons, University of Toronto. He made the extensive Rubes fonds available and assisted me in countless ways as I reviewed them. I thank Davorin Cikovic, archivist at CBC Radio, for assisting me in searching out Rubes radio shows. More thanks to Birthe Jorgenson, Canadian Opera Company archivist, who as in the past was of enormous assistance. I thank Lynda Barnett, head of the CBC Photo Stills Collection, and Jane Edmonds, archivist of the Stratford Festival, and her assistant, Ellen Charendoff, for tracking down photos and clearing them, as well as Linda Amichand, archivist of the University of Guelph Library. I also want to thank several film companies and photographers for permitting me to use their photos. They have all been credited appropriately. I thank Vaclav Taborsky, the Czech-Canadian writer, who generously translated Czech documents and films for me as needed, and John Reeves, who provided me with important background and views of Jan Rubes when I first embarked on this project.

General Thanks

I interviewed in person or by telephone or by letter Gayle Abrams, Raffi Armenian, Mario Bernardi, Tom Berry, Malcolm Black, George Bloomfield, Terrie Burt, Graeme Campbell, Mary Carr, James Coles, Ann Cooper, Robert Cooper, George Crum, Carrol Anne Curry, Merle Debusky, Margaret Dukes, Dianne Elder, Mary Lou Fallis, Victor Feldbrill, Harrison Ford, Judith Forst, Barbara Franklin, Martin Friedland, Errol Gay, Morfy Glaser, Gordon Greene, George Gross, Stuart Hamilton, Steven Henrickson, Peter Herrndorf, John Hirschfeld, Monica Simon Hofmann, Henry Ingram, Anne Jackson, Geoge Jonas, Paula Kelly, Giulio Kukurugya, James Lapine, Anne Linden, Gwenlynn Little, William Lord, Lotfi Mansouri, Donald Martin, Kelly McGillis, James and Charlotte Norcop, Christopher Plummer, Harold Redekopp, Fiona Reid, Rick Rosenthal, Saul Rubinek, Patricia Snell, Ben Steinberg, R.H. Thomson, Riki Turofsky, Karel and Tom Velan, Giles Walker, Eli Wallach, Peter Weir, Betty Jane Wylie, Margaret Zeidman, and George Zukerman. Nearly all of them are quoted in the text and/or appear in the endnotes. Others who assisted me were Chris Bell, Susan Habkirk, Allen MacInnes, Joan McCordic, and Maria Topalovich. Finally, I want to thank Kirk Howard, the president of Dundurn Press, for encouraging this biography, as well as Jennifer Gallant, who has been an admirable editor, and designer Alison Carr.

CHAPTER 1

1920–1945: Growing up in Czechoslovakia; Music studies; The Second World War

Independent Czechoslovakia arose at the end of the Great War out of the breakup of the Austro-Hungarian Empire, which had brought together Czech-speaking Bohemia, Moravia, and Silesia, and Slovak-speaking Slovakia. The long-standing nationalism of the region, especially in Bohemia and Moravia, had intensified over the preceding century, helped in no small measure by two composers — Bedřich Smetana and Antonin Dvorak — who spoke for the nation through their music.

Thomas Masaryk, a philosopher and statesman, was the driving force that brought about this independence. He was born in 1850 in humble circumstances, earned his doctorate at age twenty-six, and went on to teach at the University of Prague and write voluminously about logic and realism. His political treatises fearlessly attacked Austria-Hungary and Germany. He gained American support for his goal of independence when he visited the United States with his wife — an American — in 1918. Masaryk was elected the country's first president that same year and led the new country until his resignation in 1935.

Independence brought prosperity to Czechoslovakia. Schools and universities flourished, as did musical life. Its cities, large and small, had opera houses open year-round, much like Germany's to the west. The capital city, Prague, one of central Europe's architectural gems, had long been a great musical centre, and its national conservatory served the country's needs for trained musicians well. And it was a bilingual city, mainly Czech but with German spoken by many. It had two universities — one Czech and one German — and three opera houses — two Czech and one German.

On June 6, 1920, in Volyně, a small town of some six thousand inhabitants in Western Bohemia close to the German border, Ruzena Rubeš gave birth to a son, Jan Ladislav, named after his father, the local bank manager. Jan was Ruzena's second son, his brother Jaromir Frantisek having been born two years earlier. The family was Protestant, unlike most Czechs in Volyně and the rest of the country who were mainly Roman Catholic. There was, at least overtly, little antipathy between the two religious groups. There were also several Jewish families in the town, and Jan remembers being told not to walk past their houses, even though no explanation was given for this bizarre dictum. For Jan it meant a detour to get to places such as the town tennis courts. But there must have been some rapport too: when Jewish families were deported some years later, one of them gave the Rubešes their grand piano.

Jan Ladislav's father had shown talent in drawing and painting in his youth — enough for his work to be exhibited in Prague when he was only fourteen. He had the opportunity to enrol in the National Art Academy, but his parents showed no interest in having their son pursue the life of an artist and directed him to study the more secure profession of accountancy. And so Rubeš senior had little to do with art as an adult and,

Jan at age three with mother.

14

according to Jan, spent most evenings in the village pub playing cards quite expertly — a talent his second son inherited. Nevertheless, Rubeš senior found time to do drawings of his sons as teenagers. Two of these have stood the test of time and today hang prominently on the walls of the Rubešes' Canadian residence.

Ruzena was a highly intelligent woman who was relegated, as was the custom, to running the household. She was opinionated and bossy and seemed to favour Jan. Ruzena took solace in local theatre. Volyně staged six or seven amateur plays annually, and Ruzena played leading roles in many of them. Her efforts were recognized throughout the country in amateur drama circles and she earned awards for her work. Ruzena got her husband interested in drama too, and he also excelled in it. He even directed the occasional Volyně community theatre production. Little Jan, somewhat reluctantly, performed in plays when needed — on one occasion he was cast as a girl. He also was in several plays in his teens. Volyně had no opera.

Jan (right) in Volyně theatre.   *Jan at age twelve.*

Both the Rubeš boys did well at school, helped in no small way by the watchful Ruzena, who was determined to have her sons make more of their lives than had her gentle husband. Ruzena also urged Jan to play tennis rather than the more popular soccer, since she thought that a better class of boy took up tennis. Jan did as he was told, and by the time he reached his teens he was an outstanding player with several trophies to his credit. The older brother, Jaromir, or Mirek as he was known, did not have athletic skills beyond the ordinary, although he and Jan did, on occasion, play as a doubles team in tennis. Jan also learned to ski early on, since Volyně was only nineteen kilometres from accommodating hills, and he won all kinds of national skiing awards.

Both boys had piano lessons, with Jan's musical talent soon coming to the fore. While singing with a small group when he was fifteen, he listened attentively to a guitar player who was accompanying them and decided that he must learn to play the guitar too. However, his parents balked at buying one for him, considering the instrument more appropriate for itinerant Gypsies. Besides, they wanted him to practise the piano without the distraction of learning another instrument. Undeterred, Jan joined a small local jazz band as pianist and played for town social events — dances, parties — so that, within three months, he had earned enough money to buy a guitar on his own. He also sang in a local glee club with his father and in choirs, Catholic as well as Protestant. After his voice changed he had a full-fledged bass voice, which the glee club welcomed. Compensation came in the form of drinking good Pilsner beer with his father at the local pub after rehearsals.

As teenagers, Jan and Mirek had to travel eleven kilometres by train daily to gymnasium in Strakonice, since Volyně was too small to sustain one. (Gymnasiums in Europe extend schooling beyond that of North American high schools by a year or two.) The brothers were close and affectionate, and they continued to be so throughout their lives.

Volyně also provided them with unexpected pleasures with the opposite sex. As a teenager, Mirek had a liaison with a teacher some twelve years older than he was. Thankfully, the affair was kept quiet. Then family circumstances gave Jan the chance to discover the joys of sex. Ruzena's younger sister Bozena (Ruzena was the eldest of six sisters, Bozena was the fifth) had recently remarried and her new husband, Georges

Deymel, a wealthy Prague merchant, was not at first receptive to having a six-year-old stepson in his house. So, for nearly three years, young Henry stayed with the Rubeš household, with a string of nannies to look after him. One was a particularly comely twenty-nine-year-old, and she played a significant role in Jan's growing up. One night when Jan was sixteen, he heard a knock on his bedroom door. It was the nanny. And so Jan's sex education began. At about that time, too, he had a girlfriend who was three years older than he was. Georges, Bozena, and Henry would re-enter Jan's life, later, in Canada.

Happy as the times were, the Depression hit the country hard in the early 1930s. In 1935, Masaryk stepped down and Eduard Beneš, another Czech patriot and Masaryk's pupil and supporter, was then elected president. The country's problems with minority groups, especially the Sudeten Germans in the western part of the country where a good deal of Czech industry was located, were on the increase. The Sudetens said that the Czechs were abusing them, and, true or not, Germany supported their grievances. Other minorities — Hungarians in the south and Ruthenians and Romanians in the east — had real or manufactured grievances as well. Nor was there any love lost between Czechoslovakia and adjacent countries — Hungary, Yugoslavia, and Romania. And, of course, there was Germany to the west and the Soviet Union to the east, both coveting the highly industrialized and relatively prosperous Bohemian and Moravian regions. Slovakia, in eastern Czechoslovakia, was rich in farmland.

In 1937, Mirek completed gymnasium and enrolled in medical school in Prague, about 110 kilometres north of Volyně. Two years later, Jan followed suit, just as his parents wished him to do. The medical school had a well-known choir that welcomed Jan into its ranks. Prague, with its river, its castles, its opera houses, and its theatres, had an ambiance to rival any city in Europe. However, it was 1939. By March the Germans had taken over all of Czechoslovakia. A month later there was a protest in Prague directed against the occupiers. Students overturned cars to vent their feelings. A few days later, the Germans retaliated by executing twelve students — Mirek narrowly escaped being one of them. Then the Germans followed this heinous act by closing the universities. These were just two of many blows Czechoslovakia suffered in this sorry time. The Western powers, France and England, had abandoned the Czechs and left them at the mercy of the Third Reich. Soon after, the Soviet Union signed its infamous peace treaty with the Nazis, which enabled the two nations to carve up central and Eastern Europe as they wished, including Czechoslovakia.

So, the Rubeš brothers' stay in Prague was short-lived. With the medical school closed, they had no choice but to return to Volyně. Fortunately, storms and heavy snow prevented the Germans from entering their town until later in the spring, and this gave them time to make plans. Mirek had had enough medical training to be taken on as an intern at the local hospital, and he was able to remain there throughout the war without Nazi interference. As for Jan, at first he kept busy giving tennis lessons to the son of a wealthy family. Soon, a local choir director who knew Jan's voice heard of his plight and urged him to try for Prague's conservatory — the Germans had not closed it. His friends with whom he had sung in local cafés also encouraged him to apply. He agreed, and the choirmaster accompanied him to the audition.

Approximately 120 male singers auditioned that year for the few places in the conservatory's opera class, and all were serious young singers who knew lieder and operatic arias. Jan was completely unprepared. He had never sung serious music, operatic or otherwise. He knew only folk and popular songs — hardly appropriate audition material. Jan also knew nothing of musical theory and history and had attended only one opera in his life — when he was sixteen. And he had disliked it! The opera was none other than Smetana's *The Bartered Bride*. Its role of Kecal, the marriage broker, would have Jan's name stamped on it for the next three decades. It would be one of his best roles.

Jan started the audition with a folk song. This rather surprised the twenty-member jury. When they asked for something more substantial, he confessed that he knew nothing else. But a perceptive jury member asked him to sing scales, starting with low A and going two and a half octaves up to F-sharp. This worked. The jury saw Jan's possibilities despite his non-existent training and repertoire. He was one of only three male singers chosen for the seven-year senior course to begin in September 1940. The conservatory was clearly very selective in admitting students and Jan was proud indeed to be one of them. It worked closely with the sixteen Czech opera houses and, according to Jan, the jury's selections were based on the vocal needs of these theatres.

The conservatory correctly surmised that this twenty-year-old, who was over six feet tall, of fair complexion, and had an athlete's physique, had a fine bass voice — young basses are hard to find — and was a promising candidate for the operatic stage. Jan was assigned to Hilbert Vavra, a leading voice teacher at the school who had attended the audition. Vavra was strong on interpretation but weak on voice production, and when it came to opera, he stressed acting over singing, to help his pupils play roles convincingly. To a great extent, Jan attributes his acting successes later in life to Vavra's instruction. His persistent vocal problems, however, can also be attributed to Vavra, who did not give him sufficient grounding in vocal fundamentals.

Jan's voice teacher, Hilbert Vavra.

Vavra rushed the young Rubeš into appearing in student recitals and operatic excerpt programs. In December, the school staged excerpts from Rossini's *Il Barbiere di Siviglia*, and Jan played the wonderfully comic role of Don Basilio, the music teacher. Basilio conspires with Count Almaviva to help Almaviva win the hand of the fair Rosina, the ward of Dr. Bartolo. However, the good doctor also has designs on marrying Rosina, and so the work provides us with some of the funniest moments in early-nineteenth-century opera. It was a valuable learning experience for Jan, since he would play Basilio literally hundreds of times later in his career.

Next came a minor role, Dr. Grenvil in Verdi's *La Traviata*, performed in a local theatre. (The Czechs on occasion title this opera *Violetta*.) Based

Dnešní budova pražské státní konservatoře hudby v Trojanově ulici. - (ČTK.)

*Above: The Prague Conservatory.
Left: Jan's first Don Basilio
in Rossini's* The Barber of
Seville.

on the novel and drama *La Dame aux Camélias* by Dumas *fils*, it is a story about a noble courtesan, Violetta, who gives up her lover, Alfredo, at the urging of his father, Georges Germont. She then dies tragically. The theatre was a commercial house, at which students were forbidden to perform. Accordingly, Rubeš was listed in the cast as Jan Lŭbos. Vavra was, of course, responsible for this breach of regulations. Something of a maverick, Vavra later got himself into trouble when the National Theatre, of which Vavra was a member, found him singing operetta in a commercial theatre and cancelled his membership. Only singing in the national opera houses was permissible. A handsome man, Vavra shows a touch of whimsy in head and shoulders photos. Rubeš liked him very much.

Vavra did not neglect Mozart. By the end of 1941, Rubeš had already sung a number of Mozart arias at student recitals, including Sarastro's and Papageno's from *Die Zauberflöte* and Osmin's from the *Die Entführung aus dem Serail*. More performing went on in 1942 with the prize role of the father in Smetana's comic opera *Hubicka* (*The Kiss*). In an early 1943 recital, Rubeš sang three Michelangelo songs by Hugo Wolf and several excerpts from Monteverdi's *Orpheus*. The slim press accounts of this program said only that it appeared as if Jan was well on his way.

Then, after three years, the war caught up with Jan. The Germans closed the conservatory. His final operatic appearance was in Smetana's *Dalibor*, a typical "rescue" opera about a fifteenth-century Czech who is imprisoned because he is plotting a revolution. His loved one, Milada, is killed while leading a group to save him. The story bears a strong resemblance to Beethoven's *Fidelio*. Rubeš played Beneš the jailer, who sings one beautiful song.

The Nazi occupiers had little love for the Czechs. The assassination of the Gestapo leader Reinhold Heydrich in Lidice in 1942 by Czech partisans had led the Nazis to retaliate by slaughtering many of the town's inhabitants. The Nazis did not trust the Czechs to be soldiers for them on the Eastern Front, as they did the Hungarians and the Romanians. Instead, they gathered together all the able Czechs they could find and put them to work in factories and other settings connected with the Nazi war effort. In the meantime, Jews were quietly disappearing, with most of them taken to the concentration camp at Terezin, north of

Prague, and from there, on to Auschwitz, where they would, more than likely, perish. Rubeš remembered remorsefully, years later, how little he and other Czechs did to try to save them from this horrible fate. Before the war, the Jews in Czechoslovakia had numbered over two hundred thousand. After the war there were only fifteen thousand. Over 90 percent had perished or had fled the country.[1]

With no conservatory to attend, Rubeš was conscripted. He feared the worst, but his voice saved him. A stroke of good fortune brought him to the attention of a German arts administrator concerned with keeping Germany's cultural life alive despite the war. Jan was brought to Dresden to audition. His German auditioners were impressed and assigned him to the opera company in Görlitz and its smaller twin city, Zgorzelec, east of Dresden on the Oder-Neisse River. Görlitz, a pleasant city, was still untouched by the war.

In 1943 many of Görlitz's male singers were away fighting and dying in Eastern Europe and replacements were needed. The nationalities of the operatic conscripts were of little concern to town and company. Jan was treated as a fellow professional, this at a time when the Führer thought Slavs little better than Jews in his quest for a pure Aryan society. Jan was allowed to write letters home and even on occasion to visit his family. He spent the next year and a half (two seasons) at Görlitz, learning

The opera house in Görlitz.

22

ten roles in German and singing in the chorus. He was on stage almost every day, which in itself was valuable experience for a young singer. Jan also learned to speak German, which would, of course, be useful later. The opera house was a handsome building in the heart of the city. It seated about twelve hundred and had many of the accoutrements of a good theatre of the day. It gave two operas weekly and the standards were reasonably high. Reminiscing more than sixty years later about his stay in Görlitz, Rubeš showed little dismay and anger towards his lords and masters. He got reasonable subsistence pay and even had a girlfriend or two. In fact, there are Görlitz photos in his scrapbook that show a cheerful young man enjoying himself with colleagues. When singing a role he used the German-sounding name of Johannes Kellner, his mother's maiden name. Of special interest was the company's choice, without government objections, of Giordano's *Andrea Chénier*, an opera about the French Revolution. It was even reviewed in the local press with "French Revolution" in the headline. It deals with the poet Chénier and the events leading up to his execution. His love, Madeleine, pleads with the authorities to die with him, and she does. Jan had a minor role in the opera.

Then war-torn Europe caught up with him once more. There were several French stagehands and technical people whom the Germans had

The wartime Görlitz Opera Company on tour, 1944. Jan is kneeling, middle front.

recruited to work in the opera house. By 1944 they'd had enough and wanted to return to France — not easy to do. Rubeš and another Czech helped them to flee the city, only to be caught in the act themselves. The angry Nazis sent the two Czechs to prison. Jan's chief memory of his incarceration is of being plagued incessantly by hordes of mosquito-like insects. After a week they were allowed to go back to work. Soon after, with the Russians approaching, the city closed the opera house. The company was broken up into small musical groups and sent to entertain the military at the front. There were always guards accompanying the groups to make sure that the foreigners among them did not run away.

In early 1945, Jan's group was in Glogów in Poland. Then came a surprise. As he was leaving his hotel one day, he noted that the guards were nowhere to be seen. Taking his life in his hands, he made some minor adjustments in his papers and boarded a train back to Görlitz to collect his belongings. The city was still, relatively, intact. The infamous Nazi propaganda minister Josef Goebbels had recently spoken there and expressed his pleasure at seeing it untouched by the war. However, the bridges connecting the two cities would soon be blown up by the Germans as the Russians advanced westward. After the war, Zgorzelec became part of Poland and Görlitz became the easternmost city in Germany, the Oder-Neisse River serving as the national dividing line. To this day, the two cities still maintain close relations. Jan went on from Görlitz to Dresden by train and from there back to Volyně. Most of the train employees were Czech and they helped him to avoid the police. It was a harrowing trip. One can imagine the Gestapo searching out foreigners and army deserters and shooting them on the spot or sending them off to who knows where.

Wisely, Rubeš didn't linger long at the family home but moved on to stay with friends in the nearby hills, where he remained quietly for several months, not returning to Volyně until early May. He later recalled:

> I remember the way my village was liberated — it was the sixth of May — by Patton and the Third Army. The whole village had assembled to greet them. When the first tank rolled down the square I saw there was a white man standing in the turret. To my surprise a colored

man stood in the second tank. There were cheers, tears; the emotional impact of that moment was incredible — it was a moment you were really alive. A lot of people go through life without ever experiencing a moment like this.

Interestingly, the "colored" tank soldier spoke fluent Czech, thanks to having been brought up in a Czech community in Texas.

CHAPTER 2

1945–1948: Back to studies;
Start of a career; Escape to Canada

With the war over, Rubeš returned to the conservatory to continue his studies. Czechoslovakia was in a mood to celebrate, but it also had to deal with the aftermath of the war and the German occupation. The Czechs promptly deported 2 to 3 million Sudeten Germans to Germany and half a million Hungarians to Hungary. Those who wanted to stay had first to convince the Czechs of their loyalty to the republic.

Patriotism ran high. Postwar anti-German feeling in Prague soon led to the closing of the German-language opera house and its reopening as the State Opera House. For the first time all three opera houses were functioning in the Czech language. The National Theatre was a favoured site for Czech operas. The State and the National both seat about seventeen hundred. The third opera house, the Estates, is older and is considered one of the most beautiful smaller opera theatres in Europe. It was here that Mozart's *Don Giovanni* had been premiered in 1787. Noteworthy too were the ample funds for music and education. With three active opera houses in Prague alone, there were many opportunities for young singers.

One of the operas done at the State Opera House after the liberation was Bedřich Smetana's *Braniboři v Cechách* (*Brandenburgers in Bohemia*). Written in 1862–63, it was the first of Smetana's eight patriotic operas. The Germans had banned it in 1939 because it was an account of how the Czechs resisted the German invasion of Bohemia in 1278 and ultimately gained their independence. Rubeš alternated in two roles: Kmet, a depressed old Czech who sings a beautiful aria and prayer, and Volfram Obramovic, the mayor of Prague, which is a less interesting role. The opera was also performed in Pilsen.

Three years had gone by since Rubeš had attended the conservatory. Its restrictions on public performance persisted, but no matter, he was determined to carve out an operatic career. He continued his voice lessons with Vavra and attended classes in film techniques given by Nikolai Cherkasov, who had worked with the great Russian film director Sergei Eisenstein. These classes, open to students from a variety of performing arts courses, gave Jan insights that would serve him well in later years when acting in films would be his principal activity. He learned that, in movies, the actor thinks more than he acts and the eyes are more important than they are on stage.

Jan sang in more than one hundred performances over the next eighteen months and learned seventeen roles. In Bizet's great opera *Carmen*, he was Lieutenant Zuniga, the officer who jails Carmen. The brilliant Czech director Alfred Radok staged it. Jan had a more interesting role in Offenbach's *Tales of Hoffmann*, playing Antonia's father, Crespel, who, in despair, finally loses his daughter. Karel Ancerl, one of the few prominent Czech-Jewish musicians to survive the war, conducted. (Twenty years later, Ancerl would be the conductor of the Toronto Symphony Orchestra.) Other roles, mainly performed as part of Jan's school assignments, included the Bonze in Puccini's *Madama Butterfly* and Surin in Tchaikovsky's *The Queen of Spades*. He graduated from the conservatory with honours in 1947, receiving the equivalent of a North American MA.

Opportunities to sing bass roles in Prague were limited, since they were few in number and were usually assigned to more established singers. Accordingly, Jan moved on to the opera company in Bohemia's second city, Pilsen, west of Prague. Its opera house, the J.K. Tyl Theatre,

Jan as Kmet in Smetana's Brandenburgers in Bohemia, *Prague, 1945.*

Jan as Volfram Abramovic in Smetana's Brandenburgers in Bohemia.

had been built at the turn of the century. It had an impressive calendar of operas for 1947–48. In *Dalibor*, the story of Bohemia's legendary hero, Jan again played Beneš the jailor, and then was an enormous hit as Kecal in *The Bartered Bride*. These were two of Smetana's eight patriotic operas. *Certova Stena* (*The Devil's Wall*), in which Rubeš was cast as the hermit and the devil, was another. He also sang Vilem in Dvorak's *The Jacobin*, a bass role that suited his voice admirably. The opera takes place during the French Revolution and is principally about the Jacobin's return from political exile. Prominent before his exile, he now finds that a cousin has supplanted him in the ruling count's affections. However, with the help of the schoolmaster-organist Benda, he regains his former position in the town's hierarchy.

Rubeš was given other roles in Pilsen. One was Morie in a Czech version of Heinrich Berté's operetta *Das Dreimäderlhaus*, based on the life of Franz Schubert. When done in English it is known as *Lilac Time* — a work of questionable merit. More rewarding for Jan was the leading role of Jason in Anton Benda's *Medea* opposite the popular and beautiful soprano Marie Buresov as Medea. It was given outdoors on the Prague Castle grounds. Buresov had also sung with him in *Dalibor*. Rubeš remembers how she had walked on stage for the first performance without attending any rehearsals!

The J.K. Tyle Theatre in Pilsen.

Then came what would be one of his major roles, Figaro in *The Marriage of Figaro*. Mozart's masterpiece deals with the lecherous Count Almaviva, who plans to exercise his *droit de seigneur* with Figaro's bride-to-be, Susanna, and how the clever and resourceful Figaro thwarts him at every turn. It was clearly a Rubeš triumph. He worked well under the opera's Swiss-American conductor,

Right: Jan's first Figaro in Mozart's The Marriage of Figaro, *Pilsen, 1948.
Below: Gina Rifino (Cherubino), Walter Ducloux (conductor), and Jan Rubes (Figaro) in Mozart's* The Marriage of Figaro, *Pilsen, 1948.*

Walter Ducloux, who had served in the U.S. Army during the war and had just become the director of the Brno Opera Company. Ducloux's wife played Cherubino. Pilsen radio reviewed it and singled out Jan's performance glowingly. This led to his becoming something of a matinee idol; he received — and has kept — letters from women admirers seeking photos and perhaps more. Jan also sang Prince Gremin in Tchaikovsky's *Eugene Onegin*, a role he cherished.

That year, too, Jan Rubeš had sung competitively in the World Federation of Democratic Youth Festival in Prague. Music competitions are always popular, although they may do little for the art of music. The great Armenian composer Aram Khachaturian chaired the jury. Jan sang Dvorak's version of the Twenty-third Psalm and was ranked third in the male singer category. As a result, he was offered the opportunity to represent Czechoslovakia at the prestigious International Vocal Competition in Geneva, Switzerland, the following year, provided that he paid his own fare. (The first- and second-place winners couldn't go.) Mirek helped provide him with the necessary funds.

In the meantime there had been a political turn for the worse in Czechoslovakia. The democratically elected government, led by the communist Prime Minister Klement Gottwald, had been steadily losing popularity with voters since it took office in 1946 because of its reluctance to deal with Western countries, fearing that this would irritate the Soviet Union. Matters came to a boil in 1948 when the government removed non-communists from the police force, appointing known communists in their place. Eleven ministers promptly resigned in protest. Public opinion was such that the government feared it would lose power throughout the entire country. As a consequence, the communist police promptly stifled all public and press objections. On February 25, Gottwald set up a new communist cabinet and followed it with a *coup d'état*. The democracy of Czechoslovakia was no more; it was now a puppet of the Soviet Union. In March, Foreign Minister Jan Masaryk, Thomas's son and a non-communist, had quite mysteriously either jumped or been pushed out of a window to his death. The Western world shuddered. President Beneš opposed the communist government and refused to sign a new communist-inspired constitution in May. He died a few months later. The joys of 1945 were fast disappearing.

Before leaving for Geneva, Rubeš wrote Walter Ducloux, who had already left his post at Brno because of the new government's interference in his programs and direction, and asked his advice about shaping a career in Switzerland. Ducloux responded with an emphatic "No."[2] He said that the Swiss theatres were not well run and that the standard of musicianship was not as high as it was in Czechoslovakia. Instead, he urged Rubeš to consider going to the United States, where audiences were "wonderfully receptive and interested and not at all snobbish." A few months later Ducloux wrote a revealing account for the American *Opera News* on why he left Brno.[3] Its opera house, the second largest in Czechoslovakia, was, at the time, one of the most modern in the world, with two revolving stages, one above the other. Approximately 250 performances were given annually, and out of a population of three hundred thousand there were fifteen thousand subscribers coming from all strata of society. There were ten to twelve new productions each season and no stage set was more than six years old. But then came the *coup d'état* and the boom fell. Ducloux was no longer to conduct Czech operas, and *all* of his operatic choices needed to be approved by the communist government. This made his situation intolerable. For a young conductor

Jan with his father, his brother, Mirek, and Mirek's daughter, Eva, in 1948.

eager to build a career, Brno had become an artistic nightmare. The Iron Curtain had fallen on Czech opera. The next year Ducloux moved to America to become the CBS advisor for opera on television. Moving on, he directed opera schools, first at the University of Southern California and then at the University of Texas.

Ducloux's advice to Jan had been guarded, but the message was clear. And Mirek, anticipating his country's bleak future, convinced Jan not to return to Czechoslovakia after the Geneva competition. He had just graduated from medical school. Although he had read Marx and Engels and had joined the Czech Communist Party after the war, he was now deeply troubled by the turn of events and left the party, even though he knew that it could affect his career.[4] The brothers spoke so confidentially that they did not even tell their parents about the plan, fearing it might leak to the authorities, who, in all likelihood, would have cancelled his trip. Thus, in June 1948, Jan Rubeš left his homeland, intending not to return. It was the last time he saw his father, who died the next year of lung cancer at the age of sixty-one.

Switzerland, with all of its well-known smug conservatism, was nonetheless a welcome haven for Rubeš after the recent events in his own country. At the competition he placed fifth in the male voice category — not too disappointing, since there were singers from all over Europe and the Americas who were looking for prizes that would help them launch their careers. On the jury were such distinguished singers as Suzanne Danco and Pierre Bernac. It was at this same competition, nine years later, that the Canadian baritone James Milligan won the grand prize. Generously, Rubeš reminisced years later about the warm and tasteful singing of his fellow contestants. Jealousy was never in his makeup. Now his job was to find a way to stay on in Switzerland, since his visa stated that he must return to Czechoslovakia immediately after the competition.

Fortunately his well-to-do aunt and uncle, Bozena and Georges Deymel — the same couple who had sent young Henry to Volyně more than ten years before — now lived in Canada. They had emigrated in the early days of the Second World War, via Yugoslavia, and had crossed the Atlantic on the Cunard liner *Mauretania* without escort. Now they would help Jan enter Canada. Georges owned a women's luxury clothing store on Bloor Street, the Fifth Avenue of Toronto, and wisely surmised that an opera singer — "opera" was a foreign word to most Canadians — was hardly the kind of immigrant the conservative and unpredictable Canadian immigration department would admit. He advised Jan to apply as a tailor! In the meantime, Jan's visa had expired and the Swiss police, notorious for not tolerating unauthorized visitors, were pursuing him without let-up as he waited for his Canadian immigration papers.

He found a temporary haven at the International Refugee Centre in Berne, where he claimed to be a political refugee. There he was provided with documents that helped to placate the Swiss authorities for several months. A prosperous Swiss antiques dealer, Jean Gasser, whose secret wish was to be a singer, helped Rubeš with money, as did his Canadian uncle. Even so, he couldn't cover his expenses and had to turn to the Salvation Army to survive. Another Canadian, prominent musician John Adaskin, helped Jan's case by writing to the Canadian authorities on Jan's behalf.

The Canadian visa eventually arrived and, on December 21, 1948, Rubeš was on a train headed for Paris. He arrived in that great city at dawn the next morning and immediately took a bus to Dieppe and a ferry across the English Channel. He found his way to Southampton and there boarded the Cunard liner *Aquitania*. It had been commissioned as a luxury ship in 1914 but was converted into a troop ship in 1939 and had now become a displaced persons carrier, with six bunks to a cabin and other rudimentary accommodation for three thousand. Rubes — by now he had dropped the háček on the "s" — jokingly referred to his status not as a displaced person but rather as a "delayed pioneer."

Later in life, Jan wrote about the voyage:

> It was a trip of many firsts for me — my first glimpse of an ocean, my first trip on a ship, my first Christmas away from my country and family. I spent most of the time on deck admiring the fifty-foot waves buffeting the ship for all six days. [December is not the ideal time for a smooth Atlantic crossing.] … It was glorious, because most of the passengers were so seasick that there was only a handful of us in the huge dining room that

was set for over 2,000 people. By the end of Christmas dinner my plate was stacked with six cleaned drumsticks. It took three years before I touched turkey again. Finally at 5:30 a.m. on December 28, the dark, bleak, cold, snowy, windswept shores of my future homeland came into view. I was shockingly cold since I was still in my Czech summer clothes.[5]

It took a day to iron out Jan's immigration papers in Halifax where the boat had docked. He had thought that everyone in Canada spoke French, only to find that English prevailed. He barely knew a word of it, and stumbled along in this strange tongue as best he could. He then boarded a train for Toronto. At first he thought the journey would be just a few hours long, only to find that it would be almost two days. Luckily, his kind uncle had not only sent him a rail ticket but arranged a roomette reservation as well. "After the crowded ship here I was sitting in a little room all my own with all the worldly comforts one could wish for, including my own toilet." Impressed, he tried to settle down in his "Little Kingdom." But coming to grips with the roomette was far more challenging than he had expected:

> I pushed my suitcase to the side, for there was a mirror there and a handle below it. I pulled it and a wash basin came out of the wall. I noticed another handle on the wall. I tried that one too, and a bed came crashing down. Luckily the basin stopped the bed from crushing me to death. With great effort from a crouched position I pushed the bed up, collapsed the basin into the wall, and then jumped into the corridor and let the bed fall with a loud bang.

His troubles were still far from over. When he pulled the basin out of the wall once more, his toilet articles disappeared. In view of all these setbacks he decided to pass up wearing his nightshirt, which was in a suitcase under the bed, and decided to sleep naked. He looked out the window as the train had stopped. It was Truro, Nova Scotia, and people on the station platform were waiting to board the train. "They were laughing and pointing at this tall Czech refugee making his entry into Canada NAKED."

CHAPTER 3

1949: A new Canadian; Relaunching a career;
Forbidden Journey; Meeting Susan

Jan Rubes arrived at Toronto's impressive and cavernous Union Station at 7:30 a.m. on New Year's Day, 1949. The rail trip had taken almost two days — unheard of for someone from a small country who had never travelled such distances in the past. It was Jan's first and most lasting impression of how huge Canada is. He also realized that he had, at best, covered no more than a third of it. Georges and Bozena Deymel were on hand to meet him, and he stayed at their home in Moore Park, a pleasant upper-middle-class Toronto residential neighbourhood, for the next seven months. Half seriously, Rubes asked them on arrival, "Where is the opera house?" It was a loaded question, for, as he suspected, there wasn't one — not a promising prospect for an opera singer.

Toronto's quiet orderliness reminded him more of Geneva than of Prague or Pilsen. It was a city of banks and churches, a few high-rise buildings, a rather dreary business section, and street after street of private homes — some semi-detached and squeezed together, some small bungalows, and some magnificent mansions in affluent neighbourhoods such as Rosedale and Forest Hill. Jan thought Toronto had a small-town feeling even though its population was about six hundred thousand. And there were all kinds of "blue laws" to discourage excessive drinking at the few bars and cafés that sold alcoholic beverages. Yet one could find more drunks wandering in Toronto than in other large cities with more liberal drinking laws. Buying liquor or beer for home use was irritating. You had to go to a government store and complete a printed form stating your name and the name of the liquor, beer, or wine you wanted to purchase. Then you waited nervously for a grouchy attendant to find it and — grudgingly — hand it over. It made you feel like a criminal on the loose.

All the shops and nearly all the restaurants were closed on Sundays. Chain restaurants specializing in tasteless food were found everywhere (no wine, beer, or liquor, of course). Two department stores ruled retail sales, Eaton's and Simpson's. Streetcars noisily clanged their way up and down main thoroughfares as more cars than Rubes had ever seen before dodged around them. There was only one really large concert hall, the fifty-five-year-old Massey Hall — with a seating capacity of about three thousand — where both the Toronto Symphony Orchestra and the Toronto Mendelssohn Choir gave concerts, nearly all of them conducted by Canadian musician Sir Ernest MacMillan. Outstanding instrumentalists and singers from the U.S.A. and abroad, and occasionally from Canada, also gave recitals there. Massey Hall's severe interior — thrifty Toronto didn't feel that money should be spent on decorating a concert hall — had, fortunately, no deleterious effect on its excellent acoustics. After singing there in years to come Jan felt that, large as it was, its seating configuration helped him to "feel" the audience.

Ever resourceful, Rubes wasted no time in going to the Canadian Broadcasting Corporation (CBC) to meet people and find work. The CBC, the national radio network funded by the federal government, operated in both French and English. It was dedicated to building an effective and singularly Canadian public broadcasting network to help unify a country that covered seven thousand kilometres and six time zones. The Second World War had given the CBC a boost, and it continued to develop its thrust and programming in the postwar years. Thoughtful Canadians, inundated with commercial radio stations — Canadian and American — welcomed the CBC and its Canadian voice.

It has been said that the postwar years were rightfully the golden age of CBC Radio. This was especially true of its musical and dramatic productions. Rubes quickly convinced CBC music director Geoffrey Waddington that he was ready to do recitals on the air. Waddington, a tall handsome man from Western Canada, was committed to promoting Canadian performers. Initially a violinist, he had turned to conducting, at which he was competent but not inspiring. His artistic judgment, on the other hand, was very sound — an important attribute for a music administrator. There were several English-language CBC music producers: Norbert Bowman, Terence Gibbs, Keith MacMillan, and John Reeves. Gibbs was the most prominent during Rubes's first years in Canada. He was a cultivated musician full of enthusiasm, and his demands for quality set high standards for the CBC. Born in London in 1921, he had studied at the Guildhall School of Music and then worked for Decca Records before coming to Canada in 1948.

The other important contact that Rubes made was with the Opera School of the Royal Conservatory of Music. The conservatory had started the school in 1946, the first one of its kind in Canada.[6] By 1949, it had grown into the closest thing to an opera company Canada had. Most of its singers were mature students who had already trained vocally. One was Barbara King, who later married Henry Feith, Georges Deymel's stepson and Jan Rubes's first cousin. It was he who had been sent to stay with the Rubeses when Jan was a teenager. The school produced operas for performances at Eaton Auditorium, the Royal Alexandra Theatre, and Hart House Theatre. Eaton Auditorium, a handsome twelve-hundred-seat auditorium on the seventh floor of Eaton's College Street store, had been opened in 1931 and had been the venue for recitals by such artists as Kreisler, Flagstad, Rachmaninoff, and Björling. Unfortunately it had no orchestra pit and was, therefore, a poor substitute for an opera house. The Royal Alexandra, completed in 1907, was a fine Edwardian theatre that seated about fifteen hundred and had an orchestra pit of sorts that could, in a pinch — and by removing three rows of seats in the front of house — accommodate an orchestra of thirty musicians, with the double basses playing in a four-seat box nearby. Its acoustics were more suited to drama and musicals than to opera. Hart House Theatre was a dreary subterranean hall, dating back to 1920. It had seating for 460, with no pit, a small stage, and limited backstage facilities.

The conservatory, housed in a fifty-year-old building at the corner of College Street and University Avenue, had neither a hall to present opera nor an adequate rehearsal space. The school's basement cafeteria was the meeting place where teachers and students exchanged news of auditions and jobs. Despite the lack of facilities, two German-speaking Czechs were planting the seeds for better things to come. Arnold Walter, a pianist, composer, and critic, was the opera school's director. Knowledgeable and informed, Walter impressed Rubes a great deal. Nicholas Goldschmidt, a pianist, baritone, and conductor, was its music director. Both men were visionaries who believed that Toronto had an operatic future that needed careful nurturing. Walter was short with blond hair. He was a heavy smoker and was invariably confident that his decisions were the right ones. The tall angular Goldschmidt was less certain of his moves, but he got things done. A third new Canadian had also recently joined the school. He was Herman Geiger-Torel, an experienced stage director who had his eyes set on creating a professional opera company. Torel was of German-Jewish ancestry, of medium height, overweight, and smoked cigars incessantly. He had an almost encyclopedic grasp of the standard operatic repertoire and had definite ideas about how operas should be staged. Jan has said that he owed Torel a lot for shaping his operatic career. Torel's biggest shortcoming, according to Jan, was that he was too inflexible, too set in his ways. Torel spoke five or six languages, but his English was, at first, sketchy, and he often made hilarious linguistic gaffes. A *Toronto Telegram* columnist cited Torel using such phrases as "She has too much exclusivity," in describing a pretentious opera singer, and "Canadian singers have too many ambeetions" — he meant inhibitions — when on stage.[7]

The year before Jan arrived in Canada, the conservatory and the CBC had worked out an arrangement to produce operas jointly. Harry Boyle, an imaginative CBC executive, worked with Walter, Goldschmidt, and Torel. Together, they chose operas for broadcast. Then the school selected and trained the cast and provided the musical leadership, and the CBC did the producing. It was a daunting task on both sides. Goldschmidt was clearly delighted to have Jan Rubes on hand. Where else could he find a bass with talent and, especially, operatic experience, almost an unknown in Canada? Accordingly, he convinced Rubes to join the school, although Rubes certainly didn't need more training. Goldschmidt explained that, because of the school's arrangements with the CBC, it would be easier to cast him in CBC productions if he were a bona fide student.

And so the experienced opera singer Jan Rubes was a student once more. But there was still another caveat — the school had a tuition fee of $75. Goldschmidt, who could cope with problems at all levels, put the fee on hold until Rubes could earn some money. And so, on February 9, 1949, just over one month after his arrival in Canada, Rubes sang on the CBC for the first time. His role was Dr. Grenvil in *La Traviata*. The fee was $75. As pre-arranged, he used it to pay his school fee. Next, on April 20, he sang the Commendatore in Mozart's *Don Giovanni*. The Commendatore is killed by the Don in a duel, and eventually his ghost sets the stage for the Don's descent into hell. This time Rubes kept the fee.

Rubes's first few months of singing in Canada were not confined to CBC opera. In February, CBC producer Norbert Bowman presented him on two fifteen-minute programs of songs. The first featured Czech songs, the second, songs by Richard Strauss and Henri Duparc. Leo Barkin, a sensitive accompanist, played with him. Barkin had a rich sound that he could moderate as required, a sympathetic and unruffled temperament, and the talent to instill confidence in any soloist he accompanied. The second broadcast was part of *CBC Wednesday Night*, a weekly program created by Harry Boyle that featured music, theatre, and speakers, all done live. Unashamedly highbrow, it was a benchmark for CBC programs for many years, and at its best was in a class with the BBC's *Third Program*. Chester Duncan, a Winnipeg critic, said on the CBC after another Rubes recital, "He has quite the loveliest bass voice I have heard for ages and sang with great style and sensitiveness," and "The program hung together musically."[8]

Rubes shared a light program with three instrumentalists on a *Toronto Star* Free Concert on April 26. This concert, given at the Carlton Street United Church where Rubes was by now a soloist, was one of a series that the newspaper presented every month or so. One of the accompanists on that concert was Oskar Morawetz, a young Czech composer who had come to Canada in 1939. His compositions were mainstream and showed great craft. He was also a fine pianist and had a vast knowledge of nineteenth-century music. Rubes and Morawetz would work together several times over the coming years.

Rubes's reputation was growing rapidly, and not only because of his singing. His recent entry to Canada and the circumstances surrounding it were also generating newsworthy stories. The school was certainly keeping him busy. He sang in an excerpt program in March, and in Puccini's masterful one-act comedy *Gianni Schicchi* in April at Hart House Theatre. The plot deals with the relatives of the recently deceased and

Jan (top rear) as Betto in Puccini's Gianni Schicchi, *1949.*

wealthy Buoso Donato. Betto (Jan) is one of them. They ask the clever Gianni Schicchi to change Donato's will — Donato had donated his fortune to the church — so that they can share the inheritance. Schicchi tricks them, keeping most of the inheritance for himself, and when they find out they scream at him, "you scoundrel, you villain, you penniless impostor." George Crum, a coach, conductor, and chorus master at the opera school, has provided an example of Rubes's ribald humour.[9] The ever-playful Rubes suggested that the company sing "you scoundrel, you villain, you *penisless* impostor." Did they do it? Perhaps only in rehearsal.

Crum remembers well that everyone admired Rubes "not only for his deep velvety voice and his musicality, but also for his quiet body control and constant recognition of his position on stage, relative to the set and to other players. He knew how to use the stage, framing himself vis-à-vis the set, starting to walk with the upstage leg, and finding the lights and the mike, if any. He always looked comfortable on stage."[10] Crum, who would soon become musical director of the National Ballet of Canada, conducted Rubes in operas and was occasionally his pianist at recitals.

Rubes sang in two performances of Puccini's *La Bohème* at Eaton Auditorium in May, playing the philosopher Colline, one of a quartet

Jan on the tennis court at Balfour Manor.

of impecunious young artists and intellectuals. It was a role he would do many times. The popular opera is about Mimi and Rodolfo, Musetta and Marcello, and the Bohemian life of Paris. Mimi dies at the end of the opera in a heartbreaking scene. Rubes was behind two amusing incidents that occurred onstage when *Bohème* was done a year later at the Royal Alexandra. Always looking for a laugh, Rubes had made repeated attempts in rehearsal to throw his hat over his shoulder across the stage to land on a hat rack, only to miss every time. Impossible, said his colleagues, but he fooled them in the second performance when he actually managed to land the hat on the rack, thus stunning both cast and audience. The other laugh was during the scene when Colline arrives for supper with a fish for his hungry friends. Naturally, a prop was used, but in one case the mischievous Rubes actually got a large and smelly flounder from a fishmonger and threw it at Rodolfo — the tenor James Shields — to Rodolfo's amazement and resulting discomfort. Shields, a genial fellow as well as an excellent Rodolfo, forgave him.

Without work in July, Rubes took a job as tennis instructor and counsellor at Balfour Manor Camp in Muskoka, a mainly middle-class holiday region some 225 kilometres north of Toronto. The camp had several talented and cosmopolitan artists on staff, including the pianist Gordon MacPherson, with whom Rubes would perform two years later. Camper Martin Friedland, who would later be dean of the Faculty of Law at the University of Toronto, the author of several books, and a major figure in Canadian jurisprudence, credits Rubes with being a "defining influence" in his life. What Friedland remembers most were Rubes's values, his integrity, his passionate striving for excellence in whatever he did, and his interest in life generally. He deliberately got involved with campers in his charge — well beyond the call of duty. Together, they built a practice wall adjacent to the tennis courts. Rubes's music — he sang and played guitar around the campfires in the cool Muskoka evenings — inspired Friedland to study piano with MacPherson the following year. In fact, Friedland's life-long interest in music goes back to that summer of 1949.[11]

Then, towards the end of the summer, came a surprise phone call. Rubes was invited to Montreal for a screen test — a change of pace that would lead to the most important meeting in his life. Selkirk Productions, one of the first independent Canadian film companies, was planning to shoot a movie, *Forbidden Journey*. In it, Jan Bartik, who is from some unnamed European country, stows away on a boat headed for Canada. Once he gets to Montreal, he sets out to organize an underground to help others fleeing from his country. However, members of an enemy group (we suspect they may be communist, although it is never revealed) will have none of it and do their best to impede him and his supporters. Screenwriters Dick Jarvis and Cecil Malden used the city's streets and buildings as the settings.

Walter Schmolka, a Czech in the International Service of the CBC in Montreal, had recommended Rubes for the Bartik role. It was tailor-made for him. He was handsome, had an impressive physique, and had studied filmmaking in Czechoslovakia, and there were parallels in the film to his own coming to Canada. He did well on the screen test, and although his English was a problem at first, it improved steadily as shooting progressed. When the writers found out that they also had a singer, they convinced Jan to write two Czech folk songs into the script. Oskar Morawetz was contracted to do the film's background music. One of the visitors to the set was the outstanding Czech conductor Rafael Kubelik.

The movie was shot on a skimpy $150,000 budget, and, except for the female lead, it had an all-Canadian cast. New York actress Susan Douglas plays the young Montrealer Mary Sheritt, who had lost her boyfriend in the war. She befriends the heroic fugitive, Bartik, and falls in love with him. She was petite and beautiful, and her background, much like Rubes's, suited the film. Douglas was born Zuzka Zenta Bursteino-va in Vienna in 1925 of Czech parents, Alfred and Charlotte Burstein. While she was quite young, her family moved to a small town in central Bohemia near a ranch that her paternal grandfather owned, where she tended goats and learned to ride horses sidesaddle. On weekends the family would attend theatre and opera in Brno. On occasion they would go to Vienna, where Zuzka's maternal grandfather managed the Burg Theatre. There she attended rehearsals and performances and became immersed in theatre even before she reached her teens.

In 1939, her parents moved to Paris (they were Jewish), and from there Zuzka and Charlotte went on to New York. The U.S. government allowed foreigners to immigrate on the basis of annual quotas. Charlotte had fortuitously been born in Italy and the 1939 Italian quota had not as yet been filled. Alfred Burstein, who had been a reserve colonel in the Czech army, went to London to work with the Beneš government in exile. The separation was not painful; Zuzka's parents were incompatible. Charlotte arranged a divorce *in absentia* in Las Vegas and married Edward Weinberger, an agriculturist. Burstein returned to Czechoslovakia after the war, remarried, and, years later, moved to Toronto to be near his son, Mirek, Susan's half-brother, who had settled there.

In New York, Zuzka was determined to learn English; it would be her fourth language, after German, Czech, and French. Luckily it was July, and she had until September before registering at George Washington High School in uptown Manhattan, where many other European refugees attended.[12] She learned English very quickly by going to the movies for seven-hour stretches, often seeing the same movie three times in one day. Movies ran continuously in the 1940s, from ten o'clock in the morning. She said that she could sound like John Wayne one day and Vivien Leigh another. Known as Suzi Burstein at school, she graduated in 1943.

After studying a city phone book to find a suitable "American" name, she chose Susan Douglas. (Susan is the English version of Zuzka.) Since she had studied dance seriously as a young girl in Prague, she managed to get an

Susan as Consuela in He Who Gets Slapped, *1945.*

48

audition with the great choreographer George Balanchine, but his verdict was that her legs were too short for a career as a dancer. She next decided to try acting. After waiting four months to get her first radio audition, two came on the same day. She auditioned first for NBC, where she was told she had no talent, and then for ABC, where she was hired on the spot for the role of Beth in *Little Women*, with Katharine Hepburn as Jo. Subsequently, she played on radio opposite such actors as Rex Harrison in *Berkeley Square* and Charles Laughton in *Payment Deferred*. Susan also had a major triumph on Broadway in the Theatre Guild production of *He Who Gets Slapped*. It was based on a Leonid Andreyev comedy, and its cast included leading actors Dennis King, Stella Adler, and John Abbott. Tyrone Guthrie directed. Susan played Consuela, the circus dancer and bareback rider. She got outstanding press from the *Morning Telegraph* — "Half the audience was in love with her…. One of the most refreshingly beautiful performances that I have ever seen"[13] — and from *The New York Times* — "Graceful and light and gives the picture of wide-eyed innocence."[14] As a result Susan earned the Billboard Award for the best debut performance by an actress on Broadway for the 1945–46 season. She next played a sixteen-year-old in a Hollywood film, *The Private Affairs of Bel Ami*, with George Sanders. Susan remembers that all comely young ladies had to protect themselves from his inevitable advances, but his amorous attentions were focused at that time on Frances Dee and Marie Wilson. Sanders considered Susan too young for such goings on.

In 1947 she was cast as a teenage girl in Louis de Rochemont's landmark film *Lost Boundaries*. It dealt with a black family in Keene, New Hampshire, that "passes" for white. The father (Mel Ferrer) is the town doctor. When he voluntarily enlists during the Second World War, the navy discovers that he is black and rejects him, despite its need for physicians. The news gets back to Keene and he and his family are ostracized. This is especially painful for the teenage daugher when her boyfriend abandons her. The film is a sorry commentary on American life of the time.

In the spring of 1949, Susan's search for roles even took her to London, England, but, because she was a non-citizen, the British actors' union refused to let her audition for *Ring Around the Moon*, a new play with Paul Scofield in the leading male role. A young British actress, Clare

Bloom, got the part, and this helped launch her career. Frustrated, Susan went on a holiday to Paris. Three months later she wrote her New York agent, Milt Goldman, that she was out of money and needed work. He wrote that he could get her the Montreal assignment, which she gladly accepted. Director Dick Jarvis had seen her in *Lost Boundaries* and recognized her suitability for *Forbidden Journey*.

Jan and Susan met in a taxi on their way to the first shooting. Jan recalled that "Susan was as pleasant and bubbly as anybody is at 5:30

Jan and Susan shooting one of their twenty-seven kisses for Forbidden Journey, *1949.*

in the morning."[15] Selkirk Productions had no idea that she was Czech until they heard her conversing in Czech with Jan, after which she was ordered to speak only English with him, since he had to improve his English. There were several romantic scenes in the film, and Susan and Jan claim to have shot one kissing scene twenty-seven times because they were enjoying it so much. But Susan added that for each take she had to place one arm very uncomfortably to cover Jan's bald spot. It hadn't occurred to the inexperienced makeup director to blacken the spot prior to the shooting. The kissing scenes stretched the decency code movies endured at the time. Jan also remembers the night scene in a calèche going up Montreal's Mount Royal. "I sang her an old Czech love song. We spent the whole night riding in that calèche. It was lovely."[16] Susan has less romantic memories. The seat was hard and her behind ached by the end of the evening. Whatever, it was true love.

The film ends with an exciting chase over scaffolding in the tower of the spectacular St. Joseph's Oratory, one of the highest points in Montreal. There, members of the enemy group have a major battle to the death with Bartik and his Canadian uncle. Bartik wins. The setting was a filmmaker's dream. Bartik is eventually deported, but he has left supporters behind who will continue his work. Mary must say goodbye to Bartik but will be his contact for immigrants in the future. Perhaps he will return. With the film over, Susan told her closest high school friend, Morfy Pugh, that this was the man she would marry. And so the wedding was planned for a year hence. What Susan wanted she got! She confessed, later in life, that she had initially wanted to marry an American, since Europeans made such poor husbands. Mark Levy, a generous Torontonian, gave Jan and Susan an engagement party.

Back in Toronto, Jan continued with performances for the school, for the CBC, and for other events. Leaving no stone unturned in building his career, he met Walter Homburger, a recent émigré in his mid-twenties who was establishing himself as a concert and artist manager. At the start of the Second World War, Homburger and several hundred other young Germans, mainly Jews, had been interned, first in Britain and then in Canada. Gradually they were released into the care of Canadian guarantors, and many would become leading figures in Canada and the U.S.A. over the next half-century. The aforementioned Mark

Levy had guaranteed Homburger. According to the Rubeses, Levy had also given Homburger $10,000 to start a concert managing career. His first guest artist was the distinguished soprano Lotte Lehmann, who sang a Toronto recital in 1947. By 1949, Homburger was running an "International Artist Series," which that year included Vladimir Horowitz, Arthur Rubinstein, Marian Anderson, Kathleen Ferrier, Victor Borge, Lauritz Melchior, and Jan Rubes. Jan was in illustrious company indeed! Homburger was Glenn Gould's personal manager, and he took on the same role with Rubes.

The astute Homburger is small of stature and still speaks with a slight German accent. Not musically trained, he nevertheless has first-rate musical judgment. Rubes and Homburger became fast friends and often played poker together. Jan recalls how "Homburger scraped together a weekly allowance for me until I could earn proper fees." The following year, Homburger expanded his operations to become manager of the National Ballet of Canada and, a decade later, of the Toronto Symphony.

CHAPTER 4

1950–1954: Central American tour;
Marriage; Building a reputation

W alter Homburger lost no time in giving Rubes a place on his recital series at Eaton Auditorium. On January 30, 1950, Jan sang a serious, no-compromise program, with lieder by Schubert and Strauss, other works by Rachmaninoff, Mozart, and Verdi, and Oskar Morawetz's setting of a Tennyson poem. He also did an excerpt from Hayden's *Creation*, eight Czech songs, and Mussorgsky's "Song of the Flea." The applause elicited three encores and he had wonderful press.

A month later, the first Toronto Opera Festival was held at the Royal Alexandra Theatre. The three Middle Europeans — Walter, Goldschmidt, and Torel — chose three operas that were good box office: Verdi's *Rigoletto*, *Don Giovanni*, and *La Bohème*. Walter had promised the skeptical University of Toronto officials, to whom he reported, that there would be no deficit. The conservatory board was equally skeptical, except for its chairman, the retired general manager of the Metropolitan Opera, Edward Johnson. He firmly believed in the plans and hoped that the venture would be a significant step toward developing opera in Canada. Each opera was given three times. Rubes was Sparafucile in *Rigoletto*,

Jan (Sparafucile) in Verdi's Rigoletto, *1950.*

the Commendatore in *Don*, and Colline in *Bohème*. He was applauded
by public and press, as were all three productions. His characterization
of the assassin Sparafucile elicited glowing comments: "His voice was
rich and flexible, his enunciation admirably clear" (Rose MacDonald,
Toronto Telegram); "The most stageworthy performance of the evening"
(Herbert Whittaker, *The Globe and Mail*); "Jan Rubes sang Sparafucile,
that conspirator to end all conspirators, with a noble bass voice. This
is an experienced actor, and his presence in the company must be of
very considerable value" (Thomas Archer, *Montreal Gazette*). About the
Commendatore, MacDonald said enthusiastically, "So admirable is the
performance of Jan Rubes that one wishes the requirements of the opera
did not remove him from the stage for the greater part of the evening."
Archer didn't like the staging of the finale — the ghost of the Commendatore was pictured on the backdrop as Rubes sang the lines from
the wings. As for Colline, Archer praised his "magnificent voice and his
control and phrasing. He has a dominating stage presence." One could

not ask for more. Another highlight that spring was appearing on a *CBC Wednesday Night* doing Rocco, the kindly jailor, in *Fidelio*.

Rubes had an adventure in the summer of 1950, thanks to Herman Geiger-Torel, who had connections in South and Central America from his years directing opera in Buenos Aires, Montevideo, and Rio de Janeiro, before coming to Canada. Torel had been engaged to stage operas in Guatemala, San Salvador, and Costa Rica under the auspices of the Duno-Sandoval Opera Company, a commercial group that evidently found opera profitable in Central America. Daniel Duno, a baritone, not only ran the company but also sang leading roles with it. Miguel Sandoval was principal conductor, a post he shared with the Hungarian-American

Jan's first Colline in Puccini's La Bohème, *Costa Rica, 1950.*

Michael Kuttner. Torel recommended that the company engage Jan Rubes and Andrew MacMillan as leads and George Crum as coach — and so it did. MacMillan, who had sung in conservatory productions, was a handsome and genial war veteran. He had a limited bass-baritone voice but was a fine actor and later turned to directing.

The three men — and Torel — got along famously in this Latin setting. Unforgettably, in Guatemala they were sometimes confined to their hotel rooms to escape street gunfire. The democratic left-wing Guatemalan government was under constant attack from the opposing military. Whatever, the Canadians were unruffled by the warfare and played poker to pass the time. The trip also provided some good sightseeing. They flew over rugged mountains in small propeller planes and negotiated narrow mountain passes in aging buses with drops of several hundred metres to worry about if the bus drivers got careless. The drivers patiently and diligently dodged cattle and cowboys on horseback and stopped in primitive villages that had changed little over the centuries. There were also visits to impressive colonial and Indian sites that middle Europeans like Rubes especially appreciated. And palm trees were everywhere. Czechoslovakia seemed a million miles away.[17]

In Guatemala, Rubes sang Ramfis in Verdi's *Aida*, Fernando in Verdi's *Il Trovatore*, Méphistophélès in Gounod's *Faust*, and Raimondo in Donizetti's *Lucia di Lammermoor*, all in their original languages. The company also gave Humperdinck's *Hansel and Gretel* in Spanish. The press reflected the disturbed times in a review of the *Faust* production. "Like a sedative for the spirit, after the political events and disorders in the streets which have disturbed the vicinity [*sic*] of the city, last night's presentation of *Faust* in the Capitol Theatre confirmed again the prestige of the national opera of Guatemala…. Juan [*sic*] Rubes has a vocational talent for the theatre, besides his well balanced basso voice, and his acting as Mephistopheles was quite a creation of gestures and acts."[18] The company responded to the public's enthusiasm for the production — it was also broadcast — by doing a special repeat a few days later.

The same operas were given in San Salvador in August and Costa Rica in early September. *La Traviata* was added in San Salvador, with Rubes, as Dr. Grenvil, more or less faking the Italian. *La Bohème* was added in Costa Rica, with Rubes, as usual, singing Colline. Rubes recalled that the Costa Rican opera house, situated in the heart of the country's capital, San José, was a magnificent replica of La Scala. While there, with only four days' notice, they had to put on a command performance of *La Traviata* for the president. Rubes had barely enough time to learn his part. But there was also a long ensemble to learn. Rubes explained how he handled the challenge:

> The part is quite basic and repetitive, da, da, da, dum … da, da, da, dum, but there was no way I could learn this long ensemble part in Italian in those few short days, so I got a brilliant idea. I decided that the audience probably couldn't hear the words very clearly anyway and they were mostly Spanish speaking, so I decided to use a Czech word that sounded Italian and just repeat it. The word "dopredele" fitted perfectly into the rhythm, do-pre-del-le, do-pre-del-le. So that was what I did, with great confidence, thinking no one would know the difference. The one problem was that "dopredele" means "up your ass."
>
> As I was singing, everything seemed to be going splendidly until I looked out at the audience and saw a man in the first row killing himself with laughter. Apparently there was one person in the audience who understood Czech. After the show, this man came backstage. His name was Benny Benda. He said to me "Mr. Rubes, that was the funniest moment. I came to see a cultural event. And just at a very dramatic moment, I hear in Czech someone bellowing from the stage, 'Up your ass'!" We went out for a drink together, had a marvelous time and I finally staggered back to my hotel room totally drunk, singing "Dopredele" at the top of my lungs.[19]

In retrospect, Rubes reminisced, he and his fellow singers — from Canada, the U.S.A., and Latin America — were all competent, the performance standards were reasonable, and the orchestras were passable.

There was considerable press coverage — even a piece in New York's *Musical America* written by its representative in San Salvador.

The world premiere for *Forbidden Journey* was planned for September 22, 1950, in Montreal. The day was unforgettable for another reason: Susan Douglas and Jan Rubes were married in New York that morning, almost exactly a year after their first meeting. Presbyterian minister Cynolwyn Pugh, Morfy's father, officiated in an informal ceremony attended by Morfy (now Glaser) and her husband, Gil. Anthony Quinn's wife, Toni, Georges Deymel, Walter Homburger, and other New York friends were also present to toast the happy couple. Jan presented a charm bracelet of gold and pearls to his beautiful bride. He also observed a Czech custom, breaking a plate at the ceremony and keeping the broken pieces to bring them good luck. One of the small shattered pieces of the plate was later added to the charm bracelet, and from time to time over the years Jan would add other charms.

But there was no time to celebrate, and certainly no time for a honeymoon. They flew to Montreal in the afternoon to attend the premiere of *Forbidden Journey* at the Princess Theatre. The actor José Ferrer, as master of ceremonies, interviewed the newly married couple onstage and asked them, "What are you doing tonight?" As expected, the audience responded with loud guffaws and laughs. Ferrer's wife, the singer Rosemary Clooney, was in the audience. *Forbidden Journey* received a lot of publicity. *Saturday Night*, an important Canadian weekly magazine, made much of it, with Jan and Susan on the cover and a positive if cautious review inside.[20] The general consensus was that, as an action film, it lacked excitement, pace, and wallop. The villains were not villainous enough, and the plot was a bit tenuous. The sound was also poor. The film did a fine portrayal of Montreal and its landmarks, and the final scene at the Oratory drew wide praise. Unfortunately, the movie didn't sell well, a frequent outcome for films not made in Hollywood by a major company. Independent Canadian filmmaking still had a long way to go. Susan told a New York reporter, "The Canadians are all so delighted with their picture. It may not have the polish of a Hollywood production, but it does have a wonderful spirit. The Canadian people seem to feel that this is really their own."[21]

After their marriage, Jan and Susan settled happily in an apartment on West Seventy-second Street near Central Park in New York City. The Upper West Side, as it was known, was popular with people in the arts. The newlyweds got busy furnishing their apartment and enjoying new friends, many of whom were in theatre and films. There was Eli Wallach, at the time better known on Broadway than in the movies, and his actress wife, Anne Jackson. Others included the beautiful film star Laraine Day and her husband, Leo Durocher, manager of the New York Giants baseball team. The volatile Durocher, also known as "Lippy," had little respect for umpires and players he didn't like — and said so.

That summer and fall, Susan was involved in shooting a controversial and demanding Hollywood film, Arch Oboler's *Five*. It is a frightening tale, inspired by the increasingly ominous Cold War. After an atomic explosion, radioactive dust settles over the world and reduces its population to five people, four men and a pregnant woman, played by Susan. There are conflicts among the five survivors. In the end only Susan and the man she has fallen in love with remain alive. Her child dies. The film's thrust is unabashedly anti-war. It is eerie to see a city with buildings standing but not a living soul to be found. The cast, crew, and production

Jan (Méphistophélès) in Gounod's Faust, *Toronto, 1951.*

team were convinced of the film's importance. It was shot on Oboler's ranch in California near Los Angeles, on a remote cliff above Zuma Beach on the shores of the Pacific. According to Susan, Oboler liked living there because it was an escape from a deeply troubled world. Most of the interior action took place in Oboler's Frank Lloyd Wright house. The film didn't sell well, and critics blamed Oboler, a prominent radio producer, for having too much talk in it and for failing to realize that movies are not radio, where lots of talk is necessary. *On the Beach*, a film that dealt with a similar subject later in the 1950s, fared better.

Meanwhile, the CBC had Rubes sing the aged King Timur in its production of Puccini's *Turandot*. He also did concerts and other engagements — special events, banquets — until the second Toronto Opera Festival in February 1951. This was the first festival by what was now an independent company — the beginning of what would eventually become the Canadian Opera Company (COC). Jan shone as Méphistophélès. He was becoming more well-known. At the end of the month, he sang Simon in Haydn's *The Creation* with the Ottawa Choral Union, an accomplished amateur choir founded in 1874. Haydn had composed the work in Vienna in 1798 after his second visit to England, where he had been much impressed by Handel's oratorios, and it became one of the most popular works of its kind in the repertoire. The great Canadian soprano Lois Marshall sang Jane, and James Shields was Lucas. Singing a complete oratorio was new to Rubes and he injected a good deal of drama into his role. He would sing Simon several times over the next decade.

Now Susan had a steady job playing the lead role, Kathy Grant, in the daily American radio soap opera *The Guiding Light*. (A year later it was moved to TV.) Jan's main activities, however, were still in Canada and would continue to be so for the next eight years, with all the aggravations of commuting between New York and Toronto — storms, delays, and hairy last-minute rides to the airport. Hoping for more engagements in the U.S.A. he seized the opportunity to play Leporello, the Don's servant, in a production of *Don Giovanni* at the New Orleans Old French Opera House. The German-born Walter Herbert — he had been a Schönberg student — was company director and conductor, and Hans Busch was stage director. The Don was the Italian baritone Italo Tajo. Don Ottavio was the Canadian tenor Léopold Simoneau, whose career as a Mozart singer was just taking off. During this production, Rubes began developing his conception of Leporello as Giovanni's alter ego. Sections of the excellent New Orleans reviews found their way to Toronto: "Top honors for the night went to Jan Rubes. He was a splendid Leporello both as to voice and as to acting. He has a thorough understanding of the role and extracted from it the full measure of Mozart's delicious comedy."[22]

On he went to his first concert tour. The Celebrity Concert Series, quartered in Winnipeg, sponsored recitals for him in Regina and Yorkton, Saskatchewan; Flin Flon, Manitoba; and Kenora, Ontario. Rubes also gave an independent recital for the Calgary Women's Musical Club. And he even managed to squeeze in some skiing in Banff, his first time on skis in over two years. Whether it was skiing, tennis, or golf, Rubes always managed to fit one of his favourite recreational activities into his travels. Gordon MacPherson, his colleague from Balfour Manor Camp days, was a frequent accompanist at these recitals. Little did Jan anticipate the many times ahead when he would tour — in Eastern and Western Canada, the Far North, Alaska, and throughout the U.S.A. Rubes used almost the same recital programs for each concert, a common practice for most touring artists. He would lead off with *"Ombra mai fù"* from Handel's *Xerxes,* followed by two or three Schubert songs, and then arias from *The Magic Flute* and *Don Giovanni.* After intermission came Czech folk songs, and then Tosti's *"La Serenata,"* Tchaikovsky's "Pilgrim Song," and Mussorgsky's "The Song of the Flea" — the last two in Russian. Jan would conclude with musical comedy — "Some Enchanted Evening" from *South Pacific* or the like. For a while he included the two folk songs he had sung in *Forbidden Journey.* It was good programming with something for everybody. Such recitals helped to develop interest in good music in small communities, and Rubes, a musical populist, enjoyed it all.

Jan sang with the Winnipeg Symphony during this tour, with the competent Walter Kaufmann conducting the same Mozart arias he had sung in recitals. Kaufmann, born in Bohemia, had studied at the Berlin Hochschule für Musik with Franz Schreker and Curt Sachs. Rubes brought down the house with two of his standbys, *"Il lacerato spirito"* from Verdi's *Simon Boccanegra* and "The Death of Boris" from Mussorgsky's *Boris Godunov.* As usual, the reviews were ecstatic. Rubes now sang well

Above: Laraine Day and Jan at a New York Giants ball game, 1951. Sidney Gruson is behind Jan. Right: Jan and Spencer Tracy at a New York Giants ball game, 1951.

in four languages, Czech (and its cousin, Russian), Italian, German, and French, and he could also perform, with some hesitation, in English. Some said, jokingly, that his delightful accent was the same in all of the languages. Wherever he went he won over his audiences, thanks to his good looks, his charm, and his truly sincere wish to communicate his music to his listeners. Winnipeg booked a return engagement for November 1951 at which he sang a concert version of *Faust* with the Philharmonic Choir and Symphony. Although he had sung Méphistophélès in French and Italian, this was his first stab at the role in English. As one critic pointed out, "When Rubes sang 'What affrights you,' 'news' became 'noose,' and 'is' became 'iss'." "Singing in English," this same critic said, "inhibited his interpretation."[23]

Life in New York continued to be full of fun for Jan and Susan. Laraine Day had an afternoon radio talk show, *A Day with the Giants*, and Rubes was her guest one day. After the show she invited him to attend the game at the Polo Grounds, the home of the Giants. Rubes, who knew nothing about baseball, agreed to go. That year, the Giants were considered quite out of the race for the National League pennant, while the Brooklyn Dodgers looked like a shoo-in. No matter — the day Rubes was there, cheering with the crowd, the Giants won. The superstitious Durocher was convinced his singing friend was bringing him good luck, and he told Laraine to invite him again.

The Giants ended up winning thirty-seven of the final forty-four scheduled games to make the pennant race one of the most exciting in baseball history, and Rubes was there for all the home games, sometimes accompanied by Hollywood actors — Spencer Tracy was one. After each victory, the Durochers, the Rubeses, and other prominent guests celebrated at Toots Shors's restaurant, a favourite of show business and sporting people. Susan remembers one evening when Danny Kaye, a Giants fan, asked all present to close their eyes; he would do an imitation of Jan's speaking voice, with accent of course, and Jan would also speak the same text. "Who was Kaye? Who was Rubes?" Kaye asked the guests. An equal number got it wrong as right, such was Kaye's talent.

Then came the three-game playoff with the Dodgers. The Giants won the first game, but the Dodgers slaughtered them 10–0 in the second. It didn't look good for the Giants. In the final inning of the third game

Jan (Kecal) in Smetana's The Bartered Bride, *1952.*

the Dodgers were leading 4–2 and the Giants had two men on base. Then Bobby Thomson hit a home run, winning the pennant for the Giants. Canadian sports writer Trent Frayne wrote years later, "Luckily for Jan, the Yankees beat the Giants in the World Series or Leo might have had him sitting in the box in the Polo Grounds all winter."[24]

In January 1952, Walter Homburger called on Rubes to replace an ailing Léopold Simoneau on a western recital tour that included some of the same cities Jan had visited the preceding year. This tour was sponsored by Community Concerts, a branch of New York's Columbia Artists Management, the largest American agency for classical artists. Community Concerts was a fixture in countless North American cities at that time. Its concert clubs chose artists from Community-Columbia artist lists, but not until each club confirmed how much money it had. Thus no club would spend more than it could afford, and Community-Columbia artists would get engagements with guaranteed fees. Rubes's growing recital experience helped him when, following the tour, he gave his second Eaton Auditorium recital. He was called back for five encores!

Next came an enormous success in the 1952 Toronto Opera Festival with Jan's performance of Kecal in *The Bartered Bride*. Sung in English, it brought down the house. The following year he would sing it again with the New York City Center Opera Company and excerpts from it in Chicago's Grant Park that would bring raves from the much-feared *Chicago Tribune* critic Claudia Cassidy and the *Sun-Times* critic Felix Borowski.[25] Rubes also did Sarastro, the High Priest, in an English *Magic Flute* at the 1952 Festival, sharing the role with Russell Skitch.

In June 1952, Rubes sang again with the Duno Company, this time in Havana's beautiful opera house, the Teatro Nacional, built in 1838. He was Doctor Bartolo in *Le Nozze di Figaro* and Fernando in *Il Trovatore*. Met singers Leonard Warren, James Pease, Mario Del Monaco, and Jean Madeira had leading roles. Jan was certainly in good company. Havana was also a more than satisfactory site for Jan and Susan's belated honeymoon. The city had a population of eight hundred thousand and was a vacation paradise for wealthy Americans in pre-Castro days. Morro Castle overlooked its harbour, and the city was replete with other handsome landmarks dating from colonial times. Visitors saw little of Cuba's poverty and understood its causes even less.

Rubes's American career seemed to be moving along. The National Negro Opera Company Foundation in Washington engaged him in August to sing Méphistophélès. Jim Crow still ruled in American operatic circles, and Washington, albeit the capital of the U.S.A., was still a southern city. Rubes was one of only two white singers in the cast, which included such outstanding artists as soprano Camilla Williams and baritone Robert McFerrin. The opera was given at the Griffith Stadium, home of the Washington Senators baseball team.

Irascible *Washington Post* critic Paul Hume — it was he who had achieved notoriety by lacing into Margaret Truman's vocal recital and invoking the ire of her father, President Harry Truman — reviewed *Faust*: "Jan Rubes has not sufficient voice and is certainly no actor. Lacking these qualities, his efforts were without effect. His scene with Faust where he apparently thought he was mesmerizing the tenor into a surprise approach to Marguerite was one of the funniest and most ridiculous things ever seen on the stage."[26] As often happens, one could ask whether a second unidentified reviewer was at the same opera. "Rubes disclosed a magnificent voice ... the most finished performance ... an agility and freedom of movement rarely duplicated. He sang the role in English with excellent diction."[27] The opera had started fifty minutes late because of technical problems, which probably irritated Hume. Rubes, still in his baseball discovery mode, observed, while working on the baseball field, that it was indeed a longer throw from third base to first base than he had realized. His sports knowledge now included baseball as well as tennis, golf, and skiing.

Canada was moving more slowly than the U.S.A. in launching television because of costs and questions of policy — should it be commercial-free like CBC radio, or what? And should there be private television? Canadian audiences living near the U.S. border could get American TV, but shouldn't a sovereign nation have its own TV? The CBC finally came to grips with these questions in the summer of 1952 when Franz Kraemer produced a short experimental TV concert. This first official TV variety show was aired in September. Actor-playwright Mavor Moore was its executive producer, and Rubes was among the artists, as was the twenty-year-old pianist Glenn Gould. Each did short selections.

Jan had a change of pace when he was invited to join the cast of *Opera Backstage*, a show that Torel had conceived in 1950. It had had sporadic performances at Eaton Auditorium for its first two years and was then polished up for touring in the fall of 1952. The company's singers — Mary Morrison, Patricia Snell, Joanne Ivey, Andrew MacMillan, Ernest Adams, and now Jan Rubes, with George Crum at the piano, created an operatic caricature-burlesque that poked fun at love, death, murder, curses, and vengeance. One or another of these was standard fare in most operas. The show brought the audience backstage, figuratively speaking, to help them understand the hows and whys in preparing an opera, to avoid the clichés that mid-twentieth-century audiences must endure. It toured Western Canada and was a hit wherever it was given. Finally, it appeared on CBC television in December 1952, after which it was dropped forever.

There were three roles for Rubes in the 1953 Toronto Opera Festival at the Royal Alexandra: the Bonze in *Madama Butterfly*, Mr. Kofner in Gian Carlo-Menotti's *The Consul*, and Don Alfonso in Mozart's *Cosi fan tutte*. The story of *The Consul* was very timely. It deals with the tragic happenings of a number of sympathetic people trying to get visas in order to leave a nameless but clearly Iron Curtain country. A hit, it was repeated the next year and was also done on CBC-TV. Rubes's Don Alfonso in *Cosi* combined cynicism and humour, helped by his fine grasp of the role's vocal demands. The opera, whose title is freely translated as "women are like that," reveals the inconstancy of women in their relations with their lovers. Some consider the plot ultra-sophisticated, while others think it is flimsy and best forgotten. However, the opera has some of the most beautiful music Mozart ever wrote. The other male singers were Don Garrard and Jon Vickers. Vickers shared his role with Edward Johnson (a tenor from Hamilton). In five or six years Vickers would become one of the world's leading operatic tenors, and Garrard, a bass-baritone with a resonant low register, would also have a significant international career. Rubes thought that Garrard's voice had a darker quality than his. *Cosi* went on a short tour after a fair reception in Toronto.

Another Rubes recital that year was in Mexico City. Sidney Gruson, a *New York Times* foreign correspondent stationed in Mexico City and a good friend of the Rubeses, had arranged it — as much to play golf with Jan as to hear him sing. Gruson was married to Flora Lewis, an equally prestigious correspondent for the *Washington Post*. They often had assignments at the same location, even though they never shared information. Jan had taken golf lessons to sharpen his game and, being a talented athlete, was soon being sought after as a golfing partner. In Mexico, where labour was cheap, he had three caddies at his disposal — one to carry the clubs, one to find the balls, and one to keep the score. It made him feel quite uncomfortable. The recital went well, according to an awkwardly translated review from an unidentified Mexican newspaper. The critic made much of listening to a "real professional" while deploring the low standard of performance, generally, for song recitals in Mexico's capital city.[28]

That spring, Rubes worked with the prominent New York vocal coach Kurt Adler to prepare himself for the annual Metropolitan Opera auditions in May. He did well at his audition and earned a scholarship for several lessons with the recently retired Met baritone Herbert Janssen. He hoped that the German-American Janssen would help him to get a firmer vocal technique and a better "top." (He sometimes would ask his accompanist to transpose down a tone because he couldn't reach the high notes.) Jan was pleased with Janssen's lessons and took several more after the scholarship ran out, although they didn't solve his technical problems. The audition provided another benefit — he could attend Met rehearsals and classes during the spring and summer.

Kraemer's first substantial production on CBC-TV was aired in May 1953. It was *Don Giovanni*, with Rubes as the Commendatore. Kraemer, like Walter Homburger, had come to Canada as an interned refugee at the beginning of the war. He would produce a number of operas on CBC-TV over the next eighteen years, all of high standard. When doing operas — all of them live — he preferred to house the orchestra and the singers in separate studios, with intercom communication. It seemed to work, even though Kraemer could never explain clearly and conclusively the reasons behind this procedure.

Lest we forget, all of Rubes's Canadian activities were done while commuting weekly to New York, where he was on constant lookout for more singing opportunities. He worried chronically about not being busy enough. He gave a recital at the brand new Stratford Shakespearean Festival in the summer of 1953. Prior to the festival, Stratford — some 160 kilometres west of Toronto — had been a typical Ontario town of twenty thousand inhabitants, its main industries being furniture manufacturing and railway maintenance yards. Louis Applebaum, the unofficial head of music for the festival, presented Rubes's recital in a concert series featuring leading artists. The audiences were all small. The recitals complemented the festival's two inaugural plays, *Richard II* and *All's Well That Ends Well*. Tyrone Guthrie directed both with Alec Guinness and Irene Worth among the leading players. The specially designed tent (a few years later it would be transformed into a permanent building) and its thrust stage were unique for the time in North America. Stratford would eventually be the continent's leading theatre company. For Susan, Jan's appearance that summer brought about two reunions. She met up again with Louis Applebaum, who had written the music for *Lost Boundaries*, and with Tyrone Guthrie, who had directed her on Broadway in *He Who Gets Slapped*. Applebaum would stay with the festival for the next forty-five years. Besides writing incidental music for many of the plays, he composed the famous Stratford brass fanfares that are performed outdoors at the Festival Theatre prior to the beginning of each play and again at intermissions.

Jan Rubes had triumphed the previous winter with the Pittsburgh Opera in his seasoned role as Méphistophélès. In October 1953 he did Colline in the New York City Opera Company's production of *La Bohème*. It was his debut with the company. The *New York Times* wrote, "He had a feeling for characterization and an easy stage manner. In his one big number 'Farewell to the Coat' his voice sang out effectively — a clear, pleasant bass that has substance enough without being too dark and heavy."[29] Early in 1954, he did *Bohème* (Colline), *Rigoletto* (Sparafucile), and *The Consul* (Mr. Kofner) at the Toronto Opera Festival. He also attended Metropolitan Opera staging rehearsals, but there were no Met contracts. However, he was busy enough, singing recitals for Columbia Artists in the Southern U.S.A., hosting *Songs of My People* on the CBC (of this more soon), and doing a *Bohème* on CBC-TV in Montreal just before New Year's 1955.

With the many opportunities Rubes had in 1953 and 1954, there was one event that outshone all of them — the birth of Jan and Susan's first son, Christopher, on May 24, 1954. The Durochers were the godparents. Susan had chosen natural childbirth (no anaesthetic), still unusual in the early 1950s. To do this effectively she had to take regular classes to learn the necessary exercises and procedures. Jan was present at the birth and claims he suffered almost — but not quite — as much as Susan. It was a breech delivery and took twenty-four hours. Rubes had seen Erna Phillips, the writer and producer of *The Guiding Light*, in Chicago in 1953 and had asked her if Susan could have a baby and still remain on the show — Susan's income did much to support the two of them. The co-operative Phillips wrote the show so that Susan's character, Kathy Grant, became ill and was placed in an oxygen tent when Susan's pregnancy became visible. Kathy, however, remained healthy enough to speak her lines, the oxygen tent notwithstanding. She recovered once all signs of the birth were gone, to the relief of her thousands of followers. In the meantime Jan was into the second year of a weekly CBC radio program that would spread his name throughout Canada.

CHAPTER 5

1953–1963: *Songs of My People*

"To the people of many lands who have made Canada their home and found freedom of expression, the opportunity of hearing and singing the songs of their native lands is a priceless heritage. It is this freedom which gives new life and memory to the old songs of Europe." These were the words of CBC's vice-president Harry Boyle, the man behind the success of the CBC Opera Company and *CBC Wednesday Night*. Clichéd as the words may seem, they appropriately led off *Songs of My People*, a thirty-minute radio show that began on May 8, 1953, as a thirteen-week summer replacement. By the end of the summer, the CBC had decided to continue it on a regular basis. None of the program's principals had anticipated that it would be given weekly in the same format for the next ten years and become one of the longest running shows in CBC history.

Songs was a CBC response to the growing number of postwar immigrants in Canada, most from central and Eastern Europe. The federal government's archaic and biased immigration policies had grown more lenient in the early 1950s, if only for practical reasons — Canada needed a larger work force. As it evolved, *Songs* met the needs of both

Ivan Romanoff and Jan Rubes consider countries to feature on
Songs of My People, *1953.*

new and old Canadians through its attractive programming. That it began just as television was getting its grip on the public made its success
all the more significant.

Jan Rubes, violinist-conductor Ivan Romanoff, and Harry Boyle
came up with the idea for the show — to perform music from different
European countries, along with interesting explanatory comments. Rubes
rose to the challenge and literally *made* the show. He chose the music and

the guest soloists, wrote nearly all of the scripts, and sang many of the songs. With Romanoff, he developed a male quartet and, four months later, a larger chorus of eight to ten men. Rubes, with his warm speaking voice and enchanting accent, was also an ideal MC. Romanoff's work was equally important. He conducted a small orchestra and prepared the musical arrangements — a demanding task, since there were usually new songs to be set every week. He also selected instrumental music to complement the songs. Within a month, the meaningful, down-to-earth program had captured thousands of listeners across Canada and northern U.S.A.

The first show began with a very brief musical theme, followed by Boyle's words. Both would be repeated on every show over its ten years. Then the host appeared:

> This is Jan Rubes, and as a new Canadian I feel flattered to be allowed to step in front of this CBC microphone and announce to you the premiere of *Songs of My People*. It is four years since I timidly hugged for the first time a CBC microphone. It was during a performance of *Don Giovanni*. The broadcast was done in English, and, to be frank, at that time I really didn't know what I was singing about. Neither did I understand the friendly talk of my colleagues. Four years have passed and I am really happy to be able to understand this difficult language.

The introduction was vintage Rubes at his personal best — charming, irresistible.

Rubes started with a Slovakian folk song, explaining that it was about a boy who is being recruited into the army and is boasting about how fine he will look and how brave he will be. He then talked about the Slovakian capital, Bratislava, on the Danube, and how it was in Bratislava that he heard for the first time "a real Hungarian csárdás played by a gypsy orchestra in a wine cellar." What next? The orchestra plays a Hungarian medley. Then Rubes went on to speak sympathetically about Gypsies (Gypsies were not yet insisting on being called Romany) and how they were never a problem, at least with his family. "I saw my first real Gypsy as a very very small boy — it was a poor view. The starved thin horse dragging a painted wagon — about five dark thin children running around — a man with a moustache whipping the horse — and the goat following the wagon." Gypsies sharpened his mother's knives and mended her pots and then went on their way. This paved the way for soprano Frosia Gregory to sing "Love Comes But Once," a melancholy Gypsy song. Rubes praised Romanoff for his violin improvisations during the Gypsy piece, and more Hungarian and Ukrainian music followed. Gregory sang a French song, and then a male quartet and orchestra concluded the program.

The format — Rubes, orchestra, chorus, guest soloist — would alter little over the next decade. There would be different soloists, languages, and nationalities featured on each program. Terence Gibbs, who did so much with the CBC's Opera Company and its prestigious "Distinguished Artists" program, was its first producer. Catherine Akos, a Hungarian soprano, sang along with Rubes on the second show. This time it was German songs. The next program featured Claudette Leblanc from New Brunswick. She sang Acadian songs — and sang them beautifully. Then came Spanish-speaking Tito Fandos. Rubes sang "Grossmutterchen" in memory of his grandmother, who had died several weeks before. Talk about getting personal with your audience!

A week later, through his diligent and continuing search for singers who could do songs in lesser-known languages, he brought on a fine Estonian soprano, Irene Loosberg. Another find of his was sixteen-year-old Teresa Stratas, who sang Greek songs with exceptional sensitivity and feeling. Rubes provided Teresa with her first opportunity in a career that would ultimately mark her as one of the great singing actresses of her time. She was with the Metropolitan Opera Company for many years and played on Broadway in both straight theatre and musicals; she also appeared frequently on television and made recordings. Stratas sang on *Songs of My People* several times over the next five years, as did another excellent soprano, Mary Morrison. From Manitoba and already a prominent singer in the COC, Morrison did songs in the Gaelic she had learned from her family in her childhood. On another show, Rubes described the Norwegian soprano Selma Jetmunson as "the pretty blonde at my side." (She *was* pretty.) No one objected, although such chauvinistic language would be considered unacceptable today.

Letters poured in from the outset praising the show and its MC. Rubes happily responded by saying how pleased he was to get them. He no longer considered radio too impersonal. In his charming, folksy — but never patronizing — way, he said, "I don't feel that this microphone in front of me is a dead piece of metal, but the ear of the old English lady from Regina, the ear of the young Czech girl from Capetown. I am suddenly encircled by a friendly group of people, to whom I sing and talk — from person to person — from me to you!" Here was Jan Rubes underlining how he loved singing, how he loved sharing his songs with others, and how he wanted his listeners to enjoy it all. It said a lot about him. It also was a lesson in how to capture an audience.

In November, John Reeves took over as the show's producer. He was a cultivated musician like Terence Gibbs and took special interest in the program. Both he and Gibbs admired Rubes's approach to songs and Romanoff's arrangements and orchestrations. And they didn't object to Rubes missing the odd show because of his concert recitals and appearances with orchestras, choral societies, and operatic groups. Indeed, these in-the-flesh appearances helped consolidate the program's popularity with the public. Wherever he went over the next ten years, Rubes found that concertgoers knew him because of the show and listened to it more intently after meeting its star.

In February, Rubes, with his unfailing instinct for recognizing good talent, had soprano Milla Andrew sing on the program. In her early twenties, Milla, who had been christened Ludmila Andrejew, sang Russian-Ukrainian songs. She would have an impressive career in Canada and abroad over the next two decades. Russian, Polish, Turkish, Greek — you name it — Rubes diligently sought out songs and other material in different languages. His many songbooks, miniature histories, and folk tales stored in his archives attest to his assiduousness. On February 18, he told his audience that in the coming weeks he would crowd the calendar with important dates of other countries — independence day for Lithuania and Estonia, a Welsh national holiday, and later in March "we'll all dress up in Irish green" for St. Patrick's Day. Cleverly, he would take his listeners down the Danube to provide a setting for central and Eastern European songs. Then, when the show clearly needed some new emphasis, he had Chico Valle sing Cuban music. Rubes moved on to songs from Yorkshire and songs in Yiddish and Hebrew with local singers Evelyn Gould and Evelyn Pasen.

On the show's first anniversary — May 7, 1954 — announcer Larry Palef summed up the first year's statistics: forty-six different singers and twenty-nine different languages. Rubes himself had sung ninety-one songs in thirteen languages. Reeves, slight, slim, and intense — but always smiling — came to the microphone and said jocularly, "If I say anything Jan doesn't like, he's only got to wait fifteen minutes and then … well, he outweighs me by about eighty pounds. Still, even if he is built along the lines of a carthorse, it's a benevolent carthorse, with straight sand hair, a visible fondness for good food, and the general appearance of a tall, somnolent, and cheerful Friar Tuck." Such were the feelings of all concerned with the show.

Moving further afield, Rubes did songs of the Barbados two weeks later, featuring the black singer Isobel Lucas — her father was from the West Indies and her mother from Virginia. On July 2 he presented the Mexican singer Tito Fandos, which gave Rubes a chance to talk about his operatic experiences in Guatemala, a country whose reform government had just been overthrown by a military junta with the help of the CIA. Rubes said that "this little eye pleasing country is in turmoil again," and he told how "he was barricaded in a hotel." (Time tends to distort one's memory of personal experiences.) As always, he looked for historic incidents to give context and add dimension to the music performed. On July 23 he focused on Saskatchewan, which he knew well thanks to his concert-giving in that province. He spoke about

> a fertile piece of land, roughly in a triangle of Saskatoon, Moose Jaw to its southeast, and Swift Current to its southwest. It was exactly fifty years ago today that a group of young men from the old country set foot on this fertile soil and decided that this was going to be their home. Tonight, just at this hour, in the park of a small town called Outlook, we will join the celebrations of the life and work of a wonderful people who have merged into one beautiful family of the Maple Leaf.

Too folksy? But a growing Canada needed to know its history and its many peoples, however corny the presentation. At Outlook, said Rubes, were Slovakians from Kenaston, Norwegians from Hanley, Czechs from Glenside, "and a Polish family from Broderick trying to talk in their old language to some Yugoslavs from Conquest." Then came songs "Where Is My Home?" and "Emigrant's Complaint." Both provided nostalgia for the old and hope for the young. Rubes chose songs with great care. If his verbal accounts were, on occasion, too naive, his listeners, from the intelligentsia to the uneducated, didn't seem to mind. After a year of *Songs of My People* Jan Rubes had become one of the CBC's most popular radio artists.

On a program the next summer, he described the Prague ghetto with its "narrow and zig-zagged streets, walls without windows, dark arcades with shops, a little square where a passing streetcar looked terribly out of place. Then the little cemetery — so small that the tombstones are assembled like cards in a deck — covered with the reddish curly tiles so characteristic of Old Prague itself." He followed these words with a song, "The Roofs of Prague." Then he spoke of how the Nazis changed everything: "A friend of mine was expelled from the conservatory because his grandmother happened to be Jewish." Later, he and his friend had sung a duet in a cellar in the ghetto. "Leaving the place long after midnight, with no streetlights because of the blackout, I really felt that I was back in the thirteenth century." His friend ended the war in a concentration camp. He related how they had both met again serendipitously just the year before, backstage at the New York City Center. "There are no ghettos nowadays, or are there?" Rubes asked his listeners. Then Ivan Romanoff led his orchestra into a joyous Jewish dance, a "Freilach."

When Rubes did outside engagements that prevented him from appearing on *Songs*, he wrote the scripts and booked the vocal talent for the show well in advance. He was always meticulous and thorough. By 1955, with his reputation growing, he was as busy as any artist could be. One can't help noting again that he was still commuting back and forth weekly between Toronto and New York, where Susan was coping with her first child and appearing daily on *The Guiding Light*. Her earnings from this TV show continued to enable the Rubes family to live comfortably, since Jan's relatively meagre CBC, opera, and recital fees barely paid his commuting expenses.

And so *Songs* went on, with letters of praise arriving in a constant stream. For Romanoff there was a bonus — he met the attractive Ukrainian soprano Lesia Zubrack, who would later become his wife. She sang from time to time and also wrote the occasional script when Rubes was away or didn't have time. As for CBC management, it happily continued the show since it was relatively low budget and reached out to new audiences. When John Reeves was producing it, he gently persuaded Rubes to extend the show's parameters and Rubes had no problem doing so. One program was devoted to Australian Aboriginal music. Another featured music from Friesland, a region in northeast Holland. Consider this description after Romanoff's orchestra played a Friesland dance: "The dancers would be clad in the beautiful and elaborate burghers' costumes. No wooden shoes, but low black shoes with silver buckles, the men with frock coats and tall hats, the women in silk dresses of lovely colours, fichus of valuable white lace on their heads, closely fitted caps of real gold covered with white lace and decorated with real diamond pins." Rubes had made his point: this was hardly a tourist's image of Holland — no fishermen in baggy trousers, women in white checked shirts and white hats, and everyone wearing wooden shoes.

On another program, Roman Toi led his eighty-member Estonian male chorus in a variety of Estonian works. Now Rubes had a chance to explain — without much success — the puzzling background of the Finnish and Estonian languages and their remote links with Hungarian. In March, Teresa Stratas appeared again to sing Greek songs — she was soon to enter the Artist Diploma Course at the Royal Conservatory. Rubes related how Greece had struggled to free itself from the Ottoman Empire. The year was 1802, some twenty years before the Greeks launched their War of Independence. The men of Souli — highland villages in the northern Greek province of Epirus — were led into a trap by their Ottoman rulers and were killed or captured. The Souliote women, led by the twenty-one-year-old daughter of the local leader,

> put on for the last time their festal costumes of crimson velvet and gold, and, forming the antique circle of their

forefathers, danced a last memorable dance, and sang:

Farewell, unhappy world, farewell sweet life;
Farewell, farewell forever, our poor country.
Farewell, ye mountain springs, vales, hills and cliffs.
Farewell, farewell forever, our poor country.

With despair in their hearts, the women threw their children over the great cliff of Zalango.

To conclude this sad tale, they then, one by one, threw themselves over the cliff to certain death.

A large-scale *Songs*, titled "Music Under the Stars," was given at a Canadian National Exhibition bandshell on August 8, 1955. More than five thousand attended. There was no admission charge, thanks to a private sponsor, and the collection was donated to charity. Rubes was the MC and Romanoff conducted his male chorus and an enlarged orchestra. There were seven soloists. Several had already appeared on *Songs*, including Teresa Stratas and the Lithuanian baritone Vaclovas Verikaitis, who was also a member of the male chorus. Toronto Mayor Nathan Phillips was there and spoke briefly commending the performers and the various "racial groups" represented. The *Globe and Mail* praised all the singers.[30]

On January 13, 1956, after Rubes had sung some Newfoundland songs, he told his listeners about his narrow escape from an encounter with a Newfoundland moose and about taking his car on a Newfoundland ferry that was nothing more than "some old barrels with a few planks on them. You don't know what to do first, hold your car in place or help to pull on the thin steel wire on which the whole thing hangs — or perhaps start to take your clothes off to be ready for the swim." His stories may not have amused Newfoundlanders, but there were no complaints from them in the mail. Israeli, Maori, Ukrainian, Scandinavian, Austrian, Belarussian, Polish, Serb — you name it — followed in the weeks and months and years ahead. The South African team of Marais and Miranda sang on the show on April 6. *Songs* celebrated its third anniversary in May before a live audience of several hundred in the CBC's McGill Street Theatre in central Toronto.

Coinciding with the 1956 Melbourne Olympics, Rubes looked to Australia for music and invited Australian baritone Harry Mossfield to be soloist on the December 7 show. Mossfield was performing with the COC and had sung at the Stratford Festival the previous summer. The occasion allowed Rubes a chance to reminisce about the Czech long-distance runner Emil Zátopek's record-breaking performance at the Olympics in Oslo four years before, and about the great African-American runner Jesse Owens's triumph at Berlin in 1936: "In Europe we'll never forget the tremendous lift [Owens] gave us in the pre-war darkness." The program's ecumenical image shone brightly and clearly on January 4, 1957, when Rubes and an enlarged choir sang a shortened version of the Russian Orthodox Christmas service. Its date is set by the Julian calendar.

John Reeves wrote an article in the *CBC Times* marking the fifth year of *Songs* broadcasts, in which he summed up its impressive statistics: "The show has visited fifty-one different peoples, the chorus has sung in over thirty languages, Jan has sung several hundred songs in a much wider variety of languages than most singers would ever dream of learning, and Ivan has arranged nearly 1,100 songs and dances for his orchestra and chorus."[31] Reeves underscored the importance of Jan's other engagements, which enabled him to make personal contacts with his listeners. Rubes then added insightfully:

> Concert tours have taken me away from twenty-six shows up to now. Everywhere, I meet listeners to "Songs of My People." They are wonderful, faithful…. They always come backstage…. When I meet these people I have the feeling that we are personal friends before we even begin to talk. I've talked with Latvians in Newfoundland, with Czechoslovaks in Saskatoon. I remember a Scottish lady in New Glasgow, Nova Scotia, a French-Canadian in Ottawa, an elderly Greek in Port Angeles, Washington, and a Viennese doctor in Vermont. Then I step up to the microphone, I see them in my mind's eye and try to remember that the music we perform on the program is something shared between friends.

Some of the songs I sing on the program I learned as a child from my mother. Even then they were beginning to pass out of use and, in some cases, I've never heard anyone else sing them.... When I was at the Prague Conservatory we used to look down on folk songs as being "beneath our refined operatic dignity." Now I am finding out that certain aspects of human or national emotion cannot be better expressed than in a simple folk song; and, further, I often feel that it's more difficult for a singer to master the interpretation of a little folk song than that of any other vocal form. Some of our untrained guest folk singers are much closer to the mark than a host of trained singers who are so intent on vocal technique they forget that a folk song should be sung not with the vocal cords but with the heart. It's a question of overcoming one's inhibitions. I myself found it difficult to give a part of my heart every week to so cold an audience as a microphone; but I must say that the problem has vanished.

There were additional public *Songs* concerts in Toronto and Winnipeg, where Jan met audiences in person and cemented the program's relations with them. As always, Jan continued to heap praise on Romanoff, but in the second five years of the show producers began complaining that Romanoff was becoming dilatory in delivering musical arrangements and sometimes rehearsed haphazardly. All of this notwithstanding, Romanoff's ability to set music in so many evidently authentic and correct idioms astonished the producers. Romanoff, of Ukrainian parentage, was an excellent violinist who had trained in both Toronto and Czechoslovakia and had wide experience as a player and conductor of popular music, Russian folk music, and classical music. He married Lesia Zubrack after his second wife, Regina, died in 1960.

Reeves thought Romanoff's work with the choir was, by any measure, extraordinary. The group developed a phonetic language enabling the singers to sing in any and all of the many languages put before them, even though in many cases they had no idea *what* they were singing. It might have been sheer chance, but the choir and the orchestra numbered among their members many different nationalities. Thus *Songs* was an all-round ethnic show before "ethnic" became a popular word in the Canadian vocabulary. According to Susan Rubes, its listening audience was second in numbers only to the CBC's *Hockey Night in Canada*.

Inevitably, the *Songs of My People* concept was tried on television under a new name. Romanoff convinced CBC-TV producer Eric Till in the spring of 1958 to take on a new show titled *Rhapsody*. Romanoff would be music director. Most surprisingly, Jan Rubes was not to be its MC. Evidently, Romanoff had gone to the CBC without telling Rubes. Why, we'll never know, although there were suspicions that Romanoff wished to promote Lesia Zubrack. In any case, Rubes was very hurt by Romanoff's action. Joseph Furst, an Austrian actor who had settled in Toronto, was its host. There was solo singing, dancing, a choir, and an orchestra of twenty-four players — much larger than the *Songs* orchestra. *Rhapsody* would run in the summer, and, being TV, it would necessarily have a much larger budget than *Songs*.

Rhapsody was not a success, critically or with the public. Many of the latter, not unexpectedly, asked why Rubes wasn't on it. Romanoff and Till had no choice but to ask Rubes to join *Rhapsody* the following year. Its first show was on June 28, 1959, and it played for thirteen weeks. Now enthusiastic letters poured in from listeners. However, the dancing, an important part of this TV show, needed more rehearsing and artistry. The orchestra, too, seemed under-rehearsed. And so the show was dropped. To sum up, the more discerning watchers thought the show lightweight and poorly executed. A few years later Rubes, reminiscing, attributed the show's failure to television. The appeal of *Songs* was that listeners related to songs they knew from the past. *Seeing* them took away the powers of suggestion that came with radio.[32]

Tensions grew between Rubes and Romanoff, but they continued to work together on *Songs* for another four years. They also did a few other shows together in the ensuing years. *Songs* fizzled out in its tenth year. By then Rubes claimed that it had done songs in fifty-six languages, and that he personally had sung in twenty-seven!

CHAPTER 6

1955–1959: Recital and opera tours;
Stratford Festival; American engagements

Jan Rubes became an American citizen on June 22, 1955. (He wouldn't become a Canadian citizen until 1974.) This new status gave him pause. Was he doing as well in the U.S.A. as he was in Canada? Perhaps not. In Canada he was as much a household name as any classical singer could be, largely thanks to *Songs of My People*, but also because of other appearances on radio and television, his recital tours, and his performances in opera in Toronto. He was getting about two hundred letters a year from admirers.

True, living in New York had enabled him to audition for important conductors, and that had led to some interesting and challenging engagements. It was also true that Columbia Artists, the leading concert artist agency in North America, gave him a contract, suggesting that it thought he had a promising future. Columbia had access to all of the leading orchestras, choirs, and opera companies and, presumably, intended to promote him for appearances with them. It also worked closely with its affiliate Community Concerts, booking artists — usually the less well known ones at lower fees — for the many concert clubs in the U.S.A.

and Canada. Jan's Community Concerts career began in earnest that year, with engagements all over the continent.

Nelly Walter of Columbia handled Jan's portfolio and booked him for what seemed an endless stream of Community Concerts recitals in mainly small towns. After two years with Columbia, Rubes, additionally, hired Thea Dispeker to be his personal agent to find him more prestigious engagements. Agents such as Dispeker commanded substantial retainers. Columbia, however, still did the actual bookings for engagements found by Dispeker and charged him 20 percent commission. It charged him only 15 percent for Community engagements. In addition, artists paid for their own promotional brochures, their accompanists' fees, and their travel costs. It was not an easy way to earn money, and Rubes's net income from Columbia and Community was disappointing.

Most artists on the way up wanted to work in New York, where reputations are made, but success in that city's competitive musical environment was for the few, not the many, and Rubes was a borderline case. Nor did it help that there were so few leading roles in opera and oratorio for basses, compared to roles for higher male voices. Rubes took on bass-baritone solos more often than he should have, and then, as already noted, had trouble reaching high notes. Press reviews often noted this shortcoming.

The reviews from his touring engagements were, almost without exception, first class, although few local critics showed much knowledge of music per se. What they wrote about was a personable and talented singer with a warm voice, a fine stage presence, a charming manner, and a handsome and commanding physical appearance. His programs were catholic as always, and his interpretations were second to none. The young Canadian pianist and composer Paul McIntyre was his accompanist on most of the tours in this period. McIntyre said that Rubes meticulously prepared his programs together with his pianist.[33] He was equally meticulous when it came to the details of the concert itself: the lighting, the programming, the encores. In short, he left nothing to chance.

Rubes would begin his recitals with a spoken preamble, a kind of *Songs of My People* approach. He did this to warm up the audience, but not for too long. According to McIntyre, he had an infallible sense of timing and seemed to know when to stop talking and start singing. He was also resourceful. At a St. Patrick's Day program at Mount Holyoke College in western Massachusetts, a patron asked him to sing an Irish song — even "Danny Boy" would be acceptable, he said. Jan was stymied. He knew neither the tune nor the words, so he asked McIntyre to write out the tune for him during the intermission. He studied it quickly, added some pastoral Czech words, and then sang it as an encore, telling the audience that he would sing an Irish song in Czech! However, there was a Czech person in the house — shades of Costa Rica — who promised, fortunately, not to reveal that it was hardly a translation of "Danny Boy."

In Newfoundland, where he would have several trying experiences over the years, he gave a delayed concert in Grand Falls that endangered his making a rehearsal in New York thirty-six hours later. Luckily, he managed to book a seat on a transatlantic flight that stopped for refuelling at Gander prior to its final hop to New York. (This was still the era of propeller planes.) Getting to Gander to meet the plane, however, was no small feat. One major hurdle en route was taking a ferry whose ropes pulled the vessel from shore to shore. (He had told this same story with variations on *Songs of My People*.) It was midnight and the water was ominously black as it went rushing by. Rubes and McIntyre apprehensively

The ferry Jan took on a recital tour in Newfoundland, 1955.

asked their driver what would happen if one of the ropes broke. Fully expecting an answer that it would never happen, the driver calmly replied that it *had* happened a few months before and the ferry had drifted down the river some three kilometres before it was rescued. Rubes made the plane.

There was another suspenseful happening. McIntyre got his dates confused for a concert in Bellows Falls, Vermont — he thought it was a day later. He fortunately discovered the error on the day of the recital, flew from Toronto to Montreal, rented a car, and drove to Vermont over poor roads. He arrived at the concert hall fifteen minutes before the beginning of the recital to find Rubes thoroughly relaxed and remarkably unconcerned. Whether Paul would make the concert or not, Jan felt, was in the hands of the gods, and there was no point in fretting about it. Life with Rubes was the art of the possible, not the impossible.

Despite his successes on the Community circuit, Nelly Walter wrote Rubes in May 1957 with some advice: "Everybody complains that during your concerts you chatter too much instead of confining yourself to singing only and obtaining your success through artistic means alone. The second complaint is a minor one — people ask, since you are such a good-looking fellow, if you could keep your eyes open when singing instead of having them closed — which might sometimes be a matter for concentration."[34] So much for Rubes, the great communicator! Ms. Walter and her superior, André Mertens, were old-school German concert managers, and this showed in Walter's letter. Rubes was sufficiently incensed to write back:

> About my "chattering" during a singing recital, I can recall only one instance where the reviewer thought my talking excessive, and even this reviewer admitted it had a good effect on the audience. The overwhelming majority of reviews and letters from committee members think my approach to a recital a blessing — not cold and impersonal. Many suggested that those non-talking artists are partly responsible for the decline in subscriptions and the demand for so-called group attractions, which generally prove more entertaining.[35]

He concluded by promising to pay attention to his "chattering."

As for closing his eyes, Rubes wrote in the same letter that there are singers, like Marian Anderson, who close their eyes for the entire evening. Sometimes he closed his eyes in "SELF DEFENSE" to avoid looking at a basketball hoop (some concerts were given in gyms) or an entire first row of schoolchildren occupying themselves during the lieder group by making holes in their programs and peeking through artistically made masks. He wrote:

> The programs made beautiful material for arrows, which glide gracefully through the gym. Then you try to remember your next line in "An die Musik." Another time you try to shut from your vision the lady who came to the concert it seems for the sole purpose to finish her husband's woolen socks, or because the only light on the stage was provided by an infernally bright arch light, the kind outlawed in European theatres long ago.

Rubes spoke for a legion of artists on the Community Concert circuit.

Of course Walter had the last word. She cited one concertgoer who said Rubes talked for seven minutes and another who said that artists who talk instead of singing and playing do damage to the concert club. Ironically, fifty years later, artists who talk to audiences about their music or anything else relevant are welcomed. Rubes's attitude, his talking about the songs he would sing, was ahead of its time. The bass-baritone Steven Henrikson had heard Rubes in a Community recital in Vernon, B.C., in March 1957 when he was only fifteen, and had nothing but praise. He said that both Jan's pre-concert talk and his singing did much to influence him to study music seriously.[36] No matter, Rubes's relationship with Columbia began to cool. His contract expired in May 1959 and was not renewed. However, he didn't stop giving recitals, nor did he change his routine.

There had been other outlets for his talent. One, in 1955, was the Stratford Festival's inaugural season of music. It included George Frideric Handel's *Acis and Galatea*. Usually called a masque, it is, as the program annotator pointed out, a serenata — "a short dramatic cantata in Italian style written for a courtly celebration." Jon Vickers was Acis, Elizabeth Benson Guy was Galatea, and Evelyn Gould was Damon. Rubes sang the minor role of Polyphemus. Assisting were the Hart House Orchestra conducted by Boyd Neel and the Festival Singers conducted by Elmer Iseler. The Singers would have an illustrious career for the next fifty years as the Elmer Iseler Singers. Iseler was a magnificent choral trainer, but as a conductor he was wanting, especially in the early days of his career. The Hart House Orchestra had a checkered existence until it was dissolved in the late 1960s. The *Globe and Mail's* John Kraglund reviewed the performance harshly, and he didn't spare Rubes: "A surprisingly flexible rendition, but the range was too high for him and only the low notes were pleasant." He concluded his scolding by saying that all four soloists were miscast.[37]

However, Stratford had an undisputed triumph the following year when it mounted Benjamin Britten's *The Rape of Lucretia*. Written for a cast of eight and a chamber orchestra, it was conducted by Thomas Mayer, who had occasionally accompanied Rubes on his concert tours, and directed by Herman Geiger-Torel. The opera was done on a small, almost bare stage that suited the festival's limited facilities at the time. The story goes back to Shakespeare's *Rape of Lucrece* and before that to the Roman historian Livy's tale. Briefly, Tarquinius, the Etruscan, succeeds in raping Collatinus's wife, Lucretia, who, in shame, kills herself. This exciting opera had a superb cast, led by soprano Jennie Tourel and tenor Jon Vickers as the female and male chorus, respectively. They comment on the action in speech and in song and "act as a link between the authors and the audience."[38] Regina Resnik played Lucretia and Jan Rubes, Collatinus. Harry Mossfield outdid himself as Tarquinius, and Bernard Turgeon was Junius. Rubes had wisely recommended American soprano Adelaide Bishop, with whom he had worked, to play the maid Lucia.

John Kraglund went all out in his praise for the production in his front-page review.[39] Rubes sang the cuckolded Collatinus with understanding and compassion for Lucretia's ordeal. It was only the second time that Resnik had sung a mezzo-soprano role, and musically and dramatically she caught the essence of the enigmatic heroine. (Resnik had had a considerable reputation as a soprano and, in fact, had played

Bernard Turgeon (Junius), Harry Mossfield (Tarquinius), and Jan Rubes (Collatinus) in Britten's The Rape of Lucretia, *Stratford, 1956.*

the female chorus in the opera's North American premiere in Chicago in 1947.) The performances also served as a launching pad for Vickers and led to a contract with London's Royal Opera, Covent Garden, the next year.

Returning to Rubes's American career, Rubes sang Kecal in *The Bartered Bride* at the New York City Center in October 1955. *New York Times* critic Howard Taubman was one of the very few critics who were not overly enthusiastic about it.[40] The work was given in an English translation by Joan Cross and Eric Crozier. Julius Rudel conducted. In a performance of the same opera in Washington in May 1956, Rubes had, according to the press, stolen the show. Critic Paul Hume, who had laced into him for his Méphistophélès four years before, wasn't there.

A month after Washington, Rubes sang King Creon for the American Opera Society's production of Cherubini's *Medea*, at the prestigious Caramoor Festival outside of New York City. Rarely performed, the opera is based on the Greek legend about the sorceress who helps Jason win the Golden Fleece. Eileen Farrell, one of the finest American dramatic sopranos at the time, did the incredibly demanding title role and reaped plaudits from Howard Taubman and from just about everyone else, both press and public, who heard her. Farrell had an ample physique that could have limited her operatic career, but on the concert stage she had few equals. She was married to a Hoboken, New Jersey, police captain and was utterly without pretensions. She also had a prodigious appetite and could, within reason, eat most men under the table. According to one witness, Farrell would invariably belch loudly before going on stage. Taubman wrote that Rubes was "pleasant but not forceful enough."[41]

Rubes was Truffaldino in a concert performance of Strauss's *Ariadne auf Naxos* at New York's Carnegie Hall on January 7, 1957, presented by Thomas Scherman's enterprising Little Orchestra Society. Eileen Farrell was its Ariadne. The work was done with no prologue; orchestral pieces from the composer's music for Molière's *Le Bourgeois Gentilhomme* were substituted. Farrell's performance, good as it was, was a bit disconcerting, because she used music. The taxing role of Zerbinetta was done by another incomparable soprano, Mattiwilda Dobbs. Being black had sadly limited her operatic career. Taking part in this opera helped Jan when he staged the work himself, two decades later.

Rubes's appearance in a production of *Faust* at Bob Jones University in Greenville, South Carolina, gave him a few chuckles. Bob Jones was a Baptist university and a haven for born-again Christians — it still is — so one wonders how the audience felt about Méphistophélès and Satan. Bob Jones's theologians could have hit the ceiling when one critic went so far as to suggest that Satan "seemed a likeable fellow in spite of his motives."[42]

In May 1957, Rubes took on two important roles with the Frankfurt Opera — one of the few times he sang in Europe after 1949. The first was Osmin, the steward of Selim Pasha's palace, in *Die Entführung aus dem Serail*, conducted by Felix Prohaska. He had done it before and knew it well. The second was Prince Gremin, Tatiana's husband, in *Eugene Onegin*, conducted by Georg Solti, the director of the company. Solti went on to become the music director of Covent Garden and the Chicago Symphony. A demanding conductor, he liked Rubes's performances and suggested that he might have a future in Frankfurt. After some thought,

Rubes decided that he was not ready to give up his work in Canada and be away from his family for prolonged periods in a German resident opera company more than six thousand kilometres distant.[43] Jan Gasser, his friend from his months in Geneva in 1948, came to Frankfurt for a brief reunion. It was a happy occasion.

The sixth COC Opera Festival in 1955 had finally given Rubes the much sought after opportunity to play Figaro in *The Marriage of Figaro*. It

Jan Rubes (Osmin) and Pierrette Alarie (Blondchen) in Mozart's The Abduction from the Seraglio, *Toronto, 1957.*

was done in English in the Martin translation, unquestionably the best translation available. Rubes was in his element interpreting the role with all of his heart and mind, broadening his conception of it as he would continue to do every time he tackled it in the future. John Kraglund was more generous in his praise than usual. He commented on Rubes's "polished acting" and noted that "his rumbling voice had a touch of lyricism that heightened his performance."[44] The other local papers and the audiences cheered the brilliant singer. The *Evening Telegram*, for one, wrote that it was "vocally thrilling and visually perfect."[45] For the 1957 Festival, Rubes played Osmin, this time in English, and in the next year's festival, Schlemil and Crespin in *Tales of Hoffmann* and Padre Guardiano in Verdi's *La forza del destino*. The memorable duet with Ilona Kombrink as Leonora in Act II of the Verdi masterpiece made a lasting impression. Her rich voice, style, and beauty convinced Rubes that he should collaborate with her in the future.

The Rubes family was growing. Jonathan was born on February 16, 1956. Jan was on a concert tour in California at the time. Susan had refused to acknowledge the warning signs, so there was a rush to the hospital and the birth came quickly. The night before, John Reeves had slept on the living room couch of the Rubes's apartment en route to Europe. The twenty-four-year-old Glenn Gould was to have dinner with Susan at the apartment the next evening, but she had already left for the hospital. Gould stayed on — he liked the king-sized bed that Susan generously relinquished when he visited. He was also suffering from one of his chronic colds, real or imagined. When he phoned Susan at the hospital the next day he said that, to his great relief, his cold was better. He did not ask her how she was or if she had had a boy or a girl! The self-centred Gould had recently stunned the musical world with his recording of Bach's *Goldberg Variations* and was in New York to see about further recordings and public concerts. (It would be another eight years before he renounced public concerts.) The Rubeses, of course, knew him from Toronto and Stratford encounters.

As for *The Guiding Light*, Erna Phillips had conveniently burdened Kathy Grant (Susan) with a nervous breakdown and relegated her to a wheelchair. As after Christopher's birth, Kathy recovered once Susan's signs of childbirth were no more. When the Rubeses' third son, Anthony, was born on July 22, 1958, Kathy Grant was killed in a traffic accident and Susan left *The Guiding Light* forever. Susan recalled that some thirty-seven thousand fans (an exaggeration?) from across the United States called the station after Kathy met her fateful and sudden death — such was the power of soap operas. It happened so quickly that many thought Susan Douglas herself had died.[46] "It's funny how fans associate the actress with the role," she said. When Kathy had divorced her husband and given her child away, Susan received hundreds of letters from listeners offering her advice.[47]

The COC launched its touring company in 1958. However important singing with the COC in Toronto was for Jan, his work with the touring company was still more so. He did nearly every tour for almost two decades, singing for his audiences with great involvement and joy, and serving as a pillar of strength when things got rough for the company, as they inevitably did when touring. Opera was still little known to most Canadians when COC touring began. There were no adequately equipped opera houses of any size or importance in the country, and without CBC radio and television Canada would truly have been an operatic wasteland. The newly created Canada Council was intent on seeing *live* opera done across the country. The Canadian Opera Company — who else? — was primed to do it.

With funds promised by the council, the first opera the touring company took on the road was Rossini's *Barber of Seville* in English. A comic opera full of laughs, it is surefire with audiences, sophisticated or not. The COC assembled an excellent cast. Torel and Andrew MacMillan staged it, MacMillan sharing Fiorello with Ernest Adams, who was also company manager. Alexander Gray was Figaro, and John Arab was Almaviva (there were also alternates for these two roles). Patricia Snell and Sheila Piercey shared Rosina. There were other singers who did minor parts. Rubes played Don Basilio, one of his favourite roles dating back to his student days in Prague, and George Brough was the pianist. Critics and audiences complained, rightfully, about the lack of an orchestra, but the simple explanation was insufficient funding. It would take almost ten years, in fact, before the touring company would have one. The company gave nineteen performances of the *Barber* in Eastern Canada in November and December 1958, then five at the October 1959 Opera Festival at the Royal Alexandra, and twenty-two more in western centres in November and December 1959.[48] The *Globe and Mail*, not unexpectedly, said of Rubes's Toronto performances that he sang "with a well controlled voice and a wicked sense of humor that made his appearances among the highlights of the evening."[49]

That first eastern tour was truly a landmark in Canadian operatic history, and Jan Rubes described its trials and tribulations, especially those in Newfoundland, with sensitivity and much humour.[50] First he quoted Herman Geiger-Torel on the tour's purpose: "to operationalize tzis vast cooltural vasteland." Then Jan went on to describe the start of the trip: "It began one gray rainy morning in November, when a group of sleepy eyed men and girls quietly boarded a bus in Toronto. The sun should have smiled at us and flash bulbs of newsmen should have popped! Many important events, however, go at first unheralded — and for us it was better so. We were much too tired to care after two hard weeks of rehearsal plus four dress rehearsals in two days!"

It seemed that all went well and without mishap — for the first engagements in Ontario and the Atlantic provinces. There were, not surprisingly, the usual bad pianos, inadequate stages, and receptions with little substantial food, but the company soon learned to live with these troubles. And then came Newfoundland. Rubes wrote that taking a group of singers on a Newfoundland tour at the outset of winter was "asking for the wrath of operatic gods from Valhalla, or wherever they reside."

The company left North Sydney by boat and, from their first hour aboard until the boat landed in Port Aux Basques the next afternoon, they were hopelessly seasick. Waiting for them on arrival was what Jan called the "Newfie Bullet," a narrow gauge railway still in service in 1958. "Clean and cute, it was like looking through the wrong side of binoculars," said Jan. The cast had slept in uncomfortable bunks on the boat (when they weren't being sick on the poop deck) and now they had to sleep in equally cramped bunks on the train, which, in the case of one tenor, was virtually impossible because of his girth. After a day of train travel they were dropped off well outside the U.S. naval base at Argentia, the first stop on the tour. Their baggage and the women singers were taken to their quarters on a military bus, but the men had to walk.

They did the performance in a warehouse to an entertainment-starved naval audience who, without exception, had never before been to an opera. Then it was on to St. John's to a theatre with a stage too small to handle even the company's limited scenery. After setting aside half of it, the cast next addressed the non-existent wing space. They could not leave the stage when they weren't in on the action! It was a challenge, but there were no complaints about their solution, at least not from the audience. Basilio had a contretemps with the lieutenant-governor, who earned the distinction of being the first Queen's representative to get wet watching an opera. Seated in the first row, he was so close to the stage that the water from Basilio's hat (in the after-storm scene) splashed merrily onto his lap. His Honour said nothing. The show was such a hit that the company did an extra performance the following day, thus missing their day off.

The next leg was a half-day rail trip to Gander. There the theatre was a gymnasium, "with bleachers, showers, and the smell of unwashed socks. Rosina was waving to her Count Almaviva right under a basketball hoop." In the meantime, one of Newfoundland's famed storms was gathering strength. When the company travelled to Cornerbrook, the gale was so severe that the "Newfie Bullet" was forced to a halt and literally chained to the ground to prevent it from blowing over. After Cornerbrook came a snowstorm. At Porte Aux Basques they were told that their scheduled sailing to the mainland was delayed. And so it was back to the train, which took them to a siding where their coach was left. Soon they were out of food and there was no heat. The next day the "Newfie Bullet" reappeared with food and heat. The company cheered.

Rubes wrote, "The crossing to Newfoundland had been a 9-hour overnight boat trip, but high winds prevented the same boat from landing in Sydney on the return journey. So we squeezed onto the tiny *Cabot Straits*. Everything was scaled down on this boat, and it took six people the next morning to extricate Alan Crofoot (the sergeant and villager) from his cot."

He also commented on the Sydney performance. During the third-act duet between Dr. Bartolo and the disguised Almaviva, the audience was roaring with laughter. "The singers not performing rushed to the wings to see what magic formula provoked such an enviable response.

Well, it was no credit to the singers — without their knowledge, a little kitten had wandered onto the stage and was curiously observing these strange goings on." Rubes continued:

> Touring Canada with a full-scale production is no laughing matter, but the pioneering spirit of our Canadian forefathers helped us overcome small obstacles — hurricane winds, snowstorms, unheated dressing rooms, short hotel beds, and (the greatest nemesis of the tour) the little white sandwiches — white bread glued together with a thin layer of colored cheese or tuna fish salad at "after the performance parties." These are served to you at the moment you are dying for a steak, for you have just finished a three-hour-long performance and, with a 200-mile drive before that, you have had no time for dinner.

Jan played a big part in the company's enjoyment of the *Barber* tour. His unfailing good humour and his endless fund of games and jokes provided respite when needed. He was a morale builder when things looked darkest. As for the audiences, Bill Lord, who designed and managed many shows for the COC in those years, said that Rubes, like no other, "showed the importance of personal contact with the audience, during the show and afterwards. He was sincere about this."[51]

A year later, after the western tour of the *Barber*, Rubes remarked,

> The response to the opera in small towns and cities across Canada has been terrific. For the first ten minutes it's like a man trying out the water with his big toe. But in no time at all people throw away their inhibitions and they give. Because they have no prefabricated [*sic*] traditions they take it for what it is — entertainment. They laugh. In one performance we did for teenagers, when Rosina (the heroine) came on, they whistled. This is the kind of enthusiasm there must have been when these operas were first performed.[52]

Herman Geiger-Torel felt as Rubes did about touring. He wrote as much in his report to the Canada Council. This first tour set the stage for future tours. The response of Canadians and later Americans energized the company sufficiently for its members to overlook the long bus rides; the air, bus, and train cancellations and breakdowns; the snowstorms; the poor hotels; the doubtful food; and the inadequate stages, lighting equipment, and pianos. Rubes earned encomiums from the press across the country, for both his singing and his acting. W.J. Pitcher

Martial Singher (Jupiter) and Jan Rubes (Pluto) in Offenbach's Orpheus in the Underworld, *Stratford, 1959.*

of the *Kitchener-Waterloo Record* said perceptively, "Even if he had half the voice he has, Rubes would still carry the day with his acting."[53]

In the summer of 1959, Stratford did Offenbach's *Orpheus in the Underworld* at the Avon Theatre in an English adaptation by Robert Fulford and James Knight. It is a parody on the Orpheus legend: Orpheus descends to Hades to take his wife Eurydice back to the world on the condition that he not look back while doing so. The hilarious production was given seventeen times during the season. Rubes played Pluto. The performances were a little over the top, the director Tom Brown letting most of the cast play their roles too broadly. Herbert Whittaker, drama critic of the *Globe and Mail*, wrote, "Even Jan Rubes, whom we have always considered one of the best singing actors, lays on his Plutoisms with a trowel."[54] About the distinguished French-American baritone Martial Singher, who sang Jupiter, Whittaker wrote, "He frisks about the stage like a four-year-old showing off at a picnic. As he is dressed to resemble Napoleon III, the effect is startling." John McCollum and Irene Jordan were Orpheus and Eurydice, respectively. Hyman Goodman, the Stratford orchestra's concertmaster, played the violin for Orpheus from the pit, as McCollum mimed it on stage. George Falle gave a blistering assessment of the production in the *Canadian Music Journal*, calling it one of Stratford's more dismal efforts.[55] "It was," he wrote, "in the nature of a brassy Broadway musical comedy.... The musical excellence of the show had been sacrificed to 'entertainment value'."

The Canadian Opera Company borrowed the production to take it on tour in 1961. No less than seventy-four performances were given in Eastern and Western Canada. Rubes also did the tour, alternating performances with the bass-baritone Victor Braun. At one rehearsal, when Jan was absent, Braun did a hilarious imitation of him — accent and all. Braun might have been harbouring resentment — well-wishers would frequently tell him after a performance how good he was but how they missed the star, Jan Rubes. Braun moved on to a brilliant career in Europe and elsewhere. Phil Stark — he was outstanding — and Danny Tait alternated as Orpheus on the tour. Both played the violin on stage, as Orpheus should — a must since there was no orchestra. Herman Geiger-Torel directed. The fun was still there — Rubes in a deliberate slip called it "Orpheus in the Underground" — but things were in hand.

CHAPTER 7

1958–1963: Vancouver Festivals;
More American engagements; Montreal

Nicholas Goldschmidt had been teaching a summer opera course at the University of British Columbia in Vancouver since 1950. He had also promoted a small-scale Mozart Festival there in 1956 to commemorate the two hundredth anniversary of the composer's birth. But Goldschmidt had more far-reaching plans and was determined to realize them. And so in the summer of 1958, with Toronto behind him (he had left the Royal Conservatory and the Canadian Opera Company in 1957), he launched the first Vancouver International Festival. The esteemed eighty-year-old conductor Bruno Walter conducted the inaugural concert at the Orpheum Theatre with the Vancouver Symphony and the Canadian contralto Maureen Forrester as soloist. Thanks to Walter, whom Goldschmidt revered, the orchestra played as it never had before, and Forrester enhanced her growing reputation as one of the world's leading contraltos.[56]

Good as the opening was, it was *Don Giovanni*, conducted by Goldschmidt and staged by Günther Rennert, that was the most exciting event of that festival. It had an all-Canadian cast, save one, the Australian soprano Joan Sutherland as Donna Anna — although it was stretching it a bit to call George London (the Don) Canadian. Born in Montreal, London had moved to the U.S.A. at age fifteen, trained there, and then joined the Metropolitan Opera Company. Striving for all-Canadian casts was important as Canada sought to establish its own identity in the performing arts. The Canada Council was funding worthy Canadian musical events, artists, and groups. A strong Canadian presence was imperative; otherwise, the council might hold back its support. Rubes, predictably, was Leporello.

The opera was done in Italian, and Sutherland, making her first appearance in Canada, was stunning. The demands of singing Donna Anna posed no problems for her. John Beckwith wrote of her "superb refinement, poise and tragic dignity, combined with exceptional feeling for the Mozart style perceptible in every phrase."[57] Goldschmidt had astutely assessed Sutherland's ability when he heard her at Glyndebourne and, after a private audition, had engaged her. Bruno Walter, after hearing her at the dress rehearsal, said that she was "the best Donna Anna I have ever heard."[58] Sutherland herself said that the reviews were so good that they could go to one's head.[59] She would be one of the great sopranos of the century, who, as the years went by, sang confidently both coloratura and lyric-dramatic roles. And, along with her husband, Richard Bonynge, Sutherland struck up an enduring friendship with Jan and Susan Rubes.

How right Goldschmidt was to have chosen Rubes to do Leporello! Rubes seized the opportunity, re-studied the role carefully (as he always did) before rehearsals began, and then found that playing opposite London's Don Giovanni clarified his own view of the role even more than when he had played it with Italo Tajo eight years before in New Orleans. *Don Giovanni* got very good notices. Beckwith said London "had adopted a Rudolph Valentino moustache and a fine sneer coloured by aristocracy of bearing, vitality, insolence, and that touch of effeminacy or dandyism which seems essential to the makeup of the typical great lover."[60] The critic Irving Kolodin noted the "really creative pattern" between Giovanni and his servant:

> Utilizing the big frame and supple voice of Rubes advantageously, Rennert made him a kind of seducer's

apprentice, roistering with Zerlina's chambermaids, relishing his little ding with Elvira when disguised as his master. He was, altogether, a rougher, more robust fellow than the average Leporello cast on the Italian model, but, underneath it all a "little man," craven before the supernatural voice of the statue, seeking to atone for his cowardice with excessive attention at the supper table.[61]

An unidentified press review said Rubes's characterization was "a masterpiece of singing and pantomime, the most impressive acting of the evening." Hans Moldenhauer of Spokane, Washington, wrote, "Leporello, no mere valet and buffoon, turned into — how else could it be — the crafty disciple of his master, seeking erotic adventures of his own. Such was the entire production: a searching study and re-evaluation of Mozart's (and Lorenzo da Ponte's) masterwork, carried by the inner logic that a timeless and universal art must reach into the personal experience of every beholder."[62] Rubes, as Leporello, was atypically athletic. London understood this and played up to it. As Rubes said, "Some other Dons fail to make the most of the half-comic half-sinister relationship between the master and the servant." The men were the same height and build, and this helped the characterizations. The production was a high point for Rubes, and he would approach the role of Leporello in like fashion in future *Don Giovanni* productions.

Léopold Simoneau was vocally outstanding as Don Ottavio, as was his wife, Pierrette Alarie, as Zerlina. Rubes, who had worked with them in other operas and would work with them again in the future, never got very close to them personally, since they generally kept to themselves. The cast took several boat trips when not working, and this undoubtedly helped link them together when on stage. After all, is there a city in the world more beautiful than Vancouver, with its waterways bordered by high mountains? On the negative side, the Orpheum Theatre was a poor setting for the production, with its staging and lighting problems. The opera's ensembles also suffered because of Goldschmidt's erratic conducting. No matter, his musicianship made up for his shortcomings. And he was so pleased with Rubes's Leporello that he wrote to Nelly

Jan as Leporello in Mozart's Don Giovanni, *Vancouver, 1958
(self-portrait, left, and photo, right).*

Walter at Columbia Concerts about Jan's work, knowing that it might help his career. Goldschmidt's conscience might have been bothering him, since he had driven a hard bargain over Jan's fee. That summer, Jan found time to exercise another of his talents — this time as a visual artist. He did a fine oil portrait of himself as Leporello.

The Vancouver Festival went on for another five years, although Jan's next appearance there was not until 1961, when he played Bottom in Benjamin Britten's new opera, *A Midsummer Night's Dream*. The British press had given it mixed reviews after its premiere at Aldeburgh; it had also played at the Holland Festival and Covent Garden shortly afterwards. Goldschmidt was, naturally, delighted with the prestige it gave his festival to present the first North American production of a new work by one of the world's leading composers. As for Vancouver's *Dream*, both press and public liked it, and continuing praise has been showered upon the work. In fact, the English opera authority Lord Harewood boldly called it a work that ranked with Shakespeare's masterpiece.[63] Harry

Horner was lauded for his staging and designs, which, in the opinion of many critics, stole the show. However, Kenneth Winters wrote in no uncertain terms to the contrary in the *Canadian Music Journal*.[64] Winters had been at the Aldeburgh production and believed that Goldschmidt should have engaged a British designer and director instead of giving it to a Vienna-trained Broadway- and Hollywood-oriented director-designer. To him, the sets were too lavish and cluttered and lost Aldeburgh's feeling of the forest and the fairies' air of eerie mischief. The naughty Winters borrowed a line from the sculptor Alan Jarvis: "It was something by Reinhardt out of Disney." Rubes thought Horner did a wonderful job, both as director (a new role for him) and as designer, and found his sets vivid, imaginative, and lavish.

Rubes himself was singled out only briefly in reviews. He deserved more attention, for he gave a fine all-round performance as singer and as actor. He worked hard at his English, which was helped, he said, by Britten's using Shakespeare's text with minimum changes. Russell Oberlin, the counter-tenor who sang Oberon, got the most notice, for counter-tenors were still very new and perplexing to North American critics and listeners. (Was it Oberlin or the English counter-tenor Alfred Deller who, when asked if he was a eunuch, replied, "No, I'm unique!")

Alfred Frankenstein, long-time critic of the *San Francisco Chronicle*, attended, mainly because San Francisco was planning to include the work in its fall season. His was a mixed response, complaining that the words were no more than 10 percent intelligible, despite the reasonably good acoustics of the Queen Elizabeth Theatre: "Britten might have done more to make the text clearer, but, probably, he was not interested in tampering too much with Shakespeare."[65] Although Goldschmidt trumpeted to the press that this was the finest Vancouver Festival so far, through no real fault of his own the festival found itself in financial hot water.

It was in 1963, the festival's final year, that Rubes found himself in another juicy role — Falstaff in Otto Nicolai's *The Merry Wives of Windsor*. He interpreted it freely and with aplomb, much as he had done with Leporello five years before, claiming that he made Falstaff more of a Don Giovanni than a clown. He felt that the audience welcomed this. Rubes also liked the role because it sat so well for his voice. The opera was given five times, with Martin Rich as the able conductor. (Goldschmidt had left the festival by now.) Actually, Rubes had begun honing his Falstaff interpretation during the COC's tour of *The Merry Wives* in 1960, when it gave sixty-three performances in Eastern and Western Canada. Rubes had shared the role with Andrew MacMillan. Torel had staged the work, and Mario Bernardi had conducted it admirably at the piano.

There was also a teaching engagement in British Columbia in the summer of 1963. Both Jan and Susan had been invited to teach at the

Patricia Snell (Alice Ford), Jan Rubes (Falstaff), and Elsie Sawchuck (Meg Page) in Nicolai's Merry Wives of Windsor, *COC tour, 1960.*

Okanagan School for the Arts in Penticton, where Jan had given a recital the previous summer. Jan would teach singing, and Susan, drama. But, first, there was time, between Vancouver and Penticton, for a family holiday on the West Coast — their three little boys were now nine, seven, and five. They started with a trip to Disneyland in Southern California and a visit with Chris's godmother, Laraine Day, whose marriage to Leo Durocher had broken up. Then the five Rubeses motored up the scenic Pacific coast from Los Angeles to San Francisco. They stopped to visit the William Randolph Hearst "castle" on the way, but, unfortunately, visitor tickets to this extravagant and magnificent house were sold out that day. From San Francisco they continued north to Crater Lake and the Grand Coulee Dam, and then back to Canada and Penticton.

Steven Henrikson was one of Jan's students at Penticton that summer. He remembers Jan putting together a potpourri of Tchaikovsky songs and operatic excerpts titled *The Forest Prince*. Henrikson had been assigned only a speaking role since he had arrived late, but Rubes weakened and gave him an aria. Henrikson's gratitude knew no bounds.[66] Meanwhile, Susan, firm, strong-willed, and uncompromising, worked with students on a scene from Tennessee Williams's *Sweet Bird of Youth*. Henrikson spoke warmly of the Rubeses' hospitality. When they heard that he was sleeping in his van, they invited him to stay in their cottage in nearby Naramata and even hosted a birthday party for him, for which Jan wrote a poem. After the teaching term, Susan heroically drove the three children back across Canada and home. By this time the Rubeses were living in Toronto. Jan flew directly to Italy for a reunion with his brother — more about this later.

Engagements had been continuing in the U.S.A. In Washington he sang Rocco in *Fidelio* in 1957. He even managed to get some qualified praise from Paul Hume of the *Washington Post*: "He was sonorous as Rocco, though the top of his voice refused to give the first quartet its due. But his open knowledge of the stage and the meaning of his role was valuable all evening."[67] Hume may have forgotten that he had panned Jan five years earlier. It is only artists who remember bad notices, not critics.

In New York, Thomas Scherman's Little Orchestra Society continued to do interesting and seldom-performed works. In December 1957, it presented Berlioz's *L'Enfance du Christ* at Carnegie Hall. Rubes sang the bass role, as he would there at Christmas for the next two years. It is one of the composer's finest scores and has a uniquely serene quality. The 1959 performance, perhaps the best of the three, had Scherman conducting his orchestra and the American Concert Choir, with Jan Rubes, Martial Singher, Léopold Simoneau, and Florence Kopleff as soloists.[68] John Briggs of the *New York Times* spoke of the work's "quality of reverence and its hushed tender intimacy." The next night, Rubes, Singher, Simoneau, and Frances Bible (replacing Kopleff) sang the work at Constitution Hall in Washington. Robert Shaw led the National Symphony and the combined choirs of several local universities. Day Thorpe of the *Washington Evening Star* thought the music ravishing: "a series of vocal and orchestral cameos, each of which seems to be the perfect expression of the Biblical picture."[69] He lauded the entire quartet and singled out Simoneau for special praise. The brilliant Shaw also had much to do with the work's successful interpretation.

Paul Hume reviewed Rubes astutely in a program of operatic excerpts by the Civic Opera Society in January 1959 at Washington's Roosevelt Auditorium: "It was the evening's noblest moment in his delivery of Sarastro's 'O Isis und Osiris' from Mozart's 'Magic Flute'." Hume also commented on Rubes's "remarkably well handled Coronation Scene and Death of Boris from Moussorgsky's Boris Godounoff. It was interesting to note how warm his voice became in the second scene, which he sang in Russian, precisely as it had in the Mozart, in German."[70] Hume went on, "There are moments in the role of Boris that lie too high for Rubes to negotiate at all. But his voice in the middle and lower registers has a voluminous sound that he used with great effect. Working in front of a plain curtain in the middle of a spotlight, he yet captured the drama and tenderness, the fear and hope of the final scene with telling impact." Tenor Jacob Barkin, the brother of Toronto's Leo Barkin and cantor of a large Washington synagogue, also sang on the program.

The indefatigable Thomas Scherman conducted two other rarely performed works in which Rubes had roles. The first was Hugo Wolf's opera *Der Corregidor* (*The Magistrate*), done in concert form at Carnegie Hall in January 1959. The *New York Times* had little good to say about it: "It is flat; its characters are puppets; its music is only occasionally arresting. Wolf's tunes are not operatic. They do not characterize; they do not function dramatically or even theatrically."[71] Rubes played the mayor, Juan Lopez. A year later, Scherman tackled Berlioz's opera *Beatrice and Benedict*, in concert form at Carnegie Hall. *Beatrice* is based on Shakespeare's *Much Ado About Nothing*. The querulous *Times* critic Howard Taubman found the work lacking in humour and, despite its good choral and orchestral writing, said it was not "stageworthy."[72] There was English narration instead of French, although the musical numbers were sung in French. Taubman praised the Beatrice (Irene Jordan) and said that Rubes, who was Don Pedro, "sang creditably." Scherman's adventurous spirit in doing infrequently heard works drew few words of commendation from the critics.

There was still the occasional engagement farther afield. The Ukrainian-born conductor Igor Markevitch valued Rubes's qualities and chose him to be the bass soloist in the Verdi *Requiem* at the Palacio de Bellas Artes in Mexico City in June 1957. The next year Markevitch, who had been appointed the permanent conductor of the Montreal Symphony, did the *Requiem* at Montreal's Notre Dame Church with Rubes and three other fine soloists, Leontyne Price, Nell Rankin, and the Canadian Richard Verreau. Rubes took note of Price's voice and, quite uncharacteristically, commented on her sexiness in a phone call to Susan. Rubes said later that the great soprano was a cheerful and good-natured colleague.

Earlier that year, Markevitch, who was a rather stiff conductor, had had the same quartet of singers do Beethoven's Ninth Symphony. Rubes revealed the drama of the bass part but found its vocal demands beyond his reach. A week before the *Requiem*, Markevitch did Haydn's *The Creation* at Notre Dame. Rubes's fellow soloists were Lois Marshall and Nicolai Gedda. Marcel Laurendeau's Jeunesses Musicale Choir did the great choruses. The Haydn and Verdi works were good vehicles for Rubes. He earned panegyrics from Thomas Archer of the *Montreal Gazette* for his "noble" singing in *The Creation*: "His 'Rolling in Foaming Billows' was magnificently done, especially when he concerned himself with that gleaming stream flowing through the silent valley. I also enjoyed his manly performance of 'Now Heaven in Fullest Glory Shone'."[73]

Rubes made a major public appearance in Montreal as Osmin in eight performances of *Die Entführung aus dem Serail* at the Comédie

Canadienne in August 1960. Rather bizarrely, the opera was sung in German, but the spoken dialogue was in English. One might ask why not French dialogue in French Canada? (The 1960s would be the decade when French Canada would assert itself linguistically, change its educational system, and free itself from the Catholic Church's stranglehold on the province's life generally.) Eric McLean of the *Montreal Star* wrote, "If French-speaking opera goers felt slighted, they weren't missing much, since at least half of the English spoken was unintelligible to their English speaking compatriots."[74] That English was not the first language of four of the leads — Léopold Simoneau (Belmonte), Pierrette Alarie (Constanze), Jean-Louis Pellerin (Pedrillo), and, of course, Jan Rubes (Osmin) — partially explains the difficulty. Claude Gingras of *La Presse* thought Rubes a comic discovery and wrote that he would like to hear more of his beautiful and rich voice.[75] Whatever, the singing was excellent, and Rubes was praised for playing Osmin so well, musically and dramatically. The actor George Bloomfield — he would later be a prominent TV film director — had the speaking role of Selim Pasha and remembered, forty-five years later, how bizarre his servant Osmin looked hanging from a fig tree. He remembered, as well, his own dress (a gold costume with a gold turban and slippers that twirled at the tips) and, of course, the pretty young women of his harem.[76]

To jump ahead forty-three years to 2003, Rubes played Selim Pasha in a costumed concert version of *The Abduction* with the Toronto Philharmonia, conducted by Kerry Stratton at the admirable George Weston Recital Hall. William Littler wrote how it "triggered distant memories of one of the first real stars of the Canadian Opera Company. For those of us with lengthy teeth, Jan Rubes will always be our basso, and it was wonderful to find him back (replacing the slightly younger Gordon Pinsent) on the operatic stage."[77]

CHAPTER 8

1959–1969: Move to Canada;
Family life; Opera and musical comedy

A t the end of 1958, when the Rubeses told their New York friends that they were moving to Toronto, Eli Wallach and Anne Jackson, Leonard and Phyllis Hirschfeld, Gil and Morfy Glaser, Kim Stanley, Thomas Sherman, Mitch Miller, and the Czech pianist Rudolf Firkusny were among the well-wishers. There were three consecutive days of going-away dinners and parties. The Wallachs, the Glasers, and the Hirschfelds would remain lifelong friends. Leonard Hirschfeld, a prominent periodontist, and his wife, Phyllis, moved in elite musical circles and included violinist Isaac Stern among their close friends. They also socialized with Leonard Bernstein, Byron Janis, and Mstislav Rostropovich. The three Hirschfeld sons were roughly the same age as the Rubes boys, and the families exchanged visits at Christmas and the like. The Hirschfelds would visit the Rubeses in Canada for skiing, and on trips to New York the Rubeses would stay in the Hirschfelds' Park Avenue apartment or at their country house at New City, about an hour's drive northwest.

The move was inevitable. Much as Jan and Susan loved New York, most of Jan's work was in Canada. Furthermore, if they stayed in New

York, they would face the prospect of their children growing up in an increasingly violent city and attending schools in a deteriorating public school system. And, living in Toronto, Jan could have more family time with his wife and sons. The downside of the move was that Susan would be giving up a New York acting career, playing in top TV shows such as *Kraft Television Theatre* and *Studio One*. She could only hope that her experience would lead to work in Toronto. However, in this regard, the only encouraging words came from Esse Ljungh, a prominent CBC radio producer of drama shows.

The family's trip from New York to Toronto was hair-raising. A snowstorm forced their car to a halt in central New York State, and, unable to find accommodation, all five of them, including one-year-old Tony, had to spend the night in the car. After arriving in Toronto they moved into a temporary home on Florence Avenue in Willowdale, a suburb north of the city. Ground was broken in May for their new house, a few blocks away. It would be ready later in the year.

The Rubeses already owned a piece of Canada. On the advice of Czech-Canadian friends a few years before, they had wisely bought land on Georgian Bay west of Collingwood, some 160 kilometres north of Toronto, for just $300. A cottage of sorts was built, followed by other purchases of land in the area, including, with neighbours, a hundred-acre apple farm. Jan, credulous and trusting, listened to his friends and made some unnecessary purchases of equipment, about which he knew little. The farm didn't do well, and the Rubeses did not become apple farmers. Down the road, at the Blue Mountain ski resort, Jan would eventually buy a chalet. Of course, he taught his three sons to ski, and ski well, as was only fitting for a former junior ski champion of Czechoslovakia.

Their new Toronto home, at 59 Sumner Heights Drive, was worth waiting for — five levels built on a hill with its back perched on the edge of a steep ravine. The builders constructed a retaining wall above the ravine and then installed an outdoor swimming pool. The Sumner Heights house would be their home for more than two decades. Jan and Susan were, in many ways, ideal parents. They did not lay down strict rules of behaviour with their children. Noise was allowed in the house, except when Jan was studying a role for an opera or a play. Although Jan travelled a great deal, the boys never felt his absence. Why? Because he

The Rubes family, 1959. Jan's portrait of a neighbourhood child is on the wall.

was such an attentive father when he was home. He prepared a small puppet theatre, with puppets sent from Czechoslovakia. It was placed immediately above the television set. John Gray, who interviewed the family at their home, described how Jan used the theatre:

> … to give performances in which the characters and plots are drawn from the enchanting, violent repertory of fairy tales. One needs only to see the enthusiastic response of his children to one of these performances and the dead blank grey eye of the TV set beneath it, to understand how some of those whose youth predates such wonders as television are anxious to preserve the immediacy and the spontaneity of amusements and pleasures in which there is active participation.[78]

Rubes had enlisted the generous services of the COC costume designer Suzanne Mess to make new clothes for the puppets. Neighbourhood children would often join the Rubes boys for his shows. They stretched out on the floor on mats and applauded mightily.[79] Chris, for one, loved to sing the witch's song from Jan's version of *Hansel and Gretel*. Jan said, "I was luckily born into an era when, if we wanted music, we did it ourselves. My mother played the piano, my father the fiddle."

Jan taught his sons all the sports he knew so well, including swimming. He took them fishing and for rides on Toronto's new subway, and with Susan they went on family picnics and the like. He was also an incorrigible gamester and taught many parlour games to his boys. There were track meets, football games, and baseball games that Jan organized for all the children in the neighbourhood. He loved every minute of it. Come Easter, he would hide Easter eggs for the boys to find, and he continued to do this even after they had grown up. Working around the house was a must for Jan when he was home between engagements, and he taught his sons how to help him. Father Rubes's reputation was such that when Jonathan invited a friend for a week to the busy Collingwood cottage, the friend asked, "Are we going to have to work?" Jan always had projects in hand at home and at the cottage, and he carried them out well. According to his sons, he had the talent to build anything he wanted

— within reason. Friends of the children, impressed, would say wistfully, "I wish my father could do what your dad does." Another thing that few other fathers could do was draw and paint. Jan, talented like his father, drew several portraits of his sons. One wishes he had done more.

There were only three other houses on Sumner Heights Drive besides the Rubeses' house. A barn and a farmer's field were around the corner. It was about a mile away from the nearest primary school, and the children walked the distance unescorted. They were not pushed to study, although Jan stressed that whatever they did they were to do their best. The parents' only query about schoolwork was "Have you done your homework?" But they never checked to see if it was done. They all took music lessons but showed little or no talent. Some said jokingly that Susan's genes may have been the cause, since she was not notably musical. The children played tennis admirably as they got older, as did Susan, who, in self-defence, took up the game in her early forties — Jan was her teacher. Jonathan claims to have beaten his father when he was seventeen, but his father has not confirmed this. A typical doubles match when the boys were in their teens was Jonathan and Chris against Jan and Tony.

Jan also took the boys fishing in Georgian Bay when they were at Collingwood. They would catch the fish but Susan would clean them. Susan tells the story about Jan helping a disgruntled Tony on one fishing trip. Young Tony had caught nothing, unlike his two older brothers. Surreptitiously, Jan took a fish from the pail, swam under the boat, and hooked it on to Tony's line. Some father! Some fish story!

Adult visitors to the Sumner Heights house found it an extremely active household, with a hostess who prepared outstanding meals and a host who was hospitable to a fault. Jan would often bring his opera colleagues to the house at the end of a tour or after a run of a show. It was always a much welcomed treat for all. Altogether, family life looked up for the Rubeses in Toronto as it never had when Jan was on the New York–Toronto merry-go-round of tiresome commuting.

Susan, however, missed her work immensely. Granted, she had three children to take care of, but nevertheless she had hoped for some opportunities to act — on stage, television, radio, or in films. But nothing happened. She felt, and probably rightly, that her slight New York accent was holding her back. It was a time when Canadian theatre and broadcasting were still in the throes of trying to sound English or very cultivated North Atlantic. She tried to initiate soap operas in Canada but found no takers. It is of interest to note the many soap operas given in Canada almost sixty years later. No matter, one of Canada's undeniably leading acting talents got no work in her adopted country. She would have to look for other outlets.

Although there were rumours back in 1958 that *Songs of My People* would be dropped, it did continue, as we know, until 1963, when it was finally put to bed forever. The 1960s saw more opera for Jan. In 1960, Rubes did Figaro, one of his favourites, for the COC. The Swiss bass-baritone Heinz Rehfuss was the Count. He had appeared with several European opera companies and was one of the first international singers that the COC engaged. *Figaro* was a great success thanks to Jan's characterization. It was conducted by Walter Susskind, who had, in 1956, succeeded Sir Ernest MacMillan as conductor of the Toronto Symphony Orchestra (TSO). Jan had a similar success the next year when he did Kecal in *The Bartered Bride* in English at the COC.

It was in 1961 that the COC moved its Toronto venue to the new three-thousand-seat O'Keefe Centre. Jan was never as happy there as at the Royal Alexandra. After his operatic singing career wound down years later, he commented in retrospect that he had long been critical of the COC's move. Although the Royal Alexandra had no orchestra pit, it was, Rubes said, "wonderful for the singers…. The move did a lot of damage to young Canadian singers. Facing that huge hall makes you want to push the voice, and, if you do that, after a certain amount of time you are bound to hurt your voice." Speaking from his own experience, Rubes said, "I was brought up in the smaller opera houses of Europe, and carefully trained as a singer-actor. Position, holding your own, and preserving your vocal powers was considered far more important than running across a stage, but I had to forget about a lot of that at the O'Keefe." As for the audience, Rubes went on, "At the Royal Alex … you're never far away from the stage, no matter where you sit."[80] O'Keefe's size prevented performers from making any real contact with their audience.

Doing *The Bartered Bride* in English prompted Jan to comment favourably about doing operas in good English translations rather than in their original language.[81] Using English translations would continue to be a popular subject for debate among opera people for the next thirty years. Rubes wrote about Kecal, "My appearances last fall ... marked the fifth time I had to study this opera, which was written in my native Czech to start with. I sang it first in Czech, then in German, then in Toronto in a rather poor English translation, then in New York City Center and Washington in an even worse translation, and, finally in 1961, in the much better one at the O'Keefe Centre. Three hundred pages to be relearned five times!" Rubes went on to mention a tenor he knew of who had learned Don José for *Carmen*, first in French, then in Italian, and finally in English. Not easy.

Translating opera is fraught with peril. Rubes described his singing Raimondo in *Lucia di Lammermoor* in English at an American university:

> [In the final act] the distraught tenor [Edgar] rushes on stage inquiring about his beloved Lucy. Raimondo stops the tenor and says this immortal line — "Whither dost thou bend thy footsteps? She on earth has ceased to be." The student audience broke into laughter. A few moments later we arrived at the tragic climax in which the tenor proclaims, trembling with emotion, "Thee I follow — [meaning the deceased Lucy] — Life is hateful where she is not." Whereupon he draws his sword and fatally wounds himself. Raimondo then reacts with a long drawn-out "A-h-h" and this profound statement: "Fatal rashness." The students found it hilarious.

However, despite such sorry happenings, Rubes continued his defence of doing operas in English — if well-translated, of course — by referring to the 1958 Vancouver Festival's *Don Giovanni*, which was done in Italian. "I had some incredibly clever and funny lines ... even a few off-color jokes. Nobody in the audience laughed. Why? Quite simply, they did not understand Italian." On the other hand, for *The Barber of Seville* in English in Charlottetown, "the audience laughed with us and at us.... It was a joy to perform." As today's operagoers know, Surtitles in opera houses have made the translation issue redundant, although

English is still needed in more informal settings and schools where Surtitles are not available.

In 1962, Rubes played Hunding in Wagner's *Die Walküre*, the COC's first production of a "Ring" opera. Herman Geiger-Torel — not a Wagner fan — did his best, but the production was modest and lacked energy and passion. Rubes's Hunding received little attention in the press. The *Globe and Mail* said almost condescendingly that he was "appropriately barbarian in both appearance and voice. Indeed I have only one criticism about his strongly acted interpretation. His enunciation fell below the general standard of the production."[82] So much for Rubes, whose German was fluent. Remember Görlitz during the war? That same year he was the King of Egypt in *Aida* at the Seattle World's Fair. It was a joy for him to work with the fine cast — Irene Dalis, Gloria Davy, Sandor Konya, and Robert Merrill.

Something new was added to Jan Rubes's work in 1961 that had a favourable impact on his future — musical comedy. Winnipeg's Rainbow Theatre booked him to do the male lead in its summer outdoor production of Rodgers and Hammerstein's *South Pacific*. This marked Jan's beginning in Broadway musicals that call for a fortyish and handsome man with an indeterminate but required foreign accent. Insiders were reminded how Susan Rubes had told George Crum ten years before not to help him unduly in English — not only because she liked his accent but also because she realized that it might be useful in the future.[83] She was right.

South Pacific's principal characters are a U.S. Navy nurse, Nellie Forbush, and a middle-aged French planter, Emile de Becque. They fall in love on a Pacific island occupied by American forces during the Second World War. Significantly, the show deals with racial prejudice, a topic rarely addressed in American theatre and films at the time. De Becque, a widower, is the father of two brown-skinned Polynesian children. Nellie Forbush must come to terms with this, and she does. The colour issue arises with a different twist when a U.S. Marine lieutenant falls in love with a native girl. Both affairs drive home the message that racial tolerance and equality is the rule.

When *South Pacific* had opened on Broadway in 1949, the great operatic bass Ezio Pinza was, to everyone's surprise, cast as de Becque, and

he was unforgettable. The delightful Mary Martin played Nellie Forbush. The Broadway show ran for 1,925 performances, followed by 802
more in London's West End. Nine years later it was filmed, and the film
was as successful as the stage show.

The de Becque role was tailor-made for Jan Rubes, although it took
some years for Canadian producers to wake up to this. In the mid-1950s,
he had been offered a two-year contract to do the role on tour for an
American company while the show was still playing in New York, but it
would have meant giving up his other commitments, which, at the time,
was impossible. The Winnipeg show had only two weeks' rehearsal, but,
as Toronto's Barbara Franklin — who played Nellie — said, Rubes, as
usual, "gave a lot of himself, was emotionally involved, and inspired
others."[84] Jan loved the role and said that it needed to be done with
much passion. De Becque has only two songs, "This Nearly Was Mine"
and "Some Enchanted Evening," but what songs! The latter had been
a standard encore piece for Rubes since the show opened in New York.
Now he felt closer to it than ever. The only song in the show that actually
related to the South Pacific was "Bali Hai."

Winnipeg's response was overwhelming. *South Pacific* ran for twelve
performances in August to capacity crowds. Rubes and Franklin made a
delightful pair. A perceptive critic wrote, "Rubes's voice, big and beautiful [amplification was required for the outdoor production], caresses the
frankly sentimental lines of South Pacific's lovely tunes, and gives them
impact and freshness. Even the essentially banal character of Emile de
Becque is defeated by his personality and presence."[85]

Theatre Under the Stars in Vancouver produced *South Pacific* the
very next year, with Rubes as de Becque. Jan had recommended Barbara
Franklin for Nellie Forbush, but the producers preferred a local actress,
Barbara Jay. She was alarmingly attractive and forward, and in rehearsals
of love scenes she stirred up Rubes more than he liked. Such happenings
notwithstanding, he applauded her work in an interview with Gail McIntyre of the *Vancouver Province*: "She is delightful to play with as an actress."
The show was held over and ran for sixteen nights, with more than four
thousand in attendance for each performance. Susan visited him halfway
through the run. He had been staying at the Sylvia Hotel on English Bay,
a favourite of show business people. Jan jokingly registered her as Susan

Douglas, which caused some consternation with the front desk staff. (It was 1962, when certain protocols prevailed for hotel room occupancy.) After the matter was clarified, the cheeky desk clerk, upset over the entire matter, shouted after the two of them, just as they got into the elevator, "Certainly the nicest young lady you've had visit you this week."

Two years later, in May, Rubes did thirteen performances of *South Pacific* in Sydney, Nova Scotia. The Rotary Club was the sponsor, and a rollicking town parade launched the run. In November 1966 he did twelve more shows in Lethbridge, Alberta. D'Arcy Rickard of the *Lethbridge Herald* was completely carried away with Rubes, calling him "masterly. He is a great and wonderful performer. Perhaps you think he's too good for this cast. That's where you're wrong. He's too good for ANY cast — but you'd never know it…. He is also very humble and warm-hearted."[86]

Jan (Emile de Becque) after opening night of South Pacific, Vancouver, 1962.

Not every opera singer takes to singing pop and folk tunes as well as Jan Rubes did. John Reeves produced a summer radio show, *Cantando*, in 1965 that had Rubes back in his MC role with guest singers. He did only three of the six programs; the other three were led by the engaging Dinah Christie. Zither, harp, flute, piano, and guitar were used at one time or another on the programs. Among the singers were Margaret Rowan (later Zeidman), Mary Morrison, Kathy Newman, Maxine Miller, and Denise Angé. There was a lot of variety in the music for each show, in contrast with the well-defined themes of the now defunct *Songs of My People*. On one of Rubes's programs he sang, with some hesitation, the Paul Robeson favourite "Lindy Lou." It was a valiant effort and it came across, as it should have, as Rubes, not Robeson. Robeson, by this time — sadly — was almost a forgotten man, thanks to the Cold War. On hearing tapes of *Cantando* forty years later, one wishes it could have stayed on radio longer than it did.

The political situation in Czechoslovakia had loosened up sufficiently to permit Jan's brother, Mirek, to attend a psychiatrist's conference in Milan in July 1963. (Mirek had to leave his family behind as insurance that he would return home.) Jan sent Mirek funds to help him make the trip and then flew from Vancouver, after his work in Penticton, to join him in Milan. The devoted brothers had waited thirteen years for this reunion. Mirek was still one of Czechoslovakia's leading psychiatrists, this despite his having abandoned the Communist Party and having a brother living abroad as a political refugee. He was now in the midst of confronting the drug problem in Czechoslovakia, which the embarrassed government staunchly maintained didn't exist. After two days of conferencing, Mirek and two colleagues went on with Jan to Venice. The joyful time was over all too soon. Jan travelled back to London, saw friends there, and then, at Peter Ebert's invitation, visited Glyndebourne, where Ebert was staging Stravinsky's *The Rake's Progress*. Ebert, a fine director, did it again at the Royal Conservatory Opera School a few years later.

The following May, Jan's mother, Ruzena, now seventy-five, arrived in Toronto. Her visit got considerable press coverage. Since the Cold War had begun, few living behind the Iron Curtain had been able to travel to the West. Ruzena had been studying English using Czech television lessons and had, therefore, a rudimentary knowledge of the language. Jan, who had not seen his mother since 1948, remembered her as being on the bossy side — and she hadn't changed. Ruzena also had trouble connecting with her grandchildren. In looking back, Susan attributes this to her limited English. Susan treated her mother-in-law dutifully, as a daughter-in-law should — but warily.

Jan took Ruzena to Winnipeg in June, where the Rainbow Theatre had booked him as Baron von Trapp in Rodgers and Hammerstein's

The Sound of Music. It was in Winnipeg that Ruzena gave a cautiously optimistic report to the press on contemporary life in Czechoslovakia.[87] The reporter, Robin Taylor, wrote that Mrs. Rubes thought the majority of Czechs were better off materially than ever before. Only business-men whose enterprises were seized by the state are "distressed." There are shortages of consumer goods from the West, and not enough money generally to purchase items in the shops. Ruzena pointed out that, cul-turally, things hadn't changed since her son left the country. Every city still had its own opera house and opera company subsidized by the state. By contrast, she noted, Toronto had neither. She also said that Czechs have an uninhibited interest in Western Europe and North America — teenagers wear jackets emblazoned with "I love the Beatles" and the American Pete Seeger is one of the most popular singers on Czech ra-dio. (Right-wing Americans frowned on Seeger and his music.)

What she didn't talk about were the trials of living under commu-nism. Her granddaughter Eva would write years later about her own sheltered life in Czechoslovakia at that time and about how the news was so censored that all you got was good news.[88] "Movies were full of communist interpretations, and everyone was happy, had good jobs, and had everything they needed. That was the visible public life. At home we had other information, to be told only in the home and to trusted friends."

Ruzena had a wonderful time in Canada. When she couldn't handle a phrase in English — she evidently did quite well — Susan translated for her. She stayed with the Rubes family until the end of November, a long visit to be sure, especially for her daughter-in-law, who suffered from Ruzena's veiled — and not so veiled — criticisms of her as wife and mother.

Back to *The Sound of Music*. It is a slightly fictionalized story of the Austrian von Trapp family — the widower Baron, his seven children, and the governess-teacher, Maria, who ultimately marries the Baron. It tells how they escaped from their beloved Austria after the Nazi occupation. They then became prominent in the U.S. concert world as the Trapp Family Singers, but this is not part of the show. *The Sound of Music* opened in New York in December 1959 and ran there for 1,443 performances, followed by another 2,385 in London, and, in 1965, a film with Julie

Andrews and Christopher Plummer as the leads. The New York stage production won five Tonys.

Rodgers and Hammerstein may have been delighted with their show, but others have said that it is too lightweight, overly sentimental, and even saccharine at times. The lyrics are not substantial, and the music is good but borders on the cliché. All in all, it was a step backward, artistically, in the evolution of the American musical comedy. Clearly, the American and English public did not agree. It would be the most popular musical Rodgers and Hammerstein ever wrote, and it pleased all kinds of people. The founder of the Royal Conservatory Opera School, Arnold Walter, for one, claimed to have seen the film eleven times. (Who can forget Julie Andrews's clear and expressive voice?) Unknown to most, Plummer's songs were — over his objections — dubbed in. Plummer, a fine pianist (he almost became a concert pianist instead of an actor), could also sing well — but his singing the role was ruled out.

Winnipeg's 1964 production was only a modest success. Part of the reason was Carmel Quinn, playing Maria, who was a charming Irish actress but had a limited voice. The von Trapp children all did well. Rubes could do no wrong in Winnipeg and was received enthusiastically. Winnipeg had had a love affair with him since 1960, when he had been made an honorary citizen by the city fathers for acting as the singing host of Songs and Dances of the Nations, a major Manitoba folk festival at the Rainbow Theatre. It had featured about five hundred performers representing seventeen countries.[89] Also acknowledged in that formal recognition was his fine work on *Songs of My People*.

And then Rubes took on still a third Rodgers and Hammerstein role in 1969, the King in *The King and I*. This show had opened on Broadway two years after South Pacific and was a hit in both New York and London, thanks in many ways to brilliant casting. The memorable English actress Gertrude Lawrence played Anna — it was Lawrence who had initiated the idea of adapting a show from Margaret Landon's *Anna and the King of Siam*, an account of a young English widow who goes to Siam (Thailand) in the 1860s to teach the King's sixty-seven children. At first Lawrence wanted Cole Porter to do the music but went along with the Rodgers and Hammerstein team. In a stroke of inspiration, they cast Yul Brynner as the King.[90] So there was a fifty-plus actress playing a young woman and a young actor playing a fifty-plus man! It was a fine show; both leads won Tonys. The motion picture that followed had Deborah Kerr and, of course, Brynner, bald as ever, in the principal roles. Rubes enjoyed being the King. After shaving his head *à la* Brynner he was accused of playing the part too much as Brynner had. He certainly danced as well as Brynner had in the dance scene with Anna (Evelyne Anderson). A Winnipeg critic called him "a superb actor, he has fire, he has spirit, and an incandescent touch that lights the part."[91] It was a show for the whole family with much visual appeal: "Fireworks concluded the first act and a colorful Siamese parade wends its way through the aisles during the second act."

CHAPTER 9

1961–1968: Opera and concert tours;
National Arts Centre; Mozart at Stratford;
Expo and the Prague Spring

T here was no busier singing actor in Canada during the 1960s
and 1970s than Jan Rubes. Fearing, as always, that he would
run out of money to support his wife and children, he was still
taking on all the engagements he could find, everything from strenuous operatic tours to CBC radio and television shows and recitals. He
particularly enjoyed playing Bluebeard in an English concert version
of Bartok's *Bluebeard's Castle* in March 1961 with the TSO. Walter Susskind conducted. The opera was composed for two characters, Duke
Bluebeard and Judith, sung by Ilona Kombrink. Bluebeard begins by
showing Judith his castle and she responds lovingly, "Coming, Coming, Dearest Bluebeard," and then, "If you reject me and drive me out,
I'll never leave you, I'll perish on your icy threshold." Judith, needless
to say, suffers the same sad fate as his other loves. The work was done
effectively and was well-received. This performance led to an engagement to do a fully staged version of *Bluebeard* in French with CBC-TV
in Montreal. Here Rubes worked with another soprano, Claire Masella.
With hair dyed a light purple, he played a captivating if not bewitching
Bluebeard.

In 1962, the COC toured *La Bohème* in English in both Eastern and Western Canada, giving a total of eighty-one performances. James Craig was the pianist-conductor for both tours. He would do other COC tours in the future, spend four years with Sadler's Wells in London, and then teach at and later head the Toronto opera school. Rubes played Colline, as usual, alternating performances with one or two other basses or bass-baritones. Craig jokingly commented that he never saw a touring singer with as many friends as Jan Rubes — friends with whom he often stayed in lieu of the barely standard hotels chosen by the COC. Jan made a practice of carefully learning the names of at least ten guests at post-concert receptions and saying good night to them by name. In this way he made many friends and dropped the seeds for future engagements and hospitality. Vocally, Craig said, Jan had become expert in handling the high E-flat in Colline's aria: "He would clap his thigh loudly as he sang — or didn't sing — the note, to distract the audience."

The next year the COC toured *Cosi fan tutte* — in English. George Brough, as always solid and reliable, was the pianist. Rubes shared Don Alfonso with Peter Van Ginkel, but Van Ginkel was ill for part of the eastern tour and nearly all of the western tour and Rubes had to sing almost all fifty-three performances. Ten years had passed since he first did the opera, and he continued to question its plot, which he thought fundamentally silly. In looking back, Rubes spoke highly of his fellow singers who dealt well with the difficult ensembles of *Cosi* after tiring bus rides and unpredictable weather, the root cause of their constant colds. He, himself, had more than the usual number of singers' sore throats, and kept Toronto ear, nose, and throat specialist Dr. Douglas Snell busy helping him cope with them. Was it because he was straining his voice or singing too much?

In an interview with Thelma Dickman for the *Imperial Oil Review*, Jan's colleagues on this *Cosi* tour echoed his views about the rigours faced when touring.[92] One soprano told Dickman, "Touring company members are very rare animals. You must have the voice of a bird, hide of a buffalo, stamina of a bull, and adaptability of a chameleon." Dickman concluded that singers need poise, do-it-your-self talent, the ability to sleep anywhere, and resilience in body and spirit. Tour manager Ernest Adams added, "Touring is incredibly hard on a singer. Everything a

singer does — sleeping, eating, drinking — *everything* affects his voice....
Even in hot weather, he'll be bundled up to the eyebrows because he's
afraid of catching a cold."

The Vancouver-based management group Overture Concerts became a bright spot on the Canadian performing arts scene in the early
1960s. It was directed by the bassoonist George Zukerman. He and
Rubes soon struck up a warm professional relationship — they saw eye
to eye on bringing good music to a wider public.[93] Born in England of
American parents, Zukerman went to the High School of Music and Art
in New York and then earned an MA in music from New York's Queens
College. He was the principal bassoonist in the Vancouver Symphony
until 1963, when he decided to pursue a solo career. Imaginative and
resourceful, he developed, as an adjunct to his playing career, a large
number of concert clubs that functioned throughout Western Canada,
Northwestern U.S.A., and Alaska, much like those run by Columbia's
Community Concerts.

Overture managed both the COC's western tours and Rubes's recitals. The opera tours were demanding — there were often great distances
between performances, and, in the north, outside temperatures could
get as low as minus fifty-five degrees centigrade. Rubes remembers one
flight when, as they were debarking from the plane in frigid temperature,
the pilot warned the cast to breathe very deeply to avoid internal injury.
Schedules were tight, and days lost in travel had to be kept to a minimum. More performances in less time meant more income for the COC
— and Overture. Nevertheless, there were few complaints from COC
singers, assuredly Canada's operatic pioneers.[94] As for the Overture recitals, Zukerman did his best for his artists and for his concert clubs.

Rubes had Overture in mind when he asked the Hungarian-Canadian writer George Jonas to write an opera libretto for him. He told
Jonas, "Opera has a wide and enthusiastic audience. I think that any
genre that is sufficiently alive to be worth producing is also worth writing new contemporary pieces for. In fact, that is the only way to keep
it alive."[95] Rubes, the innovator, envisaged a light opera for a male and
female singer and a small instrumental ensemble — together they would
function as a touring group. At first, Jonas expressed ignorance as to
how to go about the assignment, but he got to work after conferring with

another Hungarian-Canadian, the composer, conductor, and pianist Tibor Polgar. Jonas, age thirty, had already written a number of radio and TV scripts for the CBC since his arrival in Canada in 1956. Polgar, thirty years Jonas's senior, had been a prominent musician in Hungary. Following the 1956 uprising in Budapest, he had gone to Germany where he conducted a group of Hungarian refugees (the Philharmonia Hungarica) for a time before moving to Toronto.

Jonas's first impression of Rubes was that he was "European, charming, sophisticated" and of Ilona Kombrink (Rubes's choice for the female lead) that she was "strikingly beautiful and, to my way of thinking, as typically American as anyone can be." His opera, titled *A European Lover; A Musical Satire Disguised as an Opera* or simply *A Musical Satire*, is an ironic commentary on how an unnamed European lover tries to seduce a beautiful North American woman. He doesn't quite succeed, despite his European ways, because her American style is a formidable obstacle. All he wants is an affair, while all she wants is a husband. Things then turn around. He wants to marry, but, alas, she doesn't, since she fears she will lose a lover and end up with a typically inferior European-style husband who neglects his wife and engages in extramarital affairs. How does it end? They look forward to a conventional marriage and a home in the suburbs.

Jonas and Polgar met with Kombrink in New York to help tailor the role for her. Polgar was a traditional composer, and he came up with attractive if ordinary music. According to Jonas, Rubes wanted the opera revised because he felt that it was not sufficiently effective and entertaining throughout its entire thirty minutes. Jonas and Polgar did as they were told.[96] The piece was designed for a small stage, and Rubes supplied the only real prop, a parking meter. A company of singers and instrumentalists was assembled and given the name Jasan Ensemble — after Jan and Susan. A full program was designed with the short opera as the main focus. Performances would start with several operatic duos with string quartet, then the opera, and, after intermission, love music and a grand finale.

A European Lover had a workshop performance at Toronto's York University in early March 1966. The *Globe and Mail*'s Kraglund was devastating: "It might have made a very funny, if not musically original, ten-minute skit. The musical influences ranged from Romberg to Gershwin — including a Nelson Eddy–Jeanette MacDonald duet called 'A New Kind of Love,' and an instrumental interlude, while the lovers retired to the bedroom, which had all the passion of an English tearoom serenade."[97] Kenneth Winters was equally critical: "Its hand-to-mouth progress up and down the chromatic scale and the draughty corridors of American musical comedy made it sound like New York dinner music at a classy restaurant in Old Budapest."[98]

Additions and cuts were made at Vancouver rehearsals in April. How did the public respond? Some thought the opera too highbrow,

Jan Rubes, Tibor Polgar, and Ilona Kombrink, The European Lover, *1966. Arthur Polson in insert.*

others too lowbrow. Yes, it *was* an urbane, sophisticated tale, and Rubes found that making some introductory remarks helped audiences to enjoy it. Arthur Polson, concertmaster of the Winnipeg Symphony, led the Jasan String Quartet, a first-class group. On a romantic note, Kombrink and the violist Istvan Jaray fell in love on the tour and later married. (Five years later Rubes would meet Jaray and Kombrink again when he was soloist with the symphony in Kenosha, Wisconsin. Jaray was its conductor and Kombrink was on the voice faculty of the University of Wisconsin in nearby Madison.)

The Jasan Ensemble tour began in earnest in British Columbia in April, and gave twenty-two performances in thirty-two days and travelled twenty-eight thousand kilometres, nearly all of it by car. Remarkably, the tour's total budget was only $15,000. The composer and librettist received $700 each, Rubes got $2,640 — including payment for all of the preliminary work he had done — and the rest of the group earned fees ranging from $1,000 to $1,650 — hardly very much money for all they did. Musical pioneers, you bet![99]

The COC continued its up-and-down existence at Toronto's O'Keefe Centre as the 1960s wore on. Geiger-Torel decided to cast a male Prince Orlovsky (Rubes) in Johann Strauss's *Die Fledermaus* for the 1964–65 season. Although Joanne Ivey had been a splendid Orlovsky at the Royal Alexandra in 1955, she had more or less retired from singing. Torel may also have surmised that, because of family obligations, she wouldn't want to tour. First there was an eastern tour, followed by the Toronto season, and then a western tour. Jan, up to the task, got good public and press response everywhere, even in Toronto, where the problems of O'Keefe's impersonal, oversized auditorium had to be addressed.

The blasé and bored Prince Orlovsky gives a lavish party in Act II. Everyone who is anybody is in attendance. At the party he sings his one major song, "Chacun à son gout." He tells his guests to drink with him and threatens to throw a bottle at them if they will not. It has become almost a tradition for Orlovsky to extend his song and comment on other worldly matters. John Kraglund, an expert in qualifying his reviews, had to admit that Rubes stole the show with his ad libbing. "He was given a chance for a bit of contemporary comment on Canadian drinking habits, biculturalism, and the flag issue."[100]

Four years later, Rubes had another opportunity to ad lib the Orlovsky aria. It started like this. In May 1969, he played in a show, *Party Day*, at the Studio Theatre of the new and breathtaking National Arts Centre (NAC) in Ottawa. The governor general, Roland Michener, and the new prime minister, Pierre Trudeau, accompanied by staff member Timothy Porteous, came backstage to congratulate the cast after the show. At that encounter Porteous got the idea of writing something for Orlovsky in the upcoming COC performances of *Fledermaus*, to be given

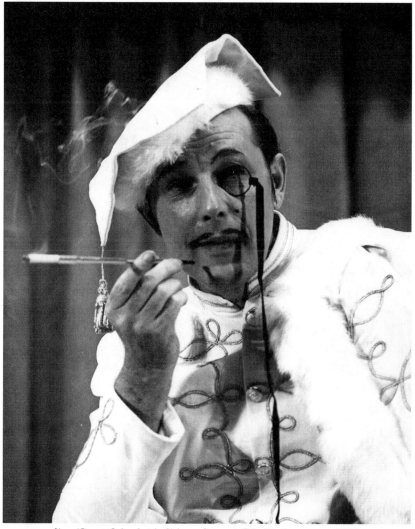

Jan (Count Orlovsky) in Johann Strauss's Die Fledermaus, *1964.*

Prime Minister Pierre Trudeau congratulates Jan after a performance of Party Girl *at the NAC, 1969. (Heath Lamberts and Jack Winter are in the background.)*

first in Toronto and then at the NAC. Porteous had been one of the writers of the hit McGill show *My Fur Lady* and was an accomplished lyricist. (He would later be the director of the Canada Council.) Rubes, pleased with the result, decided to try it out in Toronto before singing it in Ottawa.[101] He had, of course, been inserting other lyrics in previous *Fledermaus* performances. How did it go? He had what every performer dreads, a total blackout. The orchestra stopped. Rubes bit the bullet, stepped to the front of the O'Keefe stage and explained to the audience that he was trying something new for the prime minister (Trudeau was present) and asked if he could start it again. The full house applauded and urged him on. And so Rubes took on the new prime minister with Porteous's lyrics — to an appreciative public. The Toronto *Telegram* reproduced them:

Some criticize the clothes I wear,
And some the words I use,
And some the fact that I react to insults and abuse.
When people talk to me this way I tell them
"je m'en fou,
I'll say the things I want to say and do the things I do."
Society should not suppress our eccentricities,
Feel free to think and speak and dress in any way you
please.
Forget your inhibitions, do what you want to do.
There are no prohibitions.
Chacun à son gout.
Away with old traditions.
Chacun à son gout.

In clothes and cars I've always tried
Whatever has appealed.
And as for girls, I've not been tied, I like to play the
field.
So now that I'm in public life — Though critics think
it's vile,
And matrons claim I need a wife — I haven't changed
my style.
I choose a place that's far from town
Where two can quietly sup.
But long before the lights turn down,
The whole darn press turns up.
I'll ask for legislation that tells them what to do.
A man needs relaxation —
Chacun à son gout.
Leave me my recreation.
Chacun à son gout.[102]

The exuberant response prompted Rubes, now on a roll, to remove
Fifi's slipper — Orlovsky had been flirting with Fifi (the maid) — and
pour champagne into it. Then he drank the champagne from the slip-

per! Fifi (Riki Turofsky) complained that she had to walk about with a damp slipper for the rest of the act.[103]

Prince Philip was at the NAC performance that followed and met with the entire *Fledermaus* cast after the show. At first, Geiger-Torel excluded those playing minor roles, such as Fifi and Dr. Blind (Steven Henrickson), but, according to Turofsky, Rubes intervened and made the point that all members of a cast are equal and should be treated as such, which they then were. As always the generous Rubes was thinking of others. Turofsky felt that she learned more about stagecraft while working with Rubes than at any other time in her training and career.[104] As for Trudeau, he was also at the NAC. As the "wild" 1960s were drawing to a close, Canada had a prime minister who was youthful, daring, and intent on burying the image of Canada as stuffy and conservative. And he clearly liked Orlovsky's words. It was a wonderful time.

The Stratford Festival's music took some new twists after its 1959 season of *Orpheus in the Underworld*, but it was not until 1964 that Stratford's artistic director, Jean Gascon, brought opera back. He was interested in doing the three Mozart–da Ponte operas because of their dramatic qualities. The first was *The Marriage of Figaro* at the Avon Theatre, which seated about nine hundred. It had just been renovated and the orchestra pit was adequate. *Figaro* opened in early August, and Stratford watchers promptly compared it favourably to Stratford's finest musical productions of the past, *L'Histoire du Soldat* and *The Rape of Lucretia*. Rubes played Figaro and he was in his glory. Playing the show nine times allowed him to hone the role and make it his own. Cornelis Opthof, a fine baritone, joined Rubes in winning acclaim as the Count. Richard Bonynge conducted.

Even before Rubes left Stratford at the end of the run, the company's producer, John Hayes, had booked him for a repeat performance of *Figaro* in 1965. This time Stratford planned twenty-nine performances, later stretched to thirty-one. Such a long run of one opera was unheard of in operatic circles, but Stratford, with unerring instinct, went ahead with it. Rehearsals began in mid-June, and the final performance was at the end of August. There were some cast changes for the better. Lilian Sukis, just out of opera school, was a fine Countess, and even more striking was Gwenlynn Little as Susanna. Both would go on to careers

Elizabeth Mawson (Marcellina), Jan Rubes (Figaro), Howell Glynne (Dr. Bartolo), and Gwenlynn Little (Susanna) in Mozart's Marriage of Figaro, *Stratford, 1965.*

Jan Rubes (Leporello) and Cornelis Opthof (Don Giovanni) scheme in Mozart's
Don Giovanni, *Stratford, 1966.*

in Canada and abroad. The most significant change from the preceding year was Mario Bernardi as conductor. He took the work in hand at Gascon's bidding. His tempi made his version fifteen minutes shorter than Bonynge's. It was Mozart at its best.

Stratford moved on to *Don Giovanni* in the summer of 1966. Bernardi and Gascon worked together again, and Gwenlynn Little was even more beguiling as Zerlina. Kenneth Winters believed that, of the cast, she did the best singing.[105] But it was Rubes's Leporello that won the most accolades. Winters said, "He had the easiest and most practised stage deportment within the traditions and the circumstances of a famous role." Composer Lorne Betts, in the *Hamilton Spectator*, went a step further. "The word 'portrayed' is used intentionally, for Rubes does not merely sing or act. As always, he becomes the personage required ... Leporello — a comic, something of a fool, even a demeaning servant. Yet when the final scene came, he was moved to a greater stature of humanity by the inevitable result of his master's life."[106] Add this to the other critiques Rubes had earned in this role and one wishes we could have had a permanent record of it on film.

However, he did pay a price for this marathon. After twenty-nine almost daily performances he went directly into rehearsals as Méphistophélès in *Faust* at the COC. Sung out, he got poor reviews. Conductor Pierre Hétu's slow tempi didn't help. The *Globe and Mail* wrote that Rubes was the "major disappointment.... He seemed to have left his upper register in Stratford and was not even secure in his middle and lower ranges."[107] It was a bitter pill to swallow. His voice problems persisted. Accordingly, over the next few years, he took intermittent lessons with Howell Glynne, a Welsh bass who had done Baron Ochs in the COC's 1963 *Der Rosenkavalier*. Rubes explained thirty years later:

> My whole vocal production had been geared to the Czech language. That's perhaps why the great opera houses like the Met were denied to me. I would have had to study for another three or four years to switch my Slavic method to the *bel canto* method. But by that time I was thirty years old and felt the hell with it.... So, with my acting ability and my early experience, I was able to

get through many different roles, even those I had no
business singing.[108]

In the end, Glynne's instruction was no more helpful than Herbert
Janssen's a decade before.

Stratford's *Don Giovanni* had a major problem — Irene Salemka, the
Donna Elvira, became sick after opening night. The understudy, the
young soprano Carrol Anne Curry, stepped in and did the major role
the next night. (Stratford didn't give singers nights off as is usual in opera
houses.) There was a quick piano run-through of her scenes early in the
day that upset Gascon, since she was clearly nervous and acted artificially.[109] Rubes intervened and, with Gascon's permission, took her through
the rehearsal, encouraging her all the way. Thirty minutes before the
show began Jan visited Carrol Anne in her dressing room and gave her a
picture postcard of the Prague Estate Opera House. He told her that this
was where *Don Giovanni* had its premiere 180 years before. Then he said,
"Now listen to me. You will be very very good in this part. But you must
remember that we know this show and you are just starting in it. So if at
any time you don't know where you are or what to do next just stand still
and we'll adjust to you. Pay attention to Mario and sing and you will be
great." He then kissed her on the cheek and left the dressing room. The
insightful Rubes was with her on stage; she knew she could depend on
him. The same could be said about the watchful Bernardi.

Yes, she did fine for the next week and then, exhausted, asked to be
replaced. The more experienced Sylvia Grant stepped in for the remainder of the run. Curry, a leading artist manager of singers forty years
later, admired Jan for always being prepared, for being so good on stage,
and for having a truly natural instinct for performance. He never raised
his voice in rehearsal discussions and was a tower of strength generally. She thought Cornelis Opthof's Don that summer worked beautifully with Rubes's Leporello. Opthof went on to an international career,
working with Joan Sutherland, among others, as well as singing with the
COC for many years.

There remained the third of the da Ponte operas, *Così fan tutte*. It is
perhaps the most difficult of the three to stage and, as we know, not a
Rubes favourite. Stratford tackled it in English the next summer. Again,

Left: Jan Rubes (Don Alfonso) and Gwenlynn Little (Despina) in Mozart's Cosi fan tutte, *Stratford, 1967.*
Below: Jan Rubes (Pasquale) and Alexander Gray (Dr. Malatesta) in Donizetti's Don Pasquale, *COC tour, 1967.*

Bernardi conducted and Gascon directed. Kenneth Winters got to the point in one short paragraph with his comments on this problematic work of genius: "Hearing his [Mozart's] delicate score at work on da Ponte's pat vacuities is like watching a benign and magical sun change plastic flowers to real ones, or like seeing the dawn of enlightenment smooth an unlovely painted grimace into a warm, relaxed smile."[110] The cast was spotty, other than Rubes's Don Alfonso and Gwenlynn Little's Despina. Winters wrote that Little was "the ideal soubrette — prompt, brisk, bright, candid, and dazzlingly intelligible…. [She] made the maid an entirely persuasive and captivating figure." Stratford did other staged works and concerts in the ensuing years, but Rubes would not be there again until 1975.

There was perhaps an even more significant triumph the spring preceding *Cosi fan tutte*, when the COC did its most adventurous tour to date — eighty-three performances of Donizetti's comic opera *Don Pasquale*, given throughout Western Canada, the Northwest Territories, and Alaska. Ruby Mercer, the editor of *Opera Canada*, went with the group to observe it in action. She was thrilled. Mercer wrote about the company's "visit to the fox farms and the wild game reserve in Yellowknife, and shopping for mukluks, parkas, fur hats, and gloves."[111] The opera singers thus not only appeared as true citizens of the north, but more particularly were protected from the severe cold. Anchorage's leading citizens provided a sourdough pancake breakfast for the company, after which they watched a baseball game in the snow with the players wearing snowshoes. Yes, despite the cold, the company enjoyed the Far North.

This tour was especially rewarding for Rubes as Pasquale, since it gave him room to create anew the role of the old and misguided buffoon who wants to marry a young woman (Norina). His scenes, including those with his crony Malatesta, ranged from amusing to sidesplitting. Nevertheless, much as Rubes sought laughs, the opera's stock in trade, he made Pasquale a real person rather than a caricature, and brought him to life vividly for the audience. The role was also ideal for his voice. James Craig was the pianist-conductor. This was the last time the touring company used piano accompaniment. An orchestra of sixteen players did the eastern tour of *Pasquale* — thirty-three performances — from January to March 1968, with John Fenwick conducting.

More tours followed into the 1970s, with Rubes in the casts, and all done in English: *The Barber of Seville* (Don Basilio), *Orpheus in the Underworld* (Pluto), and *Cosi fan tutte* (Don Alfonso). They were even longer and more tiring tours than the early COC tours, but Rubes never flinched. Now into his fifties and older than his fellow touring members, he found poker games at the back of the bus a welcome distraction. And, as always, he enjoyed seeing old friends in towns where he had played in the past.[112] He had an attack of kidney stones in Kentucky on the *Cosi* tour and went to a hospital for relief. After a number of doctors and nurses pranced in and out of his room to study the problem, Rubes, by now totally exhausted, asked the African-American nurse sitting at the foot of his bed, "What's the big occasion? Could I please be left alone to rest?" She replied, "Oh, Mr. Roobs, just keep talking to us. We all ain't never been outa Kentucky, and this is the first time we hear a real Canadian accent!"

There were other anecdotes. Sometimes, sleep wasn't guaranteed on tour. One year Rubes had a room next door to a married couple who were also in the cast. "They had the most incredible way of making love. The first time I heard it I was going to call the police. I thought something was wrong and he was going to murder her. He was slapping her, she was screaming, and the bed kept banging against my wall. But then I realized that was their way."[113] Raffi Armenian, an Egyptian trained in Vienna, shared the conducting on the *Barber* tour with John Fenwick. He was young and new to Canada, and this was his first Canadian conducting assignment. He praised Rubes's collegiality and his kind and supportive words and deeds well beyond the call of duty.[114] Armenian later became conductor of the Kitchener-Waterloo Symphony, and he did such good work there that the city named its concert hall after him.

Meanwhile, the Rubes boys were all doing well at school. Chris, an excellent student but fiercely independent, overruled his parents' wishes and refused to apply to the University of Toronto Schools (UTS), a school for bright boys, Grades 7 to 13. (It is now coeducational.) Jonathan, more malleable, did go to UTS when his time came at the end of the 1960s. Tony went to a private school, St. George's College.

A major event in the Rubes family's life — as it was for many other Canadian families — was a trip to the Montreal Exposition (Expo). They visited it soon after it opened in the spring of 1967 and then headed for

Stratford, where Jan was singing in *Cosi*. Mirek's daughter Eva, who was twenty-two, joined them there. She had been able to travel thanks to a temporary lifting of travel restrictions by the Czech government. A psychology student at Prague's Charles University, she spoke little English. "My three cousins looked at me as if I had three heads," she said, and, by her own admission, she acted as if she was from a different planet. She got to know them all. She found that Jan had the same love and admiration for her father as he had for Jan.[115] Jan never missed an opportunity to bring Mirek into the conversation. Susan's mother, Charlotte Weinberger, her husband, Eddy, and their twenty-two-year-old son, Clem, also visited the Rubeses that summer. All of them went to Expo in October, where the wealthy and generous Velan family, also immigrants from Czechoslovakia, hosted them.

Expo was a salient event in Canadian history. Montreal's Mayor Jean Drapeau claimed that it marked Canada's arrival into "modernity" and it introduced the world to Montreal.[116] More than 50 million people visited it. The Czech Pavilion at Expo had the most impressive foreign exhibit, and those of Czech ancestry were deservedly proud. Expo spurred CBC-TV on to give a series of four half-hour musical variety programs in September devoted to Canada's many national groups. Jan Rubes was host on the fourth program, which included artists from Germany, Portugal, and Czechoslovakia. Ivan Romanoff led the orchestra and chorus.

Eva and Clem fell in love and were married the next year. Jan, as the surrogate father, gave the bride away. They spent their honeymoon at the Rubeses' Collingwood cottage. Family ties were strengthened — Susan's half-brother was united with Jan's niece. The couple has continued to see the Rubes family through the years. Eva credits Susan Rubes with being the "influential power" in her life.[117] Susan's initiatives at Young People's Theatre (more on this later) inspired Eva to start her own fitness academy in New Jersey, where she and Clem settled.

The Rubeses, encouraged by the newly relaxed communist government, visited Czechoslovakia in the spring of 1968. They met relatives and toured the country. All five of them travelled and slept in a small van. Mirek's thirteen-year-old son, Honza (Jan), went with them. After their travels in Czechoslovakia, the Rubeses joined Joan Sutherland, her husband, Richard Bonynge, and their son, Adam, on the Adriatic coast in southern Yugoslavia. Joan described the trip:

> [Jan was in] quite a high emotional state after his first visit to his homeland in many years…. The swimming was perfect, right in front of the house, and we set up tables and chairs and beach umbrellas where we played cards and mahjong and the sun worshipers took advantage of the splendid weather. One of the great delights was to hear the local fishermen calling early in the morning something that sounded like "Ree bay," which we knew meant … fresh sardines grilled on the barbecue for lunch. No matter how many, we could always have eaten more.[118]

The two families also took a sightseeing trip to the southernmost part of the country and, thanks to Bonynge's faulty navigation, nearly found themselves in unfriendly Albania.

Jan and Susan sent Honza back to Prague by air, as they headed west and home. It was about two weeks before the end of the "Prague

Jan and John Reeves at work on the CBC Czech broadcast, 1969.

Spring." Czechoslovakia stepped backwards to reintroduce bans on travel and other limitations to a freer life. Warsaw Pact countries invaded Czechoslovakia in August and the Czech government agreed to a Soviet occupation in October. The days were numbered for liberal prime minister Alexander Dubček; he was replaced by Gustav Husák the next year. It was a memorable summer in more ways than one.

The unhappy events in Czechoslovakia and the Soviet Union's occupation of the country got much attention in Canada. Radio producer John Reeves wrote a long and moving poem dedicated to the people of Czechoslovakia, with special reference to his friend Emil Zátopek, the long-distance runner who had defied the Russians. Reeves also cited the work of Federico Garcia Lorca, the Spanish poet who had died in the "service of truth." (The Falangists had killed Lorca at the beginning of the Spanish Civil War.) In rich and moving language, Reeves's poem tells how Czechoslovakia coped with the Russian invasion without losing its honour, its tolerance, and its resistance to the occupiers. Reeves read his poem in English in the summer of 1968 on the CBC. A year later, also on the CBC, Rubes read it in Czech, as translated by Josef Cermak. On the same broadcast, Hanna Malinowska read it in a Slovak translation by Kamila Strelková. Reeves wrote music for organ, two violins, and cello to accompany the readings.

CHAPTER 10

1962–1970: A film career begins;
Prologue concerts; More travels

In the middle of the hectic summer of 1962 — all of Rubes's summers were hectic at this time in his life — he got a call from Walt Disney Productions in Burbank, California, for a screen test. Two weeks after he took the test Disney cast him as the Finnish farmer in *The Incredible Journey*. The stars of the movie were a bull terrier, a Siamese cat, and a Labrador retriever! The film, based on a bestselling book by Sheila Burnford, is about three animals who trek across three hundred kilometres of Canadian wilderness to find their way home — a supposedly true story. Fletcher Markle directed and James Agar did the screenplay and production. (Disney did a second version of the film thirty years later — *Homeward Bound: The Incredible Journey*.)

The film was shot in Canada, with the Rubes scenes done in Bolton, outside of Toronto. As with his first film, *Forbidden Journey*, music found its way into the script, with Rubes singing a Finnish folk song. And, as with *Forbidden Journey*, he wasn't too happy about the sound treatment, even though it took little if anything away from the film's quality. The *New York Times* said it was "about as gentle, warm, and lively a color movie as any pet owner could wish…. Against beautiful, autumn-tinged terrain, the camera frames some of the most disarming, four-footed trouping ever filmed. The three animals are marvelous."[119] Actually, a number of cats were used during the shooting because it was difficult to get one cat that would repeat his or her actions. And, commendably, there were several leading Canadian actors in the film, although none were mentioned in the *Times* review. Rubes, the opera singer, held his own. Filmmakers took note.

In June, just prior to *The Incredible Journey*, he had sung in the prestigious Seattle opera production of *Aida*. He also did a Czech show for the CBC International Service and recorded songs by Rosy Geiger-Kullman, Herman Geiger-Torel's mother. Mrs. Kullman, a modest composer, lived in New York and periodically gave Jan her latest songs for him to study and, she hoped, perform. He was always polite and supportive — aware, of course, that her son was an important employer — but he found the songs mostly uninteresting. The recordings have remained on the shelf ever since.

For the next six years until 1969, Rubes did musicals, operas, and recitals, but no films. Then the Ontario Educational Communications Authority (OECA) asked him to play the lead in a TV film series, *Castle Zaremba*, sixteen half-hour shows with stories devised to catch the interest of new Canadians learning English. The shows dramatized real situations that new Canadians were likely to encounter — how to get a social insurance card, relations with the police, buying on an installment plan, legal marital relations, and the like. Each enactment was followed by a language lesson based on its content, with booklets and tapes to assist students. The number of Canadian immigrants was growing rapidly and many did not attend English classes. This program was a thoughtful and resourceful substitute.

Castle Zaremba was staged in a house on Walker Avenue in central Toronto. Rubes plays Kazimir Zaremba, a one-legged retired Polish army colonel who runs a rooming house where he lives with his common-law English wife, Flo. The cast included Vladimir Valenta, who had played in the memorable Czech movie *Closely Watched Trains*, and several other well-known members of the ethnic community. The series began in November 1970, and the dramatizations were first class. Conversations were slowed down slightly to help listeners understand the words.

There was an ironic twist to this worthy program. Because OECA had to answer to the CBC about its programs, they had to be strictly educational. *Zaremba* was, indeed, educational, but it was also highly entertaining. The CBC went so far as to assign TV producer Eric Koch to monitor the show — shades of Eastern European communist countries. Koch, obviously embarrassed, told Sid Adilman of the *Toronto Star*, "My point of view is not that of a middle CBC official, but that of someone who had to learn English as a second language, for I myself am an ethnic. My opinion is that *Castle Zaremba* is very original and very well done."[120] In the end, the CBC did nothing to stop the *Zaremba* programs.

Despite the unquestionable success of Rubes as a film actor in *Castle Zaremba*, it took still another four years for him to be cast in his next film, *Lions for Breakfast*. It may have been because he didn't have an agent, a must in the movie, drama, and TV world. In fact he didn't engage an agent until the late 1970s, when he signed on with first Lynne Kinney and then Gayle Abrams. Then again, he was so busy touring and had become so involved in live concerts for children, of which more below, that he didn't look too energetically for film roles.

Lions for Breakfast was, like *The Incredible Journey*, primarily a children's film. Two brothers, Zanny and Trick (why such names?), team up with an aged and eccentric drifter, Count Ivan Stroganoff (Rubes), who drives an old converted school bus and owns a piece of land in the hinterland that he won in a poker game, or so he says. Ivan adopts the two brothers, and they, in turn, adopt him. The three of them and Moby, Ivan's loyal German shepherd, go through a series of adventures as they journey to Ivan's piece of land, where they hope to find a retreat from the hectic world they live in. One adventure starts when they wake up one morning to find their bus on a lion farm, surrounded by lions.

It was a charming movie. Rubes earned the adjective "superb" from three different film critics. However, it was Clyde Gilmour of the *Toronto Star* who saw most clearly the substance in the Rubes performance:

> Made up to look much older than his off-screen appearance, Rubes earns his laughs and provides a few touching moments as well. Ivan is the sort of ageless, life-loving friend-of-humanity that Anthony Quinn tried to

copyright a decade ago in Zorba the Greek. Rubes is naturally a flamboyant performer, but he knows when to rein himself in for the intimacy of the camera. The character he depicts here is an authentic individual, not a stereotype or a cartoon.[121]

This was the multi-talented fifty-five-year-old Rubes. Perhaps his singing voice was beginning to fade, but not his grasp of film and stage, not his joy in portraying people and experiences in words and music. The full life he was leading and the children he and Susan were raising gave Rubes sagacity and judgment that could help him in new pursuits.

Now more film engagements were coming his way. The CBC-TV drama *The Day My Granddad Died* was one of the better ones. It was shot in the winter of 1975–76. The one-hour film has Rubes playing the crusty patriarch of a Polish-Canadian family living on a Manitoba farm during the Depression. He is angry that his daughter Irena eloped with a man he disapproved of. Years later she returns with her son, Alexie, to

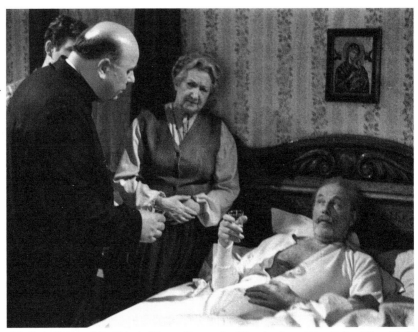

Vladimir Valenta (The Priest), Hanna Poznanska (Grandma), and Jan Rubes (Granddad)
in The Day My Granddad Died, *1976.*

meet his grandfather. Proud, stubborn, and loveable, Granddad finally makes peace with himself, his God, and his family before he dies. The film was shot in the middle of a typically frigid prairie winter. Rubes told Sid Adilman that the chill factor made it feel like sixty degrees below zero. Then, always ready with a laugh, Jan couldn't resist telling Adilman: "A makeup girl brought me inside and tucked my hand under her blouse to get rid of the frostbite. Now that's one of those unexpected nice things that can happen when you're an actor."[122] Granddad was a typical "accent" role — Jan would have many more. He played the curmudgeon so admirably that he was nominated for the annual ACTRA award for television acting. However, he lost out to Donald Sutherland, who played Norman Bethune, the great if controversial Canadian surgeon, in another CBC-TV show. Considering Sutherland's prominence in the acting world, it was an honorable defeat, especially for one whom people still considered an opera singer.

Jan and Susan were very conscious of what children want for entertainment. In 1962, when Tony was three years old, Susan, itching to get back to the theatre, began producing weekend children's dramas at the Royal Ontario Museum's Children's Theatre. She first collaborated with actor Tom Kneebone in putting together *Alice in Wonderland*. From this came more shows, until 1966, when Susan formed Young People's Theatre (YPT). She moved to the Colonnade Theatre on Bloor Street in central Toronto, and her first YPT production there was *The Looking Glass Revue*. The show called for audience participation; Susan explained that a YPT objective was to involve children in theatrical experiences. Thus members of the young audience took to the stage to create short dramas of their own. Herbert Whittaker of the *Globe and Mail* described how a four-year-old who was given a bowler hat, a plume, and a baton became a conductor. "Those who didn't make it to the stage participated by answering questions and making animal noises."[123]

Susan next sought bookings for Prologue to the Performing Arts, a non-profit organization formed in 1966 by a small group of volunteers who believed that exposing children to the performing arts should be an integral part of their education. They managed to convince school boards and arts organizations in Greater Toronto and, later, throughout Ontario to sponsor their productions. In its first season Prologue offered schools a package of three one-hour performances — a play, a ballet, and an opera — tailored for intermediate students, Grades 7 to 9. Thirty-seven schools purchased the first package — a total of 111 performances. Susan, who would soon be a driving force at Prologue, produced two one-act plays in the organization's first round. She recommended an early Tennessee Williams play, *This Property Has Been Condemned*, but school boards thought it might be a bit strong for young people. She then countered with Eugene Ionesco's *The Lesson* and Anton Chekhov's *The Marriage Proposal*, both in their own way as "strong" as the Williams play. For opera, Geiger-Torel staged Pergolesi's *buffa* eighteenth-century intermezzo *La Serva Padrona*, and Celia Franca of the National Ballet prepared a variety of dance excerpts, standard and contemporary.

A reporter took note of the children's almost unanimous approval of *La Serva Padrona*, an opera about a servant girl who lures her master into marrying her.[124] Many children were seeing opera for the first time, while others who had watched opera on TV had never been to a live performance. After the show, the cast handled questions from the audience: "How do you play a funny role and still keep a straight face?" "Is your husband jealous when you have to kiss a man on the stage?" "Can you take opera in high school?" "Does it cost much to put on an opera?" The children were clearly involved in the performances. Given good management and willing supporters, Prologue couldn't miss, and it went from strength to strength in the ensuing years. Over Prologue's first fifteen years, school boards paid about 70 percent of artist fees. The Ontario Arts Council (OAC) covered the remaining 30 percent.

Prologue soon broadened its offerings and sponsored solo artists and small groups to perform for children from pre-kindergarten to Grade 6. Jan Rubes first did a few concerts with pianist Sandra Atkinson and then worked more extensively with the soprano-pianist Margaret Zeidman, an especially able musician. She also played a small harp and learned guitar — adequately for these concerts.[125] Margaret affirmed that Jan loved to be with children, and his work with them over the next twenty years proved it. Together, they gave fourteen programs in the winter and spring of 1970 and eighteen more in the fall. Prologue's business report that year confirmed that the programs were well-received and that there were so many requests for Jan's songs that an anthology of his material was proposed. It never happened.

Mary Carr, a former high school teacher of music and member of Elmer Iseler's Festival Singers, was Prologue's first administrator. Arts writer Michael Schulman interviewed her in the spring of 1973, her fourth year with Prologue.[126] She stressed how important it was that performers like children and to find art forms to which children relate. "Audiences of children, we find, are very discriminating. Somehow, it's very hard for a performer to really fool a student audience." Carr wanted performers "to really give to the kids." Soprano Anne Linden, who did seven years of Prologue concerts with Rubes, believed that he did just that.[127] Anne had first worked with him as Diana on the 1970–71 western tour of *Orpheus in the Underworld*. When the company was stranded for two days in Ketchikan, Alaska, because of a snowstorm, a considerate local jeweller entertained them with parties two nights running. There was a lot of informal singing with Anne accompanying at the piano. She was a lovely young woman with an endearing smile, and Jan took note of her as a future partner for Prologue concerts. Anne later commented on his cheerfulness and pleasant disposition, even when he had to pick her up for concerts at 7:30 a.m. Yes, he treated the children as equals, and this helped his relations with them. It also helped that many children had seen him on TV in *Guess What?* More about this later.

Jan sang programs for pre-kindergarten, kindergarten, and early primary grades. With the youngest ones sitting in the front of the room, he would usually begin programs — no more than thirty minutes long — with folk songs, followed by something bright and sparkling. As he went on, he might move into songs in languages other than English. With two voices and two instruments there was much variety in their selections. Jan often played the guitar and, according to Anne, played it well, and the piano not so well. She related how he would tell children to take a stretch halfway through a show while she sang Gretel's dancing song from *Hansel and Gretel*. Then he would cleverly inform them that they had just taken part in an opera, and he would carry on to describe the opera using spoonerisms, such as "the bittle lird ate all the cookies." He usually concluded programs with songs from shows such as *Sound of Music* or arias such as Papageno's from *The Magic Flute*. Rubes's reputation spread.

Bermuda's educational authorities invited him and Anne Linden to give children's concerts there in April 1977. But Anne's two-week-old baby girl had just died. Heartbroken, she tried to get out of the trip, but Jan convinced her otherwise. To help her morale, her husband and three-year-old son accompanied her. Everything went well, and in fact it must have done her some good; Anne gave birth to twins nine months later.

Working with YPT led Jan to branch out into play directing. In November 1971 he directed *Seven Dreams*, based on a Hans Christian Andersen tale, at the St. Lawrence Centre's Town Hall. The centre had opened the previous year. Its Town Hall, later named the Jane Mallett Theatre, seats about 480 and is a popular concert venue. YPT did *Seven Dreams* as a black box production, a technique that uses a dark stage with light illuminating only the performers to the exclusion of everything else. Rubes, with help from an expert collaborator in black box technique, Mikulas Kravjansky, used puppets and assorted technical devices. The audience was glued to its seats.

Seven Dreams is about little Hjalmar's visit with his grandpa. Grandpa tells him he must get to bed and sings him a song about "Little Ole with his umbrella." This sets off the seven dreams in which Ole figures prominently. Hjalmar's first dream is about his lost dog and how he might get

Jan sings for children, 1971.

him back. In another, Hjalmar has to swim for his life during a hurricane, and in yet another he has a nightmare. The opening night was sold out, and Herbert Whittaker credited the interest to Jan Rubes, "whose knowledge of stagecraft has been demonstrated in almost every opera Canada has produced, and how he had joined forces with the black box technicians as director of this children's play."[128]

And now to another Prologue venture, *Il Segreto di Susanna* (*Susanna's Secret*) by Ermanno Wolf-Ferrari, a charming one-act opera premiered in Munich in 1909. Actually this intermezzo is a light-hearted copy of *La Serva Padrona*. The work is cast for two singers, Count Gil and his wife, Countess Susanna, and an amusing third character, their servant, Sante, who remains silent. It was ideal for Prologue. Robert Sherrin directed, Murray Laufer prepared a flexible set, and George Brough was the pianist-conductor. Rubes and Cornelis Opthof alternated in the Count and Sante roles. Lois Gyurica (later McDonall) was impressive as the Countess. It is a story about how the Count — a non-smoker — smells tobacco in his house and suspects his attractive wife of infidelity. (The assumption is that only men smoke.) After some marital turmoil, Gil finds that it is Susanna who smokes, and the two of them end up puffing away happily as the opera closes. It is unlikely that this kind of fun with cigarettes would be acceptable in the twenty-first century. As expected, *The Secret* (in English, of course) went over very well and by the end of April 1969 had played fifty-six times in Ontario schools. John Kraglund wrote about a question period he attended following a performance: "The students seemed more interested in operatic problems than in Susanna's secret vice of smoking."[129]

After a ten-year lapse, Rubes took on several recitals for Columbia Artists in the spring of 1969, with Tibor Polgar at the piano. Clearly, Columbia's relations with Rubes had improved. And his directing began to extend beyond YPT. Later that spring he directed Sigmund Romberg's *The Student Prince* for the Hamilton Light Opera Association. It was an amateur cast, but one of reasonable quality. At least one of the singers, according to Rubes, could have been working professionally if living in Europe.[130] Jan believed that there were insufficient opportunities in Canada for young singers. Canada needed a kind of minor league — smaller opera companies where they could gain experience. Whatever, the show sold out all six performances, in spite of almost everything going wrong during the rehearsal period. The scores arrived late and were virtually useless, the cast scrambled from one rehearsal location to another in the evenings, performers wandered in late, and the Gretchen had to be replaced twice. The cast, stage crew, and choreographer all praised Rubes: "He knows exactly what he is doing…. He understands what you are going through to learn a part…. Jan will tell them it's a tough musical but he's made it easy, he really has."[131]

He fitted in his Hamilton engagement while doing performances of *Il Segreto di Susanna* for Prologue, getting ready for *The King and I* in Winnipeg, and flying to Idaho and Wisconsin to do what had become a Rubes specialty, Cimarosa's twenty-minute one-man comedy, *Il Maestro di Capella* (*The Music Master*). He had been doing *Il Maestro* since 1964 when the Toronto Chamber Orchestra, conducted by Jacob Groob, staged it at the Royal Alexandra Theatre. John Beckwith wrote at that time that the maestro "in two accompanied recitatives and two contrasted arias, alternatively lectures, mimics, cajoles, and exults the members of his orchestra in song. Rubes's versatility made him a natural for the part, and he brought it off with secure vocal effects over a wide gamut of ranges and tones, and with a performing zest that was both tasteful and exuberant."[132]

When Rubes appeared as the maestro with the Calgary Philharmonic two years later, Jamie Portman of the *Calgary Herald* wrote, "He was the very model of a somewhat addle-brained music master attempting to conduct a chamber orchestra in rehearsal…. Mr. Rubes is a genuine personality with a marvelous stage presence and a capacity for projecting the wit and humor of his buffo portrayals … coaxing his orchestra, benignly guiding his violins and violas, and waging vocal warfare with his main enemies, the double basses."[133] His performances remained fresh. Lorne Betts, a composer and music critic of the *Hamilton Spectator*, wrote of Rubes's maestro performance in 1971: "For the solo artist it is a serious exercise in operatic know-how. The introvert, completely engrossed in what must be done, suddenly becomes the extrovert and thrusts his vast accomplishments over the footlights into one's very lap. This takes artistry of the very highest order, and this, if nothing more, is Jan Rubes's greatest skill."[134]

Jan and Margaret Zeidman did a series of concerts for Overture Concerts in April 1970 in Alberta, Saskatchewan, and Manitoba. Zeidman thought Rubes a fine travelling companion in more ways than one.[135] He laid out procedures for who pays for what, he was always prudent but not stingy when spending money, and he insisted that they carry their own baggage and use his hot plate and coffee maker for their evening meals. On free nights Jan would watch hockey games on TV and enlighten Zeidman about the game's finer points. A friend had given Jan a number of Mozart tapes and he played them so incessantly on the rented car's tape machine during their long trips from town to town that a point was reached when they both confessed that they were tiring of Mozart.

When Rubes arrived in a city or town, he promptly called friends made on previous visits. If he didn't have friends he made them. In Yorkton, Saskatchewan, they met the program co-ordinator for a children's concert, who introduced herself as Margaret Al-Deri. Rubes, curious about her surname, found that her husband was Egyptian. With his unique brand of chutzpah and charm, Rubes asked her to invite him and Zeidman to dinner, which she did. It was a great meal! Going back through Yorkton later in the tour, Rubes contacted Mrs. Al-Deri. Again she invited them to dinner, this time full of Egyptian delicacies thanks to her Egyptian sister-in-law who was visiting at the time. Earlier in the trip, less pleasurably, Rubes and Zeidman were caught in a snowstorm after leaving Fort McMurray and landed in a ditch. They were there for over half an hour when fortunately a car drove by whose occupants helped them to get their car back on the road. It was harrowing, for without assistance they could have frozen to death.

CHAPTER 11

1970–1975: *Guess What?*; STAB for schools; OPERAtion ONTARIO; A controversial director

Another Rubes venture for children was beginning to take hold in 1960, although it would be some years before it got off the ground. Louis Applebaum and three other arts-inclined entrepreneurs had formed Group Four Productions and asked Jan to prepare several television shows of stories and songs for children. This would be one of Group Four's efforts in general cultural and educational programming.[136] The initial proposal was for eighty five-minute shows, all under the rubric of *Guess What?* The catchy title was an unsolicited gift from Jan's children. They would often arrive home and blurt out "Guess what, Dad?" and then launch into an account of some unusual happening they had experienced that day. The shows would be about what, when, where, which, why, how, and who: Who made the first bicycle? Where did the first rubber ball come from? How did we tell time before clocks were invented? In sum, the shows were designed to spark children's curiosity and increase their awareness of the contributions of other cultures.[137]

But it was ten years before OECA programmed *Guess What?* on its educational television station. The five-minute shows originally proposed were changed to a more practical ten minutes, and the first few were shot in July 1971. Applebaum wrote the theme song that launched each show and Rubes delighted in singing it long after *Guess What?* had been laid to rest. This is how it goes:

> Tralala pom pom digga digga do
> Here's a question just for you
> Fuddle duddle diddle dee youpee ya you
> Where, when, which, why, how and who?
> If that's asking such a lot
> Schroom papa piddly pom, tic-tac-tot
> Then just simply: "Guess what!"

Host Rubes lives in an attic with a balcony surrounded by "fascinating items of the present and past." He begins the story for each episode immediately after the theme. Carefully, he avoids "Here, today, children, I tell you the story of…" He wrote in his notes that there should be only one "guess what?" in each show, and that he should not ask the children "Did you guess?" or "Can you guess?" Rather, he referred to things in a matter-of-fact manner, passing on information without drawing attention to it.

Rubes had no idea that he was using truly progressive techniques in teaching children. Blaik Kirby wrote in the *Globe and Mail* that the show was the best of five children's programs given by OECA.[138] Kirby had gone to the trouble of speaking with an experienced child psychologist, who said, "Mr. Rubes uses his time so well, and I like the twinkle in his eye. He projects an interpersonal relationship. It's almost as if you can talk to him on the screen." The psychologist, Freda Steinberg, compared the series favourably to a British one, also on OECA, where "the performers tend to talk to each other, rather than to the children. They were told things rather than asked. Everything was fed to them. They were not given a chance to get across their own thoughts." Jan Rubes was, as they say, a born teacher.

OECA billed *Guess What?* as social studies and ran it for over three years. It integrated study areas such as language arts, health, science, mathematics, art, and music. There were eight major sections: This and That (clocks, match, glass, umbrella), Transportation (bicycle, automobile, train), Communications (handshakes, languages, postage), School Days, Food and Eating, Games and Sports, Music and Theatre, and Special Occasions. OECA also provided guidelines for teachers using the

Jan in Guess What?, *1973.*

programs in their classrooms. Rubes wrote all of the scripts and either found or composed appropriate music to put across each story. Now, thirty years later, one can still buy a CD of songs from *Guess What?* It was and remains a major and unique triumph.

Jan Rubes rejoined his friends Richard Bonynge and Joan Sutherland in Seattle in 1971 for a production in French of Offenbach's *Les Contes d'Hoffmann*. Sutherland, La Stupenda as she was increasingly known, sang all four soprano roles — Olympia, Giulietta, Antonia, and Stella.[139] She was dazzling. Bonynge conducted. Jan played three roles — Spalanzani, Schlemil, and Crespel — a considerable challenge. There was some consternation over Bonynge's editing of the opera, and this led to baritone Norman Treigle's withdrawal as it went into rehearsal. Since Offenbach died before completing *Hoffmann*, editing it was fair game for enterprising conductors and directors. Sutherland, who valued her husband's work, liked what he did. She also said that it was challenging to get the cast to handle the French dialogue. Bliss Hebert directed, Allan Charles Klein did the sets, and Toronto's Suzanne Mess designed the costumes.

The Canadian Opera Company had some difficult times in the early 1970s. There were several reasons for this: an intransigent Herman Geiger-Torel, an ineffective board of directors with limited fundraising know-how, a querulous press, a flawed O'Keefe Centre, and a need for more international stars and a more daring choice of operas. There were also scheduling restrictions because the TSO was the opera orchestra at the time — operas had to be scheduled in September and October. In 1971, a critical Canada Council and a super-critical Ontario Arts Council together invited Lord Harewood, the British opera guru, to assess the COC — and, to make it look fair, other Canadian opera companies as well. As is usually the case, many criticisms of the company were half-truths. Its choice of operas was as daring as could be expected with the funds available, the board was conscientious if conservative, and Torel avoided using stars who refused to rehearse sufficiently for his kind of demanding direction or who asked for larger fees than he could afford.

Torel staged three of Wagner's four "Ring" operas (he skipped *Das Rheingold*) between 1971 and 1973 but earned few thanks for doing so. Rubes was Fafner the Dragon in *Siegfried* in 1972. The *Toronto Star* amusingly described how he handled the role: "To give a cave-like sound to his singing growls during his ten-minute performance ... he had to go into the washroom, the smallest room which gives the best hollow sound.... The eighty-piece orchestra was piped in to him through a public address system and he watched the conductor on closed circuit television."[140] The *Star* had a large photo of Rubes emoting in the washroom.

The COC seemed unable to please the *Globe and Mail*'s cranky John Kraglund, who did little to support the company, even when it did well. On the other hand, there was William Littler of the *Toronto Star*, who was more than reasonable in his reviews.[141] The COC suffered when its productions were compared unfavourably with the NAC's summer productions conducted by Mario Bernardi. In 1971 and 1972, the NAC did *The Marriage of Figaro*, with Rubes playing Dr. Bartolo, and, as expected, he brought much fun to the role. The NAC had the finest opera house in Canada, an excellent orchestra, and funds for first-class staging and fine singers. Was it any wonder that the COC looked like a backward child?

Rubes heroically sang in three long and strenuous COC tours from 1970 to 1974: *The Barber of Seville, Orpheus in the Underworld*, and *Così fan tutte*. He also appeared in several O'Keefe productions — Leporello in *Don Giovanni* (1970), Baron Zeta in Lehár's *The Merry Widow* (1971, 1973), Fafner in *Siegfried* (1972), and the Sacristan in Puccini's *Tosca* (1972). Some of the productions went on to the NAC. In *Tosca* he audaciously upstaged the leading tenor playing Mario Cavarodossi. He said:

> I had about two pages of music where I had to pantomime cleaning up the church. I pretend I'm chasing a mouse, and when the music ends, the mouse disappears. Well, there was a tenor whom I did not like. He'd come on stage. Couldn't give a damn about anybody, and he just stood there and belted out his aria in his beautiful voice. All this time, onstage, I'm just sitting there doing absolutely nothing. Without moving my body, I just looked and pretended to spot the mouse. The whole O'Keefe Centre knew what was going on. The tenor, of course, didn't. He was singing on and wondering why people were tittering. He checked his fly and everything.

He was so flustered. That was very cruel and since then
I have a reputation for stealing scenes.[142]

In 1972 Rubes had proposed a new program to Prologue, with the
tacit approval of the COC. It would involve an MC, four singers — soprano, tenor, alto, and bass — and a pianist. The group became known
as "STAB," an acronym of the voice types. Rubes would be the MC.
Prologue was delighted. The program was called "The Human Voice
in Three Acts." A typical episode would start off with a march and an
introduction, followed by Act 1: The Love of God; Act 2: The Love of
Song; and Act 3: The Love of Theatre; and then a finale and march to
conclude the program. A program note explains what the singing voice
means to us all:

> A baby will see and touch, eat and taste, cry and hear,
> stand up and walk long before it learns to speak. In
> the early dawn, man learned to take care of himself,
> learned to "conquer" the world before he learned to
> use his voice properly. Now our ability to speak to each
> other, to communicate and to express feelings with our
> voices sets us apart from the animals. What's more we
> SING. That's the part of God in all of us — the part we
> should know more about. Let STAB tell you!

STAB members were humorously profiled in the printed program
and introduced themselves at each show. Ann Cooper was the soprano
and played the flute. Glyn Evans was the tenor. Carrol Anne Curry sang
alto. Bass-baritone Ron Bermingham played banjo and tuba. Errol Gay,
the music director–pianist, played the trombone. Jan, in addition to being MC, was "The Man with the Guitar." William Littler described one
of the performances at the Blessed Sacrament School in Toronto: "With
the bang of a drum, the blare of a trombone, and the tootle of a flute,
six figures marched across the gymnasium floor … carrying banners
and instruments and wearing smiles."[143] He then described how Rubes
started out by quoting from the Bible: "In the beginning, God created
the world and all that was in it was good." Then, in his own words, he

explained that men and women were not so good, at least socially. "They snored, they giggled, they even belched, until one day a woman apparently heard a bird-call and attempted to reproduce it. Voila, the birth of song." As Littler pointed out, Rubes's view of music history wouldn't make *Grove's Dictionary of Music and Musicians*, but it did turn the students' facial question marks into smiles.

Next, the group encircled Carrol Anne Curry, dressed as a princess, and out came music from *Aida*. Over the next hour the group did everything from opera to gospel music to barbershop quartet. "Rubes even demonstrated the perils of singing Sweet Adeline through a layer of shaving cream." Cast members enjoyed doing the show almost as much as their audience enjoyed watching it. Rubes had warned the singers about children not always clapping at the end of a performance. "Would you believe that some children have never clapped in their lives, because they only see movies and television. I have to show them what to do at a concert…. STAB will include everything from church music to barbershop, but it is being set up to prepare them for opera…. I may end it with the quartet from *Rigoletto*. That will amaze them."[144] In April and May of 1974, STAB did fifty-seven performances throughout Ontario. The schools ate it up. Rubes temporarily left the show the following year, returning to it intermittently until 1980, when the group dissolved.

The COC touring company included a week of *Cosi fan tutte* in English at the Royal Alexandra in 1973, and the indefatigable Rubes, as Don Alfonso, did two of the performances. The small-scale setting did much to enhance the production and remind astute opera lovers that the O'Keefe Centre was indeed a mixed blessing. The next year Jan did Baron Zeta in five performances of the *The Merry Widow* with the Michigan Opera Company in Detroit. The conductor had a heart attack after the first show, and Rubes promptly recommended the Canadian Victor Feldbrill as his replacement. Feldbrill had conducted the opera for the COC in both 1971 and 1973. He attracted much attention in Detroit and commuted so frequently in the week of the performances that U.S. immigration authorities got to know him and would wave him through without questions, and with a welcoming word besides.[145]

All of Rubes's singing notwithstanding, by 1974 Torel felt, right or wrong, that his voice was no longer up to COC standards. Not one to delegate authority easily, Torel had more or less operated the company single-handedly for more than two decades. Loyal to a fault, he consulted key board members on how to keep Rubes in the company and harness his creative energy. The solution was to appoint Rubes director of touring and program development. This appointment might help Torel to consider new approaches and other innovations as well as chart a more enterprising future for the company. The COC board did not consider Rubes to be Torel's eventual replacement, as some outsiders thought, although it had made clear to Torel in 1974 that 1976 would be his last season. The board had been looking elsewhere, and eventually engaged Lotfi Mansouri to be the new COC head, and at a much larger salary than Torel's.

Jan Rubes became a Canadian citizen on November 27, 1974. His three sons, all born in the U.S.A., became Canadian citizens at the same time. However, Canadian law required that he give up his American citizenship, which he did. Two months later, in January 1975, Rubes, exercising his new mandate with the COC, laid out a blueprint for what he called OPERAtion ONTARIO. It would be a new pattern for touring. The company would spend two or three days in each community and would reach out to it more fully in new ways. Rubes chose Niagara-on-the-Lake, home of the Shaw Festival, as the training site. There the small company rehearsed, gave previews of *La Bohème*, and prepared children's programs. One was "The Sounds of Music," its objective — yet another way to introduce music to youngsters. The company also sketched out workshops for local singing and instrumental groups. One of its first tour stops was Belleville. There, Jan told John Kraglund, "If Canadian opera is to develop and to build a following, especially in the smaller communities, we have to do something more than give a performance once every couple of years. After seventeen years of touring we begin to feel we play for the same 300 people in each town. And some of our audience is beginning to die off."[146] Rubes wasn't far off the mark.

Bohème cast members valued Rubes's direction, as would singers in other operas and musicals that he would direct in the coming years. He would typically give them leeway in rehearsal to work with and adapt their styles to their fellow players and develop their roles. He did not arbitrarily impose his views upon the cast, as some directors do. The

OPERAtion ONTARIO 1975. Row 1: Deborah Jeans, Ann Cooper, Barney Ingram, Jan Rubes, Barbara Collier, John Arab, and Kathleen Ruddell. Row 2: John Leberg, Errol Gay, Avo Kittask, Peter Barcza, Herman Geiger-Torel, Tom Burrows (Shaw Festival), Phil Stark, and Glyn Evans.

tenor Henry Barney Ingram explained that Rubes wanted his players to develop a dramatic ambiance, to find their way on stage and to act intuitively.[147] Put another way, and at the risk of being repetitious, Ingram said that to Rubes acting is reacting, that performers must listen and observe what others have done in order to avoid working in a vacuum. Giulio Kukurugya, who often did Colline, echoed what Ingram and others have said about Rubes's direction. He was a bass of similar height and build to Rubes, and they often shared the same roles. His wife, Margaret Zeidman, related how Kukurugya and Rubes first met at her engagement party in 1970. They took each other's measure and, as they talked, their voices got lower and lower in pitch, as if to challenge who had the deeper, more resonant one. She called the encounter "the battle of the basses."[148] Rubes gave her two inscribed vocal scores of Czech operas as a wedding gift.

The COC had engaged Monika Simon (later Hofmann) in December 1974 to assist Rubes in his tour operations. She surmised that he wasn't interested in day-to-day administration, not unusual for an artist, and therefore dealt competently with many details.[149] Simon said that

Jan's aim was to develop a company with singers working full-time as they did in his native Czechoslovakia. She also recalled that he disliked negotiating fees, which, undeniably, was part of his job. Simon could have been overly critical, for deep down she may have felt that she was sufficiently competent to run the business end of the company without Rubes. She praised Rubes for daringly engaging Alan Lund, a prominent dance director, to direct Tibor Polgar and George Jonas's opera *The Glove* for Prologue. This Torel might never have done, because of Lund's scanty operatic background

During OPERAtion ONTARIO's stay in Kingston, Rubes scheduled some operatic excerpts and the finale of the second act of *Bohème* for inmates at the high-security Kingston Penitentiary. Carrol Anne Curry recalls how steel door after steel door slammed shut as they made their way into the prison.[150] Apprehensive, she felt as if she herself was being imprisoned. Rubes introduced the show and, to get some laughs, said he was a ski bum who had turned to singing. The male members of the cast appeared next and sang songs but got only a modest response. Then an inmate shouted, "Let's have the girls." Baritone Avo Kittask "sang the kind of song unfit for maiden aunts and Barbara Collier sizzled her way through Summertime."[151] Now they were ready for the *Bohème* excerpt. When Marcello (Kittask) picked up Musetta (Curry) the audience cheered with approval. After the show the cast shook hands with the inmates. Curry had a few words with one of them and, according to Simon, made the mistake of asking him what he was in for. "Murder," he replied. She beat a hasty retreat.

OPERAtion ONTARIO had a short but successful life. Although its members often found spending several nights in a city tiring, they admitted that choral workshops, orchestral performances, chamber music, excerpts from operas with explanations, and of course *Bohème* itself helped make a community ready for more opera. Looking back, it accomplished what it set out to do. However, Lotfi Mansouri, the new director of the COC, was critical of its performing standards. He also had other ideas about how the COC should best function when touring and thought little, it appeared, of Rubes's ideas about workshops and the like. Accordingly, Rubes's contract was not renewed and OPERAtion ONTARIO was, more or less, dissolved. To soften the blow, Jan was appointed COC

Giulio Kukurugya, Glyn Evans, Brian Roberts, Mary Lou Fallis, and Gary Relyea as Edwardian Commèdia del arte *characters in Richard Strauss's* Ariadne auf Naxos, *Stratford, 1975.*

consultant, which in reality meant nothing. He was disappointed. It did, however, leave him more time to direct and pursue other activities.

In the summer of 1975, Rubes directed Richard Strauss's *Ariadne auf Naxos* on Stratford's Third Stage. If he was looking for controversy he found it with this production. The audience sat on three sides of an elevated rectangular stage and, since there was no orchestra pit, the orchestra played under the stage and the conductor held forth at the side of the stage. Rubes omitted the opera's prologue, which some felt was essential to the audience's ability to understand and enjoy the work. His argument was that Strauss had written the prologue some five years *after* composing the opera. The show began with the *commèdia del arte–* inspired intermezzo as in traditional performances. However, the five *commèdia* characters were now Edwardian picnickers on an island dressed *à la* Pirates of Penzance. They sang in English with anglicized names — Harlequin became H. Aria Quin, and Brighella became Brig H. Ella. The unhappy Ariadne and her three nymphs sang in German, as did Bacchus, who appears later in the opera.

The physical setting — a spartan theatre with no air conditioning — made sitting through the eighty-five-minute performance an endurance test. The heat got so bad on opening night that city firemen hosed the roof with water, hoping that this would cool the theatre. It not only failed to do so but created clouds of steam everywhere. The long, narrow stage was awkward, the acoustics were poor, and the sightlines were problematic.

Musically the opera proceeded as Strauss wrote it, with conductor Raffi Armenian in firm control. As already noted, two languages were used to help the audience keep the *commèdia* and the German group apart, but it may have confused them instead. Whether Hugo von Hofmannsthal, Strauss's librettist, would have liked it is conjectural. Most of the press were so critical of the setting, the costumes, and especially the staging (which they felt too light-hearted and approaching vulgarity) that they gave little space to the music. Ariadne (Jeannette Zarou) had a beautifully mellow soprano voice and sang the text movingly, and Mary Lou Fallis handled the challenging role of Zerbinetta with confidence and style.

Herman Geiger-Torel wrote Rubes a fiercely critical letter about the production. Why no prologue? Why eliminate the *commèdia del arte* characters? "[Zerbinetta's] dress and hairdo clashed violently with the transparent music she has to sing. Strauss and Hofmannsthal visualized her as the typical Columbina. The appearance of the sailor (alias Bacchus) put me into shock. He looked like a displaced gaucho straight from the Argentinian pampas." Yet Torel had many good things to say about the singing and the orchestra. He explained his frank remarks by saying that he wanted Rubes to be a successful director.[152] None of the critics asked why the Stratford Festival, a centre of drama, didn't precede *Ariadne* with Hofmannsthal's condensed version of Molière's *Le Bourgeois Gentilhomme*, with Strauss's original incidental music. But, it would have needed a better hall.

Prior to Stratford, Jan lectured on singing and opera at Toronto's York University in the spring of 1975. He also was the narrator in two performances of Stravinsky's musical drama *L'Histoire du Soldat* at the NAC, conducted by Mario Bernardi. Nadia Potts and Frank Augustyn were the stunning dancers, and August Schellenberg was an equally exciting Devil. Eric McLean of the *Montreal Star* thought it "the most memorable performance, from every point of view, musical and visual, in my experience — which includes the one with Marcel Marceau at

Stratford many years ago."[153] He thought the music and drama were "co-equals," and he went on, "For the first time in my experience, the dancers, devil, and narrator made me feel that they were grappling with a philosophical problem of some significance — the corruption of riches and power, and the rewards of truth. Rubes gave a clear and meaningful reading." Maureen Peterson of the *Ottawa Journal* praised the show: "It was stupendous and Jan Rubes handled the narrator's role as if we were his grandchildren gathered by the fireside."[154]

Rubes went back to the NAC in July (what a busy year it was!) to direct a short piece he had created, *Cabaret Bel Canto*. The NAC wanted engaging operatic interludes to entertain the audiences before and after the main shows. The first interlude would be an "hors d'oeuvre," the second, a "snack," said Rubes. Some of his inspiration dated back to *Opera Backstage*, twenty-five years before. The show featured excerpts from mainly popular bel canto operas sung by four opera singers, with Montreal baritone Robert Savoie singing and acting as master of ceremonies. It had a short life — one summer only.

The pivotal year of 1975 had still more significant events. The family purchased a ski chalet at Blue Mountain in March, not far from their Collingwood cottage. Chris entered medical school at the University of Toronto, Jonathan was studying engineering at the University of Waterloo, and Tony, still in high school, was giving thought to a career in acting. Jan found free time to play tennis doubles with one or another of them. Jan and son usually defeated the opposition. As for Susan, her Young People's Theatre, thanks to Prologue, was making its mark in Toronto and the rest of the province. She was also looking hard for a permanent theatre in Toronto, but, as yet, had found nothing suitable.

Although this was Jan and Susan's twenty-fifth wedding anniversary year, they were both too busy to celebrate it. But there was cause for celebration of a different sort. On October 15 Susan was invested as a Member of the Order of Canada. Her YPT work had not gone unnoticed. This honour led to two grand weeks of Christmas merriment. Jan's brother and their mother arrived from Czechoslovakia and the Hirschfelds came from New York, as did Clem and Eva. YPT opened *The Popcorn Man* on December 23 — a "minor" distraction for Susan — and the New Year's Eve party was at their new chalet.

The Rubes sons — Chris, Jonathan, and Tony, 1973.

How did all of this activity affect the Rubeses' personal life? We must go back to interviews published in a Toronto regional newspaper in 1973 to shed light on their eminently successful marriage.[155] Both arrived at the same conclusion about the success of their union. "Understanding," Susan said, "comes through being in related professions." Jan said, "Because of my tours with the COC, Susan and I were often apart for perhaps half of a year. It was, I discovered later, of great value to me because it taught me not to take Susan for granted…. Our marriage, because we have been apart a lot, is still a very young one." They usually depend on one another to help solve problems. Susan suggested that Jan is meticulous in everything he does, while she isn't. She is a talker; he is a listener. The children choose different times to speak with one or another of their parents. "Jan has a great sense of humour," Susan noted, "which is probably the greatest quality for keeping our marriage together. My sense of humour is not so great, but at least I appreciate his." Anyway, their marriage was working, although both were in a profession notorious for marriages that didn't last.

CHAPTER 12

1976–1982: Young People's Theatre; Opera and musicals; Children's concerts

S usan Rubes had become a major figure in Toronto's theatrical life. In 1975, she received the Toronto Drama Beach Award, in addition to the Order of Canada, and took YPT to London in co-operation with its English counterpart, the Unicorn Theatre. The company did Henry Beissel's *Inook and the Sea*, and it went over extremely well with English children, who, Susan observed, did not seem as overwhelmed as Canadian children about going to the theatre.[156]

Susan had another dream that needed fulfilling — to have her own theatre for YPT — but where was the money to do it? In 1977, this determined and quite remarkable woman enlisted help from governments, foundations, corporations, philanthropists, and ordinary citizens; went after press and TV publicity; and campaigned with anyone who would listen to her. Now, in her early fifties, she spoke convincingly and photographed well, especially when she wore a workman's helmet to clue in the public about the building she wanted.

And she found it, an old building at the southeast corner of Frederick and Front Streets in downtown Toronto that could be converted into a theatre. It had been erected in 1881 and in its early years was a stable for horse-drawn streetcars. Beginning in the 1890s, it became a generating station for transit vehicles that had shifted to electric power. The building had been empty since 1929, and the Toronto Transit Commission couldn't sell it because it was a historic landmark — it was the oldest building in Toronto related to public transit. Then along came YPT. Susan had architect Eb Zeidler draw up a plan for a theatre and drama school, even though the popular mayor, John Sewell, was against converting the building. He feared that the city would be stuck with a white elephant if the venture didn't succeed. Failure was not a word in Susan's vocabulary, but to please Sewell she quickly had Zeidler draw up new plans so that the building could be reverted to who knows what. Thus seats and risers were to be movable, which, as it turned out, encouraged flexible and imaginative staging. Sewell finally gave the go-ahead. YPT had what it wanted, a central location and space to do its work.

As expected, all kinds of problems arose as renovations got underway. There were structural faults and water seepage from nearby Lake Ontario. Then came an electricians' strike that lasted eleven weeks and caused further delays. Costs climbed to over $2 million. This meant that Susan had to scramble for more money. In the end, it all turned out well, and the new building opened its doors as scheduled on December 22, 1977. It had a 350-seat theatre, a smaller studio theatre named after the frequently querulous *Toronto Star* drama critic Nathan Cohen, a production workshop, a film workshop, a snack bar, and two lobbies for mini performances.

Bryan Johnson of the *Globe and Mail* was elated. He called it "an absolute wonder for kids anywhere, an event to be celebrated with cheers and hosannas all around. The place is a marvel of warmth and enthusiasm, all carpets and cosiness where once there was a cold brick ruin. Young people are treated like little princes and princesses. And with their champion, the indomitable Mrs. Rubes, at the helm, they seem bound to have their own little theatrical wonderland for years — let's hope decades — to come."[157] Gina Mallet of the *Toronto Star* also gave kudos to Susan for her tenacity and quoted a telling one-liner by another Rubes admirer, David Silcox, then Metropolitan Toronto arts officer: "I think of her as pumice stone. She grinds at people."[158] Because of this neverending fundraising, the Rubeses' social life had suffered. Jan wistfully

noted how few dinner invitations they were getting during that year because Susan couldn't resist using the dinner table to pester other guests
for money for YPT.

Yes, Susan was very busy. YPT had produced *Joey the Clown* at the
St. Lawrence Centre, and it ran weekends from Christmas 1976 until
the end of January 1977. Peter White of the *Globe and Mail* described
the black box technique used in the show: "The actors and sets are all in
black. The stage is bathed in ultra-violet light so that all that is actually
seen is costumes and props."[159] Later, he pointed out, "It is completely
without the whacking violence of much television fare aimed at this age
group." He found *Joey* hard to resist, as did Gina Mallet, who called it "a
humdinger of a kids show."[160]

Clark Gesner's *You're a Good Man Charlie Brown* was also done over
Christmas, followed by Len Peterson's *Etienne Brulé* in March. Brulé came
to Canada as a member of Champlain's expedition in the early sev-
enteenth century. He soon took off on his own, living among Indians,
exploring the Great Lakes, and going as far south as Florida. Betty Jane
Wylie's *The Old Woman and the Peddler*, a play for very young children, was
next. The audience helps the old woman to rediscover her identity after
a peddler takes it from her. Still another show given during the year was
W.O. Mitchell's *Cabin Fever*, an adaptation of his CBC radio series *Jake
and the Kid*, for ten- to twelve-year-olds. As usual, Prologue toured all
these YPT plays. Susan vetted them carefully, since she wanted them
both to entertain and to involve children and, in the end, show them
what live theatre as a depiction of life was all about. To put it another
way, she saw YPT as a learning laboratory to assist young people in their
cultural growth through contact with the creative process. It had come a
long way since the Museum Theatre days. As a feature of its fundraising
program, YTP claimed that four hundred thousand had viewed its productions in schools and elsewhere in 1976. Quite an achievement!

The careers of Susan and Jan were intersecting more frequently,
thanks to YPT. Jan played several crucial roles in opening YPT's new
building. They chose the Czech Laterna Magica production of *The
Lost Fairy Tale* to launch the theatre in December 1977. Laterna Magica's technique had been unveiled at the Brussels World's Fair in 1958,
but its origins go back to the Second World War. With many of their

opera houses bombed, the Germans had taken their sophisticated theatre equipment, including mirror projections, to relatively unharmed Prague for safekeeping. After their defeat they left their equipment behind for Czech theatres to use. Rubes, when he returned to Prague in 1945, met three brilliant stage artists, Josef Svoboda, Vaclav Kaslik, and Alfred Radok, and kept in touch with them and their work over the ensuing years.[161] Radok and Svoboda synthesized and fused film, slide, and sound with live acting using this German equipment, while developing still more advanced equipment on their own. The Czech National Theatre supported Laterna Magica and took it to the 1967 Montreal Exposition. Josef Svoboda was its principal creative force. *The Lost Fairy Tale*, whose origins go back to Svoboda, used mixed media — black box techniques, music, film, mime, and dance.

To prepare for the YPT opening, the film sections of *The Lost Fairy Tale* had to be dubbed into English. Accordingly, the Rubeses sent Billie May Richards to Prague — she had been the voice of the Kid in the CBC's radio show *Jake and the Kid* — to dub the voice of the little

The Lost Fairy Tale, *1978.*

girl already on film (Alzbeta Mjartanova). Ken Wickes was also sent to Prague to dub the voice of the old man (Ladislav Pesek). Jan Rubes went to Prague at the end of May, where he worked closely with the two director-technicians who would do the show in Toronto. He also translated the text from Czech to English for the dubbing. He explained how he tried "to match all the Ps and Ts and Ms so it could be lip synched. My biggest problem was that in Czech, 'Yes' is 'Ano'. In every second sentence the girl on the screen says 'Ano'. Finally, after many sleepless nights, I suddenly realized that 'Ano' matches 'Oh, no' and, because the character who asks her the questions is the live narrator in the show, I reversed all the questions so that the girl on the screen could answer 'Oh, no' instead of 'Yes'."[162]

Jan was the narrator, the only principal actor on stage. He explained to the audience that the show was a dreamland story for children and adults, an adventure of a grandfather and his granddaughter in an old clock from which time has run away. The two find themselves in constantly changing and difficult situations, but there is a happy ending. Rubes alerted the audience to the play's magic and sorcery, to vanishing and reappearing objects, to a speaking apple, and to the effects of a magic comb and mirror. They meet Red Riding Hood and the Wolf and see Snow White and the Sleeping Beauty. They follow a magic egg and hear a mysterious watchmaker playing the violin, as well as the yearning voice of a speaking bird. A turtledove is in danger but recovers its freedom.

The Lost Fairy Tale was one of YPT's most popular ventures and Rubes narrated whenever he was free. (There was an alternate narrator.) Its opening run, following the grand opening in December, began in January 1978 and played twenty-three times. There was a horrendous snowstorm the night of the final performance, and there were only eleven hardy souls in the audience. The actors' union Equity specifies that if there are fewer than twelve in attendance a show can been cancelled. However, this didn't stop the company from doing the show. They felt that the eleven who braved the storm deserved it. There were another twenty-three performances in the summer, and it played again in the fall. It went on to Vancouver for Christmas 1978 and returned to YPT in January and February 1979. Next, it toured Northeastern U.S.A., including five performances in the Kaufmann Auditorium at New York's 92nd Street

YMHA. One American critic wrote about audience behaviour: "There were no dawdlers. You didn't dare drop your program for fear you'd miss a flying chair or the great egg chase or the veil of invisibility." The same critic went on: "The film broke — or stopped — or perhaps was lost like the fairy tale. Rubes was left on stage without his pre-recorded wonders. But never fear. Rubes is above all a performer, and he entertained the audience with a wonder all his own until technical things could be set straight. Rubes is programmed to be wonderful. So is the show."[163]

The second Rubes contribution to the new theatre was a short story he had written back in 1976, more than a year before the building opened. It is about an old knife sharpener who is squatting in the cellar of the transit building. When Susan Rubes and the transit authorities turn up to inspect the building, the knife sharpener panics, fearing that they plan to tear it down. With the help of a neighbourhood boy, Jamie, he finds that the building will stay where it is. The old man gets involved in the renovation, and the story ends with the theatre giving him a job. The CBC agreed to produce the story as a TV drama, aptly named *The House on Front Street*. Rubes is the knife sharpener, and Susan and her YPT colleagues play themselves in the half-hour show. George Jonas produced it, and, after many shootings, it was aired in March 1978.

And still a third contribution of Jan's to YPT in its first season on Frederick Street was his revival, in January, of the 1971 production of *Seven Dreams*. Bryan Johnson wrote:

> Puppeteers disappear, and fluorescent objects sail magically around the stage…. Alphabet letters come pouring out of books, dance around the stage, and end up eating each other. Fluorescent pastel building blocks pop suddenly into existence and pile themselves up to make a castle. The three blind mice dance on stage and become ferociously bloated…. The audience, composed entirely of school kids and their teachers, clearly adore the show.[164]

How satisfying it was to see children by the hundreds file into the theatre every day until the end of April, when the show closed. They paid one dollar to attend, but those who didn't have the money were admitted anyway.

On February 17, 1978, YPT opened *The Diary of Anne Frank*. Eyebrows were raised about the show's suitability for children, but Susan Rubes's vision prevailed. Her close friends in New York, superb actors all, played the show. Eli Wallach was Anne's father; his wife, Anne Jackson, her mother; and their twenty-two-year-old daughter, Roberta, the thirteen-year-old Anne. No less admirable were Toronto's Kate Reid and August Schellenberg, who played the Van Daans. Susan had literally twisted the Wallachs' arms to get them to do the show in the first instance, but what is friendship for? The Wallachs performed for minimum fees. Their compensation was limousine service to and from the theatre on a daily basis, donated by a friend of Susan's. Children attended in force, but some caused a small problem — their sucking lollipops and unwrapping candy was distracting the actors. Anne Jackson asked the children before the second performance began to refrain from sucking candy and suggested that they bring the candy to the stage where it would be held until the final curtain. Only one little boy did so, but all the children stopped sucking candy.

Anne Frank was a great hit. It ran for four weeks, and then was held over for another week. Toronto had witnessed "unforgettable" drama, and the consensus was that YPT was a now a major theatrical enterprise.[165] There were many tears shed in the audience when Otto Frank closed his daughter's diary and the wonderful cast took its curtain calls. The Wallachs then took the show to Off-Broadway in New York, where it ran for close to a year. In the New York production, their younger daughter Kathryn played Anne's older sister Margot.

Returning to May 1976, the opera singer Rubes again played Baron Zeta in *The Merry Widow*, this time for the Vancouver Opera Association (VOA). Joan Sutherland was the Widow, Bonynge conducted, and Lotfi Mansouri directed. All of the performances were completely sold out. It was a happy time and a suitable prelude for what was to come in the autumn when Rubes staged *La Bohème* for the VOA. Ray Chatelin of the *Vancouver Province* wrote the kind of review performers and directors pine for but rarely get:

We saw a *La Bohème* that was a joy, an exclamation of
life, a sense of pure lyrical beauty, the likes of which
have not been seen here in years.... Intricate care in
characterization, movement, and action led to a dramatic study into personalities, and the singing reflected
these tiny nuances.... A truly remarkable insight into the
human condition marked this *La Bohème*.... One could
become totally involved with an operatic, living experience rather than mere musical entertainment. Under
director Jan Rubes's guidance, it has a sense of dramatic
impact that grows from within. Rubes balances the staging so that one set of emotions is constantly in contra-
diction with another.[166]

Shall we go on? No one knew the opera better than he did; he had
played Colline many, many times. Obviously this was his chance to stage

Jan Rubes (Baron Zeta) and Joan Sutherland (Anna Glawari) offstage at Lehár's The
Merry Widow, *Vancouver, 1976.*

the opera in a good theatre, and memorable it must have been. Incidentally, Rubes was on stage in Act II playing the doddering Alcindoro.

With such a production, Vancouver couldn't wait for his *Fledermaus*. The VOA mounted it in March 1977, but Rubes's broad interpretation of the work did not please Susan Mertens of the *Vancouver Sun*, who wrote that his direction "can only be called unabashed and heavy-handed. Rubes makes the implicit become explicit and the explicit become self-evident. At times — particularly in the over-worked third act — the

Jan as The Maestro in Cimarosa's The Music Master, *1976.*

dizziness of decadence becomes the drunkenness of desperation."[167] This same critic, clearly an expert in alliteration, accused Rubes, who played Frosh, a speaking role, of overdoing the slapstick, as so often happens in *Fledermaus* productions.

Despite cognoscenti frowns, the show went off well, and Mary Costa was an engaging Rosalinda. This negative press came on top of a poor review by John Kraglund of Rubes's semi-staged version of Domenico Cimarosa's *The Music Master* (*Il Maestro di Capella*) at a TSO Young People's concert, given two months before at Massey Hall. Rubes did a skit to help the musical presentation, which Kraglund stuffily frowned upon.[168] Jan's taste, his humour, and his imagination resulted in unconventional approaches to standard works and undoubtedly raised many an eyebrow. The conductor, Victor Feldbrill, also a favourite Kraglund whipping boy, received his share of negative criticism.

Taking the long view, Rubes was not thrown excessively by poor and intemperate reviews. If he wanted to direct innovative productions, then he must take the bitter with the sweet. Things went better on the tennis court. For a change of pace and with just a bit more time on his hands, he won both the singles and doubles Ontario tennis championships in his age category in July 1977. And in December he flew with conductor Raffi Armenian to Regina to do *Il Maestro di Cappella* with the symphony there. It was a smash hit. But the handwriting was on the wall. He could still do limited singing roles, but it was acting and directing that would be taking over.

Then, in February 1978, Rubes was cast in a TV drama, *Catsplay*, based on a play by the Hungarian István Örkény and adapted for TV by Timothy Findley. The show starred the remarkable Helen Burns as Mrs. Orban, a confused and pathetic widow of sixty-five who is in love with a retired, unattractive, and disinterested opera singer (Jan Rubes). She had done the role on stage in Minneapolis and Washington, and it was very much her show. The rest of the cast was excellent and the show got very good press from the *Globe and Mail*'s Blaik Kirby.[169] Kirby wrote:

> [Mrs. Orban is] a rumpled disorganized, undignified
> widow of 65, full of tempestuous life and busy having
> her heart broken. Refusing to act her age or to live

anything less than to the full, she is passionately in love with a gluttonous old roué (Rubes) who is stolen from her by a "friend." She gives us emotional storms of fury and pitiable weakness as she stands vigil in the rain outside her lover's window, and a warm reality to her actions even though they are those of a fool, designed to make us guffaw…. As Hollywood and fiction almost never tell us, love is not the exclusive preserve of the callow.

Kirby's sagacity in this unusually insightful review came to the fore when he mused, "On TV we are so used to comic characters who are no more than outlines, with no inner detail, that one like Mrs. Orban comes as a jarring shock. We hardly know how to react. This is about a *real* person, not an empty shell. Are we really supposed to laugh at her? Suddenly we see how much more could be done if TV drama and its audience wanted to do it." Rubes must have had a laugh when Kirby noted that the script had erroneously described the aging opera singer as "fat," which Rubes certainly was not.

As if he wasn't busy enough, Rubes went to Fredericton in September 1978 to play in the Leigh-Darion-Wasserman musical *Man of La Mancha*, based on the Cervantes masterpiece *Don Quixote*. Rubes was stunning as the foolish dreamer, the idealist, the knight

Jan plays The Man of La Mancha, *Fredericton, 1978.*

errant when knighthood and chivalry had almost disappeared. He plays three roles: the author Cervantes, then the mad knight, and finally Don Quixote, now sane and back at his home in La Mancha. It is, as readers of the novel know, the time of the Inquisition, and Quixote leads a tortured existence. Yet he does not lose his faith in humankind and his ability to dream "the impossible dream." From this comes the unforgettable song that Rubes sang so beautifully in the play, and had sung countless times at recitals and other musical events.

Theatre New Brunswick is housed in Fredericton's charming Playhouse on the banks of the Saint John River. Built in 1964 with a gift from New Brunswick's Lord Beaverbrook (Max Aitken) and recently renovated, it seated around seven hundred. In 1978 it had a nucleus of several good semi-professional actors, with top professionals imported for shows when needed. Malcolm Black, the director in charge at the time, was so taken with Rubes that in his book of fifty different Don Quixote images, he said jokingly, "they now all look like Jan Rubes."[170] In rehearsals, Jan's thorough knowledge of his lines, coupled with his immersion in the role, set the company's tone and standard for all that followed. Evidently, when the stage crew heard Rubes sing his death song in rehearsal they wept openly.[171] Sharon Halley, the choreographer and principal dancer (Fermina), had been in the original New York production. Carolyn Turney of the *Fredericton Gleaner* wrote that Rubes's interpretation "was sensitive and articulate, and his presentation of Don Quixote as an old man just prior to his death is just one of many beautiful moments experienced during the performance. The timbre of his voice suited the part perfectly and his musical interpretations were superb."[172]

La Mancha ran for nineteen performances, including several in other New Brunswick centres. Some of the venues were not set up for a musical. They had no pits for the ten-piece orchestra, conducted by Barbara Spence. It had to play just off-stage, unseen by the audience. This was barely adequate; a pit would have helped immeasurably. Wherever they went, Rubes got standing ovations, which were unusual at the time for Canadian audiences. In Jan's view, Quixote in many ways eclipsed all of the operatic roles he had done.[173] Carried away, he said, "I think that the American musical is the pinnacle of theatrical creation on this continent. You not only have to be a singer but also an actor, much more than in an opera. In opera the composer has done seventy percent of the work for you. All you have to do is strike a good posture, and the music completes the picture, especially in the good old standards we were doing in Toronto." Too simplistic?

Three years later, Rubes staged an abbreviated version of *La Mancha* for Prologue. He put together an excellent cast and had Margaret Zeidman as pianist-conductor (there was no orchestra). It opened in March 1981 and gave eighty-nine performances! Rubes had warned his colleagues, as in the past, not to expect much applause, because young audiences were increasingly passive when responding to live entertainment. Be that as it may, the show was an enormous success. Zeidman recalled that when Jan, in his final scene, gazed into the distance, his movement and expression were so powerful, so compelling, that the engrossed audience of young people turned their heads and looked with him.[174]

Rubes was doing Prologue shows whenever he had an open date in his calendar, from 1978 to 1982. He also played two cameo roles, Captain Truls and Holm, in YPT's *Hans Christian Andersen*, directed by

Bruce Wilson (sailor), Jan Rubes (Captain Truls), Tom Kneebone (Andersen), and crew in Hans Christian Andersen, *1979.*

Brian MacDonald. Based on the film starring Danny Kaye, the show had thirty performances before it closed at the beginning of July 1979. The skilled Tom Kneebone played the storyteller, and Veronica Tennant and Annette av Paul shared the role of the beautiful ballerina. Gina Mallet savaged the production, especially the dancing. She also said it was the third YPT production of the season "to be scuppered by an ill-chosen director." Ray Conlogue of the *Globe and Mail* also had reservations about the show, although he was not as destructive in his review.[175] Myron Galloway, who saw the show later in the run, praised it and said that the children seemed to love it.[176] In the course of his lengthy review, he quoted Susan on how to keep the children interested: "We have to give them a lot of excitement, color and action on stage, and lots and lots of people." Susan also related to Galloway some of YPT's horrendous facts of life — that it paid the city an annual rent of $15,000 and taxes of $25,000 and got back $6,000 in grants. Fortunately, Young Variety, an international organization, had made an outright donation of $100,000 the previous week, enabling YPT to pay off its building deficit.

Then, in October, Susan Rubes left YPT to move on to the CBC and direct its radio drama section. At a press conference, Susan said, "There isn't enough money to run the theatre, present a season, keep the schools' touring program, and turn the theatre into a seven-day-a-week entertainment place."[177] Heating and cooling the old TTC building was also a burden. Nonetheless, YPT found the wherewithal to continue without her. She said that she planned to revitalize radio drama in her new post and would receive a reasonable salary for her efforts, unlike at YPT where she earned next to nothing. She would also be allowed to take acting roles during holiday periods if they did not conflict with her CBC work.

In 1979 Jan, too, was assessing his career. He told Michael Schulman that he was unconcerned that his operatic career was gradually fading away.[178] Was he trying to soften the blow of being an aging singer? He stated that, since leaving the COC in 1976, he had made more money doing things on TV, radio, stage, and for Prologue than if he had stayed with the COC. Although he didn't mention it, he was approaching sixty with no appreciable retirement money, so larger fees were welcomed. Later in the interview, Rubes put his foot into it discussing the role of the Canada Council. "Now we have massive government support for the arts," he said, "but without anyone sitting up there in the government making the necessary judgments about *quality*." This was unfair and he should have known better, for the council had expert juries recommending grants. Speaking about commissioning composers, and the problems arising from it, Jan suggested that there be a "special concert hall or opera house for the performance of experimental works, to give the composer a chance to see and hear his work performed and to learn from his mistakes." He urged that there should be grant money allotted

Claudia Cummings (Lulu) and Jan Rubes (Schigolch) in Berg's Lulu, *1980.*

for singers who must learn the often difficult roles of contemporary music without having sufficient time to do so properly. He may have been anticipating what was to come next.

There was still another job for him with the COC. Lotfi Mansouri, who questioned Jan's voice but valued his acting, invited him to do, or, should we say, talked him into doing, the difficult role of Schigolch in Alban Berg's *Lulu* in October 1980. Berg died before finishing the final act of his dodecaphonic opera, although he had left sketches for its completion. Frederic Cerha finally completed it satisfactorily in 1979, more than forty years after Berg's death. The COC's production was the third given anywhere with Cerha's conclusion, and it attracted international attention. *Lulu* is a landmark in operatic composition, both for its music *and* for its drama. It is based on two erotic stories by the dramatist Frank Wedekind that spark Lulu's adventures and her eventual downfall. Playing the part of an old man with a mysterious attachment to Lulu — he could be a former lover but actually is her father — gave Rubes room to develop the part. But what Mansouri hadn't told the unsuspecting Jan initially was that learning to sing a twelve-tone role takes a lot of work, even for a fast learner. Rubes said later that it took him six months to get it under his belt. Nevertheless it was worth doing, since he contributed a great deal to one of the COC's finest and most adventurous productions.

While Rubes was getting ready for *Lulu*, he took the lead in a CBC radio five-installment show, *Second Time Lucky*, a comedy about Czechs in Toronto and their times at the (fictitious) Café Wunderbar. He plays the role of Jaromir and even sings a rough version of the "Beer Barrel Polka." Jon Ancevich, who wrote *Castle Zaremba*, did the show's script. Rubes worked with a seasoned group of radio actors: Barbara Hamilton, Eric House, and Ruth Springford. In an interview with Don Harron on the CBC show *Morningside*, Rubes called it a soap opera and said that Susan Rubes was pleased that it was being done. The head honcho of radio drama at the CBC still firmly believed in soap operas.

Earlier that year, Limelight Dinner Theatre did a production of *South Pacific*, with Rubes playing Emile de Becque. Two Czechs, Adolf Toman and Vladimir (Mirek) Burstein (Susan's half-brother), had been operating the theatre for two years. Toman had trained at the Prague

Academy for Theatre Arts and had appeared with Czechoslovakia's National Theatre Company. He had been stranded in Paris after the Prague Spring of 1968 and came to Canada the next year. After working to establish a Czech theatre and the Aladdin Theatre for children, he opened Limelight. Toman was its producer-director and Burstein took care of its business. Limelight was located on north Yonge Street, some distance from downtown. It could seat more than two hundred and had had much success staging several Broadway musicals in its first two years. However, none of them matched the reception to *South Pacific*. (Now, in 2007, Toman is minister of culture in the Czech Republic.)

It had been almost twenty years since Rubes had first done it, but he still could produce sufficient ardour to play the middle-aged lover convincingly. He was happy, too, that the small, comfortable, two-tier stage and pleasant setting allowed him to relate easily to his audience. MacKenzie Porter, a bright, unpredictable, and opinionated writer, loved it. He wrote, "That rich, dark oak voice in such memorable numbers as 'Some Enchanted Evening' and 'This Nearly Was Mine' fills the room with romance."[179] The cast, smaller than for the original production, sang and acted attractively. There were few complaints that a piano was used instead of an orchestra. The restaurant's "house special" was roast beef, chicken Bali Hai, sole Polynesian, and South Seas platter. The diners were somewhat surprised when the sailors and other ensemble members served as waiters before the show and during intermissions. The musical ran until August — 103 shows. Rubes missed only four of them.

In December, Limelight, enjoying the sweet smell of success, staged *The Sound of Music*, also with Rubes. As in years back, he played von Trapp. There was a standing ovation at opening night. However, Bob Pennington of the *Toronto Star* was less than thrilled with the production and the food. He said "Rubes stumbled over snippets of dialogue, made a dubious transition from staid widower to swooning lover, and should pack in the guitar playing."[180] MacKenzie Porter voiced a quite contrary opinion, writing that the show was an "artistic knockout." The audience gave it a standing ovation when the curtain came down.[181] While doing the show, Jan commuted almost daily to Kitchener, where he was shooting a film called *Utilities*! That's what being busy is all about.

CHAPTER 13

1980–1985: More acting, less singing; University
teacher; Tennis champion; TV, radio, and stage roles

In 1980, the sixty-year-old Rubes was no longer an opera singer
who also acted, but now an actor who could also sing. In March,
CBC-TV aired a one-hour docudrama called *Harvest* as part of its
"For the Record" series. The opening credits noted that it was a fictional
story set in Saskatchewan. It was, however, inspired by a real and ongo-
ing controversy. Officials of the Saskatchewan Economic Development
Corporation (SEDCO) offered farmers northeast of Saskatoon generous sums for their land in order to create a satellite city. But, in truth,
SEDCO wanted the land for a uranium refinery. Caught in the act, the
government turned over its plans to an arm's-length private company to
negotiate the sales.

In the film, Carl Weschel (Rubes), a Mennonite farmer, unlike his
fellow farmers in the area, refuses to sell his land. He doesn't trust the
private company any more than the government agency that initially
tried to trick him and other farmers. He gets evasive answers when he
asks company officials if nuclear power is necessary and what are the effects of radiation. The officials fail to understand that Weschel's problem
is moral, not financial. Is nuclear power good or bad? "I don't love the

land, but we have always got along," he says. Carl's son David, a member of the provincial legislature, doesn't completely agree with his father, and rifts flare up between father and son, as they do between Carl and his fellow farmers. The family rift is resolved, and David helps Carl bring in the harvest because his angry neighbours, who disagree with him, refuse to help him. However, thanks to Carl, the future of the refinery remains in doubt. In reality, most of the farmers opposed the refinery, and

Jan Rubes (Carl Weschel) and David McIlwraith (Weschel's son David)
in Harvest, *1981.*

it remained an issue when the film was shown. However, they eventually caved in and sold their farms.

There were reservations about the way film writer Rob Forsythe tampered with the facts to make a good story. Certainly he was looking for trouble when he identified SEDCO by name, but he did this because he felt strongly about its improper behaviour. As for the show itself and the cast, there was little criticism. One critic wrote, "Rubes is ideal in the central role of Carl with his slightly stubborn old-world ways, his accent, unshaven face and wind blown hair."[182] More specific praise came from James Nelson of *Canadian Press*: "When the land developers first visit Weschel's farm with an offer to buy two quarter sections of land, the look in Rubes's eyes has all the suspicion, uncertainty, and mistrust thousands of farmers must have felt. And when father and son are divided on principle, Rubes's acting maintains the fatherly love and respect he has for his son. What Rubes does with the part makes it a fascinating hour of television."[183] A third critic thought that Rubes "brings a powerful sense of humanity to his role…. He's not a fanatic, merely a deeply religious man who is troubled by the few facts he discovers about nuclear power. You can't help liking and admiring the man, and this adds charm to the film."[184]

A more controversial point of view was expressed by Ron Base of the *Toronto Star* — he was known as the loose cannon among Toronto film critics — who called it "an updated version of Ibsen's *Enemy of the People*." He wrote that Rubes "would have been right at home in a John Ford western. Instead he grimly tends to his wheat on a Saskatchewan farm." Base's condescending outlook rears up again at the end of his review, when he describes Weschel as "a one-note samba who dances strictly to a monotonous tune called Grim and Determined. Jan Rubes is a fine opera singer, but he's no Gary Cooper and *Harvest* isn't the *High Noon* of the nuclear energy controversy."[185]

Nothing Base wrote could have been further from the truth. Rubes's characterization unmasked a wide variety of facial expressions, his walk was determined, he was tolerant, and his demeanour was rich in substance. It was, to be sure, his finest dramatic effort to date. At first, the film's young director, Giles Walker, had difficulty toning down Rubes, whose broad style unnerved him. But, when the takes were reviewed and the best ones chosen, Walker admitted that Rubes was all a director could ask for. His craggy and implacable presence and imposing integrity did much to enhance the show's credibility.[186]

Harvest was shot in October 1979. Rubes appeared in Saskatoon in a Celebrity Series concert three months later. A Saskatoon favourite and an honorary citizen of the city, he called his show "An Evening at Home." He sang and told stories and, the next day, gave a five-hour vocal workshop.[187] As his voice was not what it used to be, he no longer gave full recitals and avoided singing operatic arias. Although it had not yet been released, word had already leaked out about *Harvest*'s content. The *Saskatoon Star-Phoenix*, in an article on Rubes, mentioned that *Harvest* did indeed deal with Saskatchewan's dispute about uranium and would soon be shown on television. Three months after the film's release in March, the CBC revealed that it had pulled *Harvest* from a package of ten shows it had sold to the U.S. Public Broadcasting System (PBS).[188] Evidently CBC president Al Johnson and Saskatchewan Premier Alan Blakeney were very unhappy about the film. Johnson, who had been a deputy minister in the Saskatchewan government before assuming his CBC post, followed Blakeney's lead on this. Also, there seems to have been a threat of a lawsuit if *Harvest* was shown again anywhere. In retrospect, that it was shown at all, given the CBC's unpredictable behaviour and fear of controversy, was a bit of a miracle. For this we must thank general manager Peter Herrndorf, who overruled CBC higher-ups.

Rubes appeared in several other films in the next few years — some for movie houses, some for TV. *Mr. Patman*, featuring James Coburn and Kate Nelligan, was screened at the 1980 Toronto Film Festival. Shot in Vancouver, it is a confusing movie about a male nurse in a mental hospital who gradually loses his mind. Rubes had a minor role as the menacing Vrakettas, who helps drive Patman to paranoia. The film had little success and limited circulation.

In 1981, Rubes was in the Canadian-produced *The Amateur*, a Cold War movie with John Savage, Christopher Plummer, and Marthe Keller. Based on a popular novel by Robert Littell, the thriller was shot in Toronto, Vienna, Washington, and Munich. Terrorists kill photo-journalist Sarah Kaplan. Her fiancé, Heller (Savage), a CIA computer programmer, vows to get the killers after meeting with Sarah's father, Sam

Kaplan (Rubes), who had lost his first wife and two children in Nazi death camps and had sought out their killers after the war to get his revenge. When Heller says, "But it didn't bring them back from the dead," Kaplan replies, "It brought me back from the dead." Heller finally plants explosives to go off when the villainous terrorist leader Botaro goes for his morning swim. The explosion not only mortally wounds Botaro but also, breathtakingly, blows him out of the pool to his death. Plummer is a Czech Elizabethan scholar who moonlights for the KGB, and Keller is an attractive CIA agent. The film was reviewed widely and favourably, and the *Los Angeles Times* and other journals singled out Rubes for special praise in his small but pivotal role. His reputation was growing.

Wilfrid Laurier University appointed Rubes artist-in-residence in October 1981. This kept him on campus one day a week working with vocal students on the fundamentals of opera — interpretation, stage movement, theatre technique, and production. According to Dean Gordon Greene, Laurier had already developed a strong vocal program. He praised Jan:

> Rubes concentrated on pushing our young singers to understand the words they sang in whatever language — to create the story, the emotion, and the events of the text through the music as they sang. Oh, yes, he would shout intemperately on occasion at a lackluster performance, but behind his shout was a twinkle. No one could take personal offence because the ultimate issue for Jan was always the music. He stressed putting your ego aside, addressing the text, the story, the role in opera, the poetry in lieder. And I recall his saying that you grow by putting everyone else before you. We must serve the composer and the music.[189]

Jan concluded his stay at the university by devising and directing a student program of vocal excerpts titled "History of the Human Voice." This was a prelude to a student production of *Man of La Mancha* on December 4 and 5. His raison d'être as teacher was in the printed program and might well be read by other opera school directors: "It was my wish to make my young colleagues aware of the fact that a singer in today's world of electronic media can not just be a 'singer' anymore. He has to be a complete performer — so with the help of my students we have devised an evening when and where we would exercise all our skills as performers." Rubes qualified the results by noting that rehearsal time had been limited, but what he relished was "the unbounded joy and help and talent of these young artists. I thank them for making this evening possible." Lucky students.

In a change of pace, the Rubeses' genial friends, the Velans of Montreal, hosted them for almost two weeks in St. Moritz, Switzerland, in March 1981, where they skied to their hearts' content. Karel and Olga Velan had emigrated from Czechoslovakia in 1949. Karel had started an industrial valve corporation that flourished, and subsequently he contributed large sums to needy Czechs and Czech organizations. After the 1989 Velvet Revolution, he set up a foundation in the name of Olga Havel, the wife of the president of Czechoslovakia. Karel was the president of both the Czech Canadian Association and the Czech American Association, and he continues to hold the latter post in 2007. The Rubeses were frequent visitors at the Velan house in Montreal and at their country place in Sutton, Quebec.

Jan's brother, Mirek, and his wife, Jarica, visited the U.S.A. in the spring of 1981 to see their daughter, Eva, and son-in-law, Clem. Then they moved on to Canada, spent time at Collingwood, and went to Stratford to be with Jan and Susan. That summer, Jan did fifty-one performances of *South Pacific* in Thunder Bay. Tony Rubes, now twenty-three and on the threshold of an acting career, played Buzz Adams in the show. Perhaps Jan took on the assignment to give himself the opportunity to bond with his youngest son. As if he hadn't had enough of *South Pacific*, Jan did another thirty-four performances of it at Limelight in the fall, followed by a TV show, *From Now On*. Tony gave his parents much pleasure by playing the role of a student in Barbra Streisand's film *Yentl*. Part of it was shot in Czechoslovakia, which gave Tony a chance to see his Czech relatives.[190]

The always accommodating Jan Rubes had agreed to play a leading role in a new work, *The Barnardo Boy*, in Kingston, Ontario, in May of 1981. Staged by an amateur theatre company, it would be given at the Grand Theatre, an attractive Victorian structure built in 1879 and renovated several times since then. The city had taken it over in 1962. *The Barnardo Boy* is a fictionalized tale about the work of Dr. Thomas John Barnardo, a turn-of-the-century English physician who helped bring thousands of poor English orphans from the streets of London to relatively prosperous Canada, where they would have a chance for a better life. Rubes played Albert Ashby, a Barnardo boy now in his old age. Ashby tells the audience about his life, first as an orphan in England and then in Canada. Clifford Crawley composed the music for the show with a libretto by David Helwig, who was also directing. The Barnardo boys are a significant footnote in Canadian history.

Rubes examined Crawley's music before accepting the job but did not anticipate the difficulties in store for him in doing the actual show. The inexperienced director didn't see eye to eye with Rubes on a number of matters and, in the end, made Rubes nervous. Conductor James Coles and the orchestra — most of them were professional — got along better with Rubes, although Coles said that Rubes seemed aloof and even a bit patronizing.[191] The *Kingston Whig-Standard* — the Davies family had made it one of Canada's finest newspapers at the time — gave the show immense coverage. There was a gala opening night and the houses were good for all four shows. Critic David Barber was carried away by it, calling the production "masterful."[192] As Ashby, "Rubes sings for half an hour about his mother," wrote reporter Bill Hutchison.[193] Rubes told him that the words and feelings of the opera were very close to his own when he left his mother behind in 1948. There was much praise for Jan's performance in the show, but no mention was made of his accent, hardly suitable for the English-born Ashby.

In 1982, Rubes went to Vancouver to film a CBC show, *Play Gypsies*. It celebrated the one hundredth anniversary of the birth of the Hungarian composer Emerich Kalman, a master of the middle European operetta. Rubes plays the aging virtuoso Gypsy violinist Racz Pali, who has trouble deciding which comes first, women or his violin.[194] Rubes thought the lyrics of the two songs Racz sings "terribly British" and not suited for his Czech accent. They had also been written for a typical "spiel-tenor," so the range would have to be lowered about a fourth. The "Dear Old Stradivari" begins with the line "A woman or a violin, that's a choice to ponder." The other song, "Time, Oh Time," is all about Racz's aging. The verse begins, "There I was so young, so handsome, seems like only yesterday, on each arm ten girls and then some — reigning monarch of the day." Otto Lowy, a Czech who ran a popular weekly radio program of mostly ethnic recorded music, helped convince the CBC to do the show. Although well intended, it lacked style and finesse.

Tony Rubes graduated in theatre arts from York University on June 10, 1982. Six weeks later, Jonathan, now a mechanical engineer, married Judith Gilman. Susan had met her at a tennis clinic and led her on to Jonathan. An interior designer and a woman of considerable charm and personality, she hit it off well with her future in-laws. The nuptials took place at the Rubes house. Jonathan, who strongly resembles his father, called it "a homemade wedding" with a delightful air of informality. Guests brought food and Chris baked the wedding cake. Riki Turofsky sang "There Is Love" and there were the usual speeches. Jonathan spoke in praise of his mother and said, jokingly, "Whoever I married I know would have been introduced to me by my mother." The balcony over-looking the pool was the site for formalities and speeches, with the approximately 120 guests in the garden below. After the formalities, there was much frivolity and some guests even went swimming.

That August, the competitive Jan Rubes won the national tennis crown for over sixties at the annual Canada tournament held in Montreal. Jan and Susan sold 55 Sumner Heights in the fall and moved to an apartment in the Colonnade on Bloor Street, in central Toronto. They moved again the next year to the Manulife Centre, a towering skyscraper on nearby Charles Street. They had also discovered Pelican Cove in Sarasota, Florida, an attractive escape from Canadian winters, where they have been going annually ever since. Dr. Chris Rubes, now head of emergency at Toronto General Hospital, was the admitting physician when a comatose Glenn Gould was brought to him on October 4. Gould died soon afterwards.

America's favourite prime-time TV soap operas in the 1980s were *Dynasty* and *Dallas*. Why not a Canadian show celebrating — if that is the right word — Canadian capitalism and its complex if not nefarious activities? The CBC responded with *Vanderberg*, a six-part miniseries

Soprano Kiri Te Kanawa and Jan after a round of tennis, 1985.

Jan's backhand at age fifty-seven.

shot in the summer of 1983 about Hank Vanderberg (Michael Hogan), a Calgary tycoon with business and private life problems, and his wife, Elizabeth (Hogan's wife, Susan), who is restless and seeking fulfilment. Jan Rubes is Lewis Vanderberg, Hank's father, the conservative founder of the company now successfully run by his son. Hank plans to make millions internationally. Michael Durland of *Canadian Cinema* wrote that *Vanderberg* was "the dramatic face of Canada's corporate age."[195]

This wasn't far from the truth. Certainly the show had lots of sheen — beautiful scenery provided by the Rockies, planes, and fast cars. The young women were good-looking, and young Vanderberg was brash, egotistical, and not very likable. The series was well-received in some quarters and considered pap in others. Lorraine La Page of the *Montreal Standard* thought Rubes played the elder Vanderberg "with a genteel urbaneness that adds much to the dimensions of the family relationships."[196]

The CBC did not renew the series. According to Susan Rubes, CBC-TV was ineffectual when it came to mounting an extended series: it didn't prepare scripts or book actors well enough in advance of the dates required, it didn't use the same crew throughout the series, and it failed to engage alternate directors so that one could work on the next show while the other was directing the one being shot. She felt that the CBC preferred doing individual shows that appear to be unique and demonstrably creative.

John Reeves enters our story again. In addition to being a writer, composer, radio producer, and long-distance runner, Reeves was a staunch advocate for a free and democratic Czechoslovakia — witness his poem following the Prague Spring of 1968. Before 1968, he had worked hard to smuggle scripts of dramas and documentaries out of Czechoslovakia to broadcast on the CBC. He had also set two of his detective novels in Czechoslovakia. In February 1980, Reeves produced a radio drama — one in a series of three shows about three religious leaders who shared the name of John — on the trial and death of the fifteenth-century Czech religious leader Jan Hus, with Jan Rubes playing Hus. Among his efforts to bring the church closer to the people, Hus had used the vernacular instead of Latin in his services. As a result, the Church Council at Constance accused Hus of heresy. Several well-planned traps were laid for him, in what would later be called a "vicious judicial murder." Since Hus refused to recant he was stripped of his priesthood, had to wear a dunce's hat, and was burned to death at the stake. As the flames crept up to his chest and face, Hus prayed joyfully, secure in his beliefs. It was an unforgettable show.

The Hus show was one of several CBC radio shows in which Rubes was cast in the early 1980s. Three others were *The Prime Minister and the Angel*, *Stagford*, and *40 Zlosynù*. *Stagford*, a Czech play produced by Reeves, takes place during the Soviet occupation. Several people, including a Russian soldier, have disappeared after getting lost in a remote forest. They eventually turn up in Stagford, a make-believe town whose description sounds like science fiction. There is a chairman of the town (Rubes) who is not politically appointed and who really seems to know nothing about the Soviet grip on the country and cares even less. Government officers are thwarted since they expect a *political* chairman to run things, not someone who picks strawberries and makes wine for a living. The prosperous Utopian town lives in peace and harmony — there are no cars and all eat well.

John Reeves, a Cambridge graduate, was truly a Renaissance man who included serious composition in his creative work. In January 1983, Elmer Iseler conducted his three-act opera-oratorio, *Salvator Mundi*. There were a number of fine vocal soloists, including Rubes as Pontius Pilate. Given at the St. James Cathedral in Toronto, the three-and-a-half-hour work is about Christ's last days. In spite of competent performances by choir, soloists, and several organists — a pre-recorded section by a chamber choir was included — the piece was too long and the script and music needed more drama. Reeves licked his wounds and moved on to other challenges.

The Peddler of Fortune, a winsome show, was given on a CBC radio series, "Saturday Stereo Theatre," in April 1983. Based on the stage play *Mendel Fish*, it was adapted for radio by Aviva Ravel and takes place in Montreal during the Depression. A benevolent if enigmatic character, Mendel Fish (Rubes), enters a poor Jewish community and soon reveals that he has the power to change misfortune to fortune. He sings, "Take what you need, but give what you can." Philosophy is important, he says: "Without food for thought a man is no better than a cow in pasture." Mendel Fish produces several small miracles, becomes an alderman, and makes as if he wants to marry the poor but beautiful Rachel who is half his age, rather than — and more appropriately — Rachel's widowed mother. Finally, he arranges — or so it seems — to get killed in a street accident. He has completed his work. We ask, will Mendel Fish turn up in still another poor neighbourhood in the future? Perhaps.

The next year Rubes was the narrator on a CBC radio adaptation of Hans Christian Andersen's *The Nightingale*. It is a musical geared to the whole family, with an original score by John Robey. It takes place in a mythical far-off country where a nightingale enchants all of those who hear her sing. People capture her in order to enjoy her singing even more, and then sadly abandon her in favour of a jewelled replica. The CBC also did a CD of the fifty-five-minute show, and YPT co-produced a slightly longer version for the stage.

And then, in February 1985, the popular *Morningside* radio program aired a series of five shows, each fifteen minutes long, titled "Yalta — Decisions that Changed the World." Rubes played Stalin, one of the three principals, the others, of course, being Roosevelt and Churchill. A good many interesting radio shows were being produced, thanks to Susan Rubes. She had taken on the CBC post in order to revive radio drama, and she had, to an extent, done just that. If she rubbed a few of her colleagues the wrong way it was the price one often pays for making progress. As she had done at YPT, she got to the people who could help her — sometimes without going through proper channels — and, with their support, did what was best for the art.[197]

In 1983, Jan Rubes produced a new kind of show for Prologue. Titled *Quiet*, it deals with a young five-member rock band whose leader, Peter, is losing his hearing. The band's music is high voltage and the more Peter surrounds himself with it the deafer he gets. *Quiet* addresses the impact of electronic instruments on music, comparable to the effect of the combustion engine on man's mode and speed of travel. Peter is thoroughly demoralized. His career as a leader and composer appears over, but Jan Czarnowski, a music professor played by Rubes, saves him by showing Peter and his band how dangerous extremely amplified music can be. Rubes based his short play on his real-life experiences. He felt strongly about how such music attacks young people's senses, and about how they self-destruct by playing and listening to it. *Quiet* also showed in its own small way how Rubes was not only keeping up with the times but also exploring new areas. It played in twenty-three Ontario centres.

Still another change of pace was Rubes's involvement in Benjamin Britten's *Noyes Fludde* at a TSO Young People's Concert, conducted by Andrew Davis at Roy Thomson Hall in April 1983. Forty-five minutes long, the work was given twice on the same day. It uses adult professional singers as the principals, several advanced teenaged singers, and a small professional instrumental core that plays together with a large children's orchestra. About one hundred children are dressed as animals and sing as they board the Ark. There is, finally, an invisible God, whose resonant speaking voice rings out over everything else as the drama proceeds. God must match his text with the music. Jan Rubes played God! The Toronto Symphony Youth Orchestra and the Canadian Children's Opera Chorus, along with children from several local churches and schools, were also involved. The audience becomes part of the action as it joins the chorus to sing two hymns. Britten envisaged *Noyes Fludde*, which is more of a pageant than an opera, as a community effort to be done in a church. Roy Thomson Hall was a valiant attempt to prove otherwise. The local press had divided opinions about the performance. No matter, the performers and the audience enjoyed it immensely.

In June 1983, the St. Lawrence Centre produced the popular Broadway version of *Cabaret*. The press reaction was mixed. Gina Mallet of the *Toronto Star* didn't like it very much — "too long, poorly cast, very un-Broadwayish."[198] The Jewish Herr Schultz (Rubes) has an affair with the Gentile Fraulein Schneider (Sylvia Lennick). Mallet thought the affair too sentimental and overdone; others disagreed. There were thirty-seven performances.

On June 1, the night before *Cabaret* opened, Guelph University awarded Jan Rubes an Honorary Doctorate of Letters. The university president introduced him at convocation and, in summing up Jan's life, made an irritating number of factual errors. This might have been because he had been given faulty or incomplete information. Then Jan said a few typical words to the graduates about aspiring to great heights and achieving success, which for him, he said, was due to Mozart. He then proceeded to sing Sarastro's aria from *The Magic Flute*, first in German and then in English. He was not in good voice, and there were moments that made one squirm. He said a few words about Don Quixote and then sang "The Impossible Dream" from *Man of La Mancha* — marginally better than the Mozart aria. In his final remarks, he thanked his wife for her support, acknowledged the presence of his brother, Mirek, who had come from Czechoslovakia for the event, and corrected the

Mirek, Jan, and Tony at the Guelph Convocation, 1983.

president — humorously — for saying that he was the Ontario senior tennis champion when he was, in fact, the Canadian champion. It was a well-deserved and memorable occasion.

In the fall, Jan had a key role in a CBC-TV drama, *Charlie Grant's War*. It was shot in just twenty-four days but wasn't shown until fourteen

Dr. Jan Rubes at the Guelph convocation, 1983.

months later, in January 1985. One of the CBC's finest efforts, *Charlie Grant* was written by Anna Sandor, the daughter of a Hungarian Holocaust survivor and the writer of the CBC's popular *King of Kensington* series. It tells the true story of Charlie Grant (R.H. Thomson), a member of an upper-crust Vancouver family who convinces his mother and uncle that he wants to see the world before joining his uncle's business. He ends up in Vienna in 1932. Thanks to a Jewish diamond dealer, Grant enters the diamond business and inherits the firm when the owner dies. He is also befriended by a retired opera singer, Jacob Goldmann (Jan Rubes), and his wife, Elizabeth (Joan Orenstein), who practically adopt him. Goldmann is Jewish, and Grant is appalled when, following the Anschluss, the German SS beat him in a totally mindless attack simply because he is a Jew.

A decent, caring man, Charlie Grant soon realizes that an awful fate is in store for the Jews of Europe. A sympathetic Austrian government official helps Grant negotiate a fake passport for a Jewish family. Grant is soon doing the same for others. After much effort, he convinces the reluctant Goldmanns to leave Austria. Grant is determined to get them to Canada, but the Canadian office in Vienna doesn't co-operate. Deeply troubled, he writes his mother (Marigold Charlesworth) to ask her to use her influence to convince the Canadian government to open its doors more widely to refugee Jews, and, in this case, the Goldmanns. Of course she fails — Canada had one of the most dismal records in saving Jews from the Holocaust of any Western nation; it accepted a mere five thousand. Mrs. Grant's meetings with the infamous Minister of Immigration F.C. Blair and Prime Minister King are chilling. King, Mrs. Grant's old friend, tells her that his Liberal Party is in trouble in Quebec and would be destroyed if Jews "flooded the country." The show's depth of sophistication is further revealed as Mrs. Grant shows herself susceptible to the prevailing genteel anti-Semitism of the time. She tells the Prime Minister that it is one thing to keep Jews out of "our clubs," but another to keep them out of Canada with the Nazis at their heels. As for Blair, her meeting with him yielded nothing but the fact that he detested Jews.

Grant is eventually found out and imprisoned in a concentration camp. He meets Goldmann there just before Goldmann dies — his wife

Jan (Jacob Goldmann) being harassed by two SS men in Charlie Grant's War, *1984.*

had already died at Auschwitz. Thomson and Rubes are both eminently convincing in their roles, and show by their faces alone their characters' suffering. Grant survives, unlike his Swedish counterpart Raoul Wallenberg, who disappeared after the Soviet liberation. In all, Charlie Grant is credited with saving six hundred Jews.

Thomson, an articulate spokesman for the film, told Donald Martin:

> It's vital for a nation's identity to have its own heroes setting its own standards. I didn't know a thing about Charlie Grant before making this film — but I knew everything about Davy Crockett. We spend so much of our time trying to cut everything, the politicians, the bureaucrats, the CBC — we're in a very cynical time. I don't think a country can make much progress if it's so cynical toward itself. We need to aspire toward greatness, and Charlie Grant was a great man.[199]

Rick Groen of the *Globe and Mail* subtly compared Grant's actions with Canada's: "The story of an ordinary man who made a difference and an ordinary nation that didn't."

The film also had special meaning for Susan Rubes. She had lost her four grandparents to the Nazis. Her paternal grandparents perished in a Nazi death camp. Her maternal grandparents managed to survive at Terezin, but when liberation was imminent they were put in a sealed boxcar, where they died. A fellow prisoner related this to Susan years later. There was no formal record of this heinous act. *Charlie Grant's War* was almost two and a half hours in length and earned six ACTRA nominations, more than any other TV show that year. Rubes was one of the nominees. It could have been coincidence, but the book *None Is Too Many: Canada and the Jews of Europe 1933–1948*, an indictment of Canadian policy towards European Jews, was published the same year that the CBC shot *Charlie Grant*.

Blame it on the times, but the attacks on human dignity and the hardships and worse that beset people in different parts of the world were increasingly capturing the attention of Canadian creative artists. The Toronto Workshop Theatre's director, George Luscombe, long a theatrical spokesman for the Canadian left, staged one such work, *Victor Jara Alive!*, in March 1984. A dramatic musical by writer Ken Gass and composer John Mills-Cockell, it deals with the life of Victor Jara, one of Chile's most popular composers. Jara, played by Frank Moore, was a fervent supporter of Salvator Allende, one of the first freely elected presidents in Latin America. Rubes did several roles in the show, including Allende, whose last utterances were recorded before he was silenced forever in a military coup led by General Augustus Pinochet. Here is an excerpt from Allende's final speech that Rubes recites in the play:

> This will probably be the last opportunity I have to address you. The air force has already bombed the towers of our Radio Corporation. But my words are not spoken in bitterness, but rather in disappointment. Let there be a moral judgment on those who have betrayed the oath they took as Chilean soldiers and loyalty to the Commander in Chief.
>
> In the face of these events, all that remains for me

to say is — I shall not surrender. I will pay with my life for the loyalty of the people. MY PEOPLE. The peasant women who believed in us, the working women, the mothers who knew of our concern for their children, the men of Chile, the worker, the peasant, the intellectual. Many of you will be persecuted ... I am certain that the seed which has been planted in the conscience of thousands and thousands of Chileans shall not be uprooted. Avenues shall again be opened and free men shall march toward a better society.

Rubes also sang some of Jara's attractive songs, accompanying himself with his guitar. Here are the first two verses of the five-verse song "Stand Up! Arise!" It is sung at the beginning of the play at a demonstration in Argentina in support of Chile's exiles ten years after the fascist coup:

Stand up! Arise!
And look toward the mountain.
Source of the wind, the sun, and the water.
You who have carved out the rivers and valleys
Planting the seeds of flight within your spirit.

Stand up! Arise!
And look toward your brother.
Stretch out your hand and build the chain together.
United in blood, and united in history
Now is the time, the beginning of tomorrow.

Jara is political drama, and the play's script may have been so intent on getting across its message that it left little room to bring the characters to life and act out the story convincingly. The daily press was generally critical for this reason, in spite of the play's good intentions. Both Allende and Jara had been brutally murdered — the CIA is reputed to have had a role in this — yet Canada had conveniently forgotten about these sad events for eleven years.

CHAPTER 14

1982–1986: *Witness* and other films; TV and stage plays

J ust before Jonathan's wedding, Rubes was engaged to play the fatherly role of Dr. Oscar Schloss in a CBS TV drama, *Little Gloria, Happy at Last*. Based on the bestselling book by Barbara Goldsmith, it is an account of the complicated custody case of the young heiress Gloria Vanderbilt in the 1930s. It had a stellar cast, including Angela Lansbury, Christopher Plummer, Maureen Stapleton, and Martin Balsam. Dr. Schloss, a prominent pediatrician, had looked after Gloria from birth. Since the two-part miniseries played on a leading U.S. network, it attracted considerable attention.

Peter Weir, the Australian film director of *Gallipoli*, *The Year of Living Dangerously*, and, most brilliantly, *Picnic at Hanging Rock*, was planning to direct a new film, *Witness*, and saw Rubes in *Little Gloria*. Weir, envisaging him for the doctor role in *Witness*, promptly brought him to New York for a screen test and was so impressed with the results that he called Jan back to read for the more significant role of the grandfather. Although it was rumoured that Weir had considered Max von Sydow for the role, not only did it go to Rubes, but Weir, after discussions with Harrison

Jan (The Grandfather) in Witness, *1985.*

Ford, who would have the lead in the film, enlarged the part to give Jan more scope.

The Amish people in Lancaster, Pennsylvania, are central to the film. They are a religious sect, mainly farmers who spurn nearly all worldly goods. They forbid photography, do not attend movies and stage plays, drive only horse-drawn buggies, dress simply, are non-violent, and keep away from outsiders whom they call "the English." Weir wrote two decades later about the Amish and about the challenge in casting the film.

> Although American born, and living in the U.S. for generations, they speak with a German-tinged accent and exist in a kind of living museum of nineteenth century rural life. The way they look, the way they move, their existence without the conveniences of modern life has produced a very different and fascinating group of people. How to cast them convincingly? My first thought was to cast Europeans. This plan finally proved unnecessary but it did bring Jan Rubes to my attention.

In casting a role, you're always looking beyond the reading of lines at an audition, looking for what the individual before you will bring to the part that is uniquely their own — their spirit, their life experience, something, that when combined with the part as written will give greater richness to the character. Jan was hardly like a nineteenth century farmer but he had a demeanour that was not just European, but seemingly from another era. I never really considered anybody else for that part and was delighted with the result. His own qualities gave the character authenticity, which combined with his performance made for a highly credible portrait of an Amish elder.[200]

The conscientious and prescient Weir brought the entire cast to Lancaster in May 1984, ten days before shooting, to acquaint them with Amish ways. He, on his own, had already studied them extensively. Yet the Amish barely co-operated in making the film, despite Weir's efforts to convince them that he had no intention of interfering with their way of life. It didn't help when a Temple University professor accused Weir of not showing sufficient respect for the Amish, and this raised the hackles of Weir and the entire company. A Mennonite house near the Amish settlement was used in shooting the film because the Amish refused to make one of theirs available. The Mennonites, whose beliefs resemble those of the Amish, co-operated fully.

Witness begins with Rachael Lapp, a young Amish widow (Kelly McGillis), and Samuel, her eight-year-old son (Lukas Haas), preparing to board a train in the Philadelphia railway station. Samuel goes to a restroom and witnesses the murder of a narcotics policeman. He then identifies the killer to Detective John Book (Harrison Ford), who has been assigned to the case. Book reports this to his superior, who, it is revealed, was in on the murder. Book is shot at and injured by a fellow policeman. He flees with Rachel and Samuel and takes refuge in the Amish community, where he is cared for and recovers. Book falls in love with Rachel. Her father-in-law (Rubes), suspecting that she is returning Book's love, criticizes her. Rachel's feelings are simply and quietly revealed — looks and gestures prevail more than the spoken word, with several scenes wonderfully erotic by implication, not action. According to Rubes, McGillis started out badly — she was Weir's, not Ford's, choice for the widow — but the chemistry between her and Ford improved as the filming progressed. After the murder is solved, Book leaves the widow, their love unrequited.

Harrison Ford did a lot of homework with the Philadelphia police force and its homicide division to prepare for his role. Coming across as an authentic detective was important. Although he had little contact with Rubes on camera, he commented recently on Rubes's fine acting in the film and how impressed he was with the "poignant" way in which Jan handled the gun scene with young Samuel, his grandson. Altogether, Ford retains fond memories of the film, the director, and Rubes.[201]

Sylvia Train of Toronto interviewed Rubes on location and reported how he talked about everyone else but himself.[202] He praised Weir, who brought the cast in every day to see the previous day's rushes. The cast became so interested in the production that even those who were not in a shoot stood by to watch what was happening. Rubes also liked doing the film because the shooting "followed the script chronologically, so it was like being on stage. We went from one sequence to the next." He took Train to meet Kelly McGillis — Jan liked McGillis and the feeling was mutual. McGillis thought Jan "a beautiful spirit."[203] Reflecting on their work together more than two decades later she felt that he could be very serious and, at other times, very silly. Jan's fun-loving nature prevailed no matter where he was and what he was doing. Rubes and Train visited the makeup man who was doing McGillis for the next shoot; he was also the one who did Rubes's artificial beard. Jan later told a CBC interviewer that he had to remove the beard when he ate, and that it took an hour to put back on.

Later that summer Rubes spoke with Peter Gzowski on CBC radio. He complained that his work on *Witness* had kept him away from tennis for six weeks and that he couldn't wait to enter the national tennis competitions. Then he got down to the substantive part of the interview: the Amish. In trying to understand them, he had done chores with their animals, taken daily walks through piles of manure, visited Amish congregations, and listened carefully to their traditional chants. When he went to Hollywood for some final shoots, he sang some of the chants from memory for the noted film composer Maurice Jarre, who was doing the music for the film. Jarre included them in a fugue he wrote for the barn-raising scene. Rubes also talked with Gzowski about how today's singers, some of whom he had taught, had to be aware that television brought facial expressions and even thoughts under closer scrutiny than did the stage. Film acting, he suggested, is more difficult than operatic acting, since in opera, as he had said in the past, the timing is supplied by the music and this determines what you can or cannot do. In film, acting is more in the abstract — the actor has to create his actions mentally at every shooting. He concluded the interview by stating how grateful he was for *Witness*, because it opened up his chances for roles other than prairie farmers and Jewish refugees.

Rubes couldn't put *Witness* aside. Over a year later he told Ruth M. Kelly that "Peter Weir believed the film could explore Amish culture. I think that's why it turned out to be so marvelous. It was a voyage of discovery for everyone involved in the production as well as the audience."[204] Kelly wrote that "Rubes reached back into his experience as 'CBC's token ethnic farmer' to provide the cadences of speech and physical stances required. He also researched Amish history and came away awed by their beliefs." Rubes said:

> I feel that their survival here is a great tribute to our society. It's a testament to our tolerance to have allowed them to live a completely different style of life. They were completely wiped out in Europe due to religious persecution. The strength of their beliefs is truly amazing. When the Indians attacked them when they first settled in North America, they just put their heads down and were slaughtered. I think Peter Weir put it very nicely when he said "I admire them but I don't understand them."

The film was a box-office winner, receiving eight Academy Award nominations and winning two — for editing and screenplay. In an interview with Sid Adilman in February 1985, just before *Witness* opened in Toronto, an elated Rubes said, "I've acted extensively the last three years. The biggest personal difference for me is that I don't have to be in shape for singing and that lifts a tremendous burden. I can play tennis, I can get colds, I can eat what I want — and still act. I couldn't do any of that when I was singing full-time."[205] And then he added, "Peter says I could make a lot of money playing the kind of parts von Sydow does. Wouldn't that be terrific, and at my age!'"

And so his film career as an older man, as a patriarch who is either loved or hated, developed rapidly. His life had been one of great variety, but now, when he was at so-called retirement age, he had more work, more travelling, more meetings with interesting people than ever before. In 1985 he appeared in no less than eight TV dramas — for CBC, CTV, ABC, and CBS — some involving extensive shooting. CBC's miniseries *Crossing* required him to travel to Paris and, later, Los Angeles. It is a Second World War epic featuring Rubes as a Viennese violin virtuoso. One of the leads in the series was his old friend Christopher Plummer. Their paths were continuing to converge.

To fill out 1985–86, the indefatigable Rubes appeared in five radio dramas and hosted five CBC-TV opera programs. Joan Irwin of the *Toronto Star* thought Rubes an inspired choice for the opera shows and "marvelously seductive" in enticing listeners to stay with opera, rather than changing channels.[206] Jan embellished his remarks with personal experiences and anecdotes about the operas being given. He also earned applause when he played a heavily bearded Santa Claus in Disney's film *One Magic Christmas*. He told Craig McInnis that he played a European-style Santa Claus. "In Czechoslovakia, St. Nicholas played a large part in our life. We celebrated St. Nicholas's birthday on Dec. 6, and it was much like Christmas is here, with gift-giving and all the rest. Philip Borsos [the director] let me create my part along the lines of what I thought I was best able to do. At the first meeting we had, I said: 'No ho-ho-hos'!"[207]

One Magic Christmas was a Canadian film promoted as a Christmas show for adults. It opened in November in Toronto and subsequently played profitably in movie houses throughout North America. The Graingers, Ginny (Mary Steenburgen) and Jack (Gary Basaraba), are stretched financially — he has been out of work for six months and she is a poorly paid checkout clerk in a supermarket. Their two children have little to look forward to at Christmas. Along comes Gideon, an angel in a long black coat and black hat — one naughty reviewer said that he looked like a child molester — who creates miracles for all of them. One is a trip to the North Pole to meet Santa (Rubes) in his factory. The film is thus about dreams that can come true and how the Christmas spirit, in the best sense, prevails. Janet Maslin of the *New York Times* called it "a modern film with a gratifyingly old-fashioned feeling, some of which is a matter of its unselfconscious plainness. The Graingers look, sound, and dress like real people, which on the screen becomes considerably more remarkable than it sounds."[208] The film was nominated for seven Genies, including Rubes for supporting actor. (Genies are annual movie awards given by the Academy of Canadian Cinema and Television. Juries select the nominees and academy members vote for the winners. They are, in effect, Canadian "Oscars.")

The pressure of conflicting obligations was brought home to Jan one wintry night when he was driving from Toronto's airport to a teaching commitment at the University of Windsor. He was coming from New York, where he had been fitted for a wig and clothing for *One Magic Christmas*. Windsor is 380 kilometres from Toronto, and Jan was tired. Alas, he fell asleep at the wheel! "I went through the median and the next thing I know I'm going the wrong way on the 401 [a major superhighway]."[209] After narrowly missing three oncoming cars, he collided head-on with a truck. Both drivers were miraculously unharmed. It was Jan's sense of duty that had brought about the accident in the first place. "[It] just forced me to reiterate my original thinking that one has to be tremendously lucky to have a fruitful, successful life," he said. Rubes had taken on the Windsor teaching post for 1984–85, replacing Steven Henrikson, who was on sabbatical leave. It involved monthly visits of several days at a time. Windsor had a musical theatre program that Rubes took to considerable heights. He concluded the year, as at Wilfrid Laurier, by directing a production of *Man of La Mancha*.

As if he didn't have enough on his platter, the week after the McInnes interview about *One Magic Christmas*, Rubes narrated "Music in the Romantic Era," one of a series given by Preview Concerts at Harbourfront on Lake Ontario. He also hosted a CBC-TV cultural show, *Thursday Night*, as well as the Sunday opera series. Hosting shows about music, thanks to his warm, mellifluous speaking voice, brought him much work.

When TVO aired *Heimat*, a German series of thirteen episodes, in 1986, Rubes was invited to introduce each show. It chronicled six generations of a German family in a Rhineland village up to and including the Second World War. Eight years later he would do the same for another series, *Heimat II*, about a young composer and his fellow students — actors, writers, film producers — studying in Munich in the 1960s.

Vocally, Rubes still seemed up to doing Sancho Panza in an Opera In Concert production of Massenet's *Don Quichotte* at Toronto's Jane Mallet Theatre in March 1986. Thanks to the direction of the inspired Stuart Hamilton, a pianist and vocal coach, Opera In Concert had won a large following. The productions were not staged and had only piano accompaniment. Hamilton was especially at home with nineteenth-century romantic French operas, and his expertise showed in his work. Giulio Kukurugya played the Don, as he had in Hamilton's 1976 production of the same work, and Jean Stilwell was an enchanting Dulcinée. Hamilton felt, like so many others, that Jan sang remarkably well for one who was at the end of his singing career, and that, as always, he was the consummate professional.[210] Actually, Jan was also in the midst of playing a major role in the movie *Dead of Winter*, but playing two roles at the same time didn't seem to bother him. It was being shot in Toronto, and he was so enthusiastic about *Don Quichotte* that he invited his movie colleagues, including director Arthur Penn, to attend the opera. Its success even earned Rubes a few kind if typically qualified words from John Kraglund: "Although he retired from opera several seasons ago, his interpretation of this multi-faceted role proved that his vocal and dramatic art are still of enviable high quality — more than enough to make up for the decline of a voice that is still securely controlled."[211]

Whether it was films, television, radio, stage, musicals, or opera, Rubes was prepared to take it on. He generously used a sliding fee scale for financially strapped local groups like Opera In Concert — he charged it $1,000 for rehearsals and the performance. Yet, in movies, he would receive upwards of $2,500 for a day or $12,500 for a week. He would, when possible, write in an additional percentage of the profits in his contract. His fees continued to grow well into the 1990s.

Dead of Winter was a suspenseful murder mystery. Rubes plays a major role, Dr. Joseph Lewis, an eccentric and slightly mad wheelchair-ridden psychiatrist-producer with sinister intentions. Lewis's equally sinister sidekick, Mr. Murray, is played by Roddy McDowall. Mary Steenburgen plays three roles: Julie, a woman murdered early in the film; Katie, an actress who is held hostage by Lewis and Murray; and Evelyn, a murderous woman. She is excellent in all three. There is a lot of implausible action that is hard to take seriously, yet the suspense is occasionally gripping; as the climax approaches, watchers are on the edge of their seats, riveted by what is basically a very campy film. It was unusual to have Rubes playing the villain instead of the nice old man from somewhere in Europe. There would be more such roles to come. He was now, by any standard, a first-class character actor.

Rubes enjoyed doing *Kay O'Brien*, a weekly CBS TV hospital series shot in the summer of 1986. He was Dr. Joseph Wallach, head of surgery at a New York hospital. Interior scenes were mainly filmed at the Toronto General Hospital, where Dr. Chris Rubes was an emergency room specialist, and, incidentally, an unofficial consultant for the producers. The hospital was only a short walk from the Rubes apartment,

Jan Rubes (Dr. Joseph Lewis) and Roddy McDowall (Mr. Murray) greet Mary Steenburgen (Katie McGovern) in Dead of Winter, *1987.*

which made doing the show even more attractive.

CBS gave a lavish kickoff party for the series in New York with lots of press coverage. Producer Bill Asher explained that he had chosen Toronto because no space was available at New York hospitals. He added, "In Toronto they are not quite as violent. They are a happier lot. You don't hear all those horns. You feel more relaxed and it's reflected in the activity in the emergency rooms. Twenty-six of the twenty-eight operating rooms were empty on weekends."[212] An article by Canadian Jim Slotek suggested that Asher "in describing this idyllic land [Canada] sounded like Margaret Mead reporting on the doings of blissful aborigines.[213] Yet this was the first time that a major prime-time American series was shot in Toronto, although exterior shots were done in New York. Nevertheless, Canadian film aficionados beat their chests with pride — few noting that Rubes was the only Canadian in a major role.

Kay O'Brien (Patricia Kalember) is an attractive resident surgeon who gets enmeshed in problems, romantic and otherwise, in and out of the hospital. It was a formula show with attractive moments and predictable outcomes. Dr. Wallach lectured resident doctors in the hospital's lecture hall — the same lecture hall that Chris used with his residents and interns. Jan, in his doctor's white coat, looked so much the part that he could move freely around the hospital. Wanting to visit a hospitalized friend, he even used the staff-only connecting tunnel to the adjacent Mount Sinai Hospital without having to identify himself. Unfortunately for Jan, the show was dropped after a few weeks because of low ratings. It had been competing with NBC's popular *Hill Street Blues* and ABC's special Thursday night programs.

While shooting *Kay O'Brien*, Rubes took on the stage role of the alcoholic farmer, George, in a popular comedy thriller by Peter Colley, *I'll Be Back Before Midnight*. It played at the St. Lawrence Centre's Bluma Appel Theatre in June. In an interview on CTV he said that he enjoyed acting in theatre more than anything else and loved doing this play. What he didn't say was that he had accepted only $3,500 per week for seven shows, far less than he was earning for *Kay O'Brien*. *Midnight* is about a young scientist, Greg (Jack Wetherall), and his wife, Jan (Fiona Reid), who is recovering from a mental illness. He brings her to a rented farmhouse for peace and quiet, but he also brings along his "sister," Laura

(Charlotte Moore), who is actually Greg's former girlfriend. Greg has an unusual relationship with Laura and seems to be out to destroy his wife. George complicates matters by dropping in regularly to tell stories about local murders. Greg's wife does not recover. The show opened at the Blythe Festival in Southwestern Ontario and has since been staged in many different locations in North America and abroad, ample evidence of its popularity. In view of this continuing exposure, it would be unfair to give away the play's ingenious conclusion!

Henry Mietkiewicz of the *Toronto Star* wrote, "Rubes creates a character of uncommon malevolence by emphasizing idiosyncratic, grandfatherly friendliness. Appearing to have nothing to hide, he alone makes us wonder about the possibility of double or triple crosses."[214] Bob Pennington said his "delight in drollery and bawdy sense of humor" added much to the role. "After a slow first act, the second act grips the audience sufficiently to take the comedy seriously and the horror not so seriously."[215] It ran for fifty performances.

The gifted Fiona Reid knew of Rubes as an opera singer and was at first skeptical that he was up to a difficult stage role.[216] It didn't take long for her to see that, as any good actor would, he married his own instincts with the character he was playing. "Rubes was clearly comfortable in his own skin." She thought his sense of timing was excellent and speculated that this was probably due to his musical background. Because Jan was still shooting *Kay O'Brien* while doing *Midnight*, he had an understudy in case the film's demands kept him later than the eight o'clock curtain. One night he didn't turn up until the actual curtain time, so the producer held up the show while Jan caught his breath and dressed for the play. Playing two very different roles on the same day was, as we have seen, not unusual for Rubes. The understudy never did the role on stage.

In January 1985 the Canadian Radio-television and Telecommunications Commission (CRTC) was considering several applications from television companies for a pay-TV children's channel. Susan Rubes, no longer at the CBC, had tentatively accepted the part-time presidency of the Family Channel (TFC), one of the more promising applicants for the pay-TV licence. The TFC board wanted her badly because of her background with YPT and Prologue. Susan made her acceptance of a full-time position conditional on TFC winning the CRTC licence.[217] In July the CRTC, unable to make up its mind, decided, in classic Canadian fashion, to establish a task force to review the applications and submit its recommendations in January 1986. By this time there were seven applicants for the one licence. Nothing happened. Susan continued her relationship with TFC and signed a binding contract as consulting president in July 1987. Shortly afterwards, the CRTC finally awarded the licence to TFC. It was more than two years since the CRTC had addressed the matter. Such are the ways of Canadian bureaucracy.

Susan unveiled some of her TFC plans in an interview with Stephen Nichols of Canadian Press.[218] Her goal was to present programs that would be watched by the entire family. TFC would give eighteen hours daily of animated and live action shows with no sex and no violence. Approximately 60 percent of the shows would be American, especially Disney films with characters such as Mickey Mouse and Donald Duck, 25 percent would be Canadian, and the rest European. It was a money-making scheme that TFC hoped would work. Not surprisingly, Susan left the organization in 1989. She had done her job. TFC was moving along, and Susan wanted to return to her first love — acting.

CHAPTER 15

1987–1990: *Max Glick, Something About Love, Two Men;* Gemini Award; Opera directing

Jan and Susan Rubes were together in a film, *The Outside Chance of Maximilian Glick*, in late autumn 1987. The movie was based on a Morley Torgov novel that had won the 1983 Stephen Leacock Medal for Humour. It takes place in the small prairie town of Beausejour, near Winnipeg, and is a warm, funny, and occasionally wry story about a twelve-year-old Jewish boy who is preparing for his bar mitzvah. He is also preparing to enter a provincial piano competition, and his piano teacher is confident he will win first prize and the scholarship that goes with it. Along comes an attractive new girl in town, Celia, who is about his age, takes piano lessons from the same teacher, and plays as well as he does. Their teacher decides that it would be best for them to play four-hand piano music, for if they win in this category they will *both* get scholarships. There is, however, an unforeseen problem — Celia isn't Jewish. It couldn't matter less to her family that Max is Jewish — they even invite Max to help decorate their Christmas tree — but it matters a great deal to Max's family, who eventually forbid him to play piano with her.

Max befriends Beausejour's new rabbi, who has a long beard, curly sideburns, and wears a black coat and hat. Rabbi Teitelman, played superbly by Saul Rubinek, irritates the Glick family and other Jews because he looks *so* Jewish, and, to make it worse, he has a few untraditional views about Judaism. Beausejour Jews want their Jewishness concealed and yet their traditions upheld. The rabbi has his own demons; he sometimes thinks he should have been a stand-up comedian instead of a man of the cloth. When Max explains his piano-playing problem to Teitelman, the rabbi consoles him as best he can and tells him to talk it through with his parents. It doesn't work. In the end, Max says no to the bar mitzvah unless they let him play with Celia in the competition. Predictably, all ends well. There is a bar mitzvah at which Max tells his parents and other Jews present how off-base they are, the two young people play in the competition, and, later, they see Cam Title, formerly Rabbi Teitelman, telling jokes on a television talent show.

The entire cast is excellent in this family film, especially the two children, Noam Zylberman (Max) and Fairuza Balk (Celia). Rubes plays the boorish grandfather who is constantly telling the boy about what it means to be a Jew even though his views on Judaism are a maze of contradictions. Susan Rubes is a Jewish granny (Bubby) to beat all such grannies, always ready to take Max's temperature and give him an enema when the boy feels low. The piano teacher, Derek Blackthorn, deals with the competition problem well, as does his Japanese-Canadian wife, who wisely tells Max not to let other people's limitations become his limitations. "Open yourself up to life, Mr. Glick," she tells him. In the end, Max gets his parents and grandparents to confront their own racism.

There are a few funny one-liners. One is a flashback early in the film when Max, several days old, is circumcised. He comments wryly twelve years later that Jewish parents spend the rest of their lives trying to cut off the rest of it. Max also observes that "Jewish parents never let their children grow up. I guess that's why they are called the Children of Israel." One critic said whimsically that Max was a cross between Huck Finn and Woody Allen.

Screenwriter Phil Savath had Max Glick tell his story through his own eyes using voice-over narration technique. In essence, his most important observations and actions throughout the movie are his bar mitzvah speech. His family is a captive audience who must listen to his point of view and come to realize that he is right and they are wrong. Saul

Rubinek liked the script so much that he did the film for far less than his usual fee. *Maximilian Glick* received five Genie nominations, including one for Susan Rubes. It didn't win any. Initially, the film had had trouble getting funding. Finally, several groups came through — the National Film Board, the CBC, Telefilm Canada, the Manitoba Cultural Industries Development Office, and Film BC. It was the first feature movie shot totally in Manitoba, a rather historic event.

Earlier in the same year, Jan and Susan spent almost a month in Sydney on Cape Breton Island, Nova Scotia, where, years back, Jan had appeared with the COC in *The Barber of Seville* and also in *South Pacific*. Now they went to this bleak and yet beautiful place to film *Something About Love*, a classic small movie. Wally Olynyk (Stefan Wodoslawsky), a thriving Hollywood movie producer who had left Sydney fifteen years before, is called back to visit his father, Stan Olynyk (Jan Rubes), a mortician who is going downhill mentally. We find, eventually, that he has the beginnings of Alzheimer's disease. Returning home is not easy for Wally. His father had never shown much affection for him in the past, and there had been other vexing differences. On top of these personal problems, being Ukrainian in a basically Scottish-Irish settlement made Wally feel like an outsider in his hometown. And now Wally must cope with his father's illness. However, the film proves that you *can* go home again. Stan, cranky and disagreeable, loves his son, but is too rigid, obstinate, and reserved to show it. It becomes a voyage of discovery for both of them.

Wally's brother and sister ask Wally to help them deal with their father's illness. Wally extends his visit. He sees his old girlfriend Bobbie (Jennifer Dale), now divorced, and they talk about his having left Sydney years before. Bobbie tells Wally "everyone on the island has a story about the time they almost left," although few actually do. About his father one reviewer put it well: "Wally and his father cannot magically heal a lifetime of shared emotional strain, but they are both given an opportunity to reveal the depth and breadth of their difficult love for each other…. They learn something about love and this simple lesson makes for a gratifying two hours at the movies."[219]

One thing that makes the film exceptional is how Wally and Stan search for ways to forgive one another. Stan, too proud to apologize to

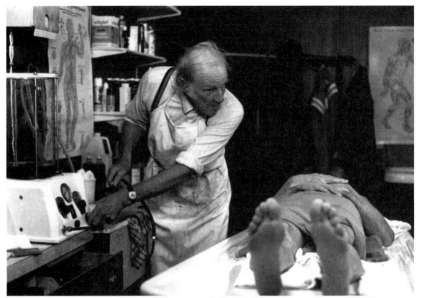

Jan (Stan Olynyk) embalms a corpse in Something About Love, *1985.*

his son for not showing him enough love when he was a youth, employs a subtle change in tone with Wally that speaks louder than words. Stan may be angry and dysfunctional but you understand why. When a neurologist (Susan Rubes) confirms that Stan has Alzheimer's, he presses on to rediscover the son he loves. This done, the proud man decides that he will not be a burden to his family, and drives his car over a cliff to certain death.

Something About Love was screened at the 1988 Montreal Film Festival, and Rubes earned all kinds of kudos. John Griffin of the *Montreal Gazette* wrote, "There are just enough cracks in Stan's crustiness to show great reserves of love, pride, and pain. The final opening-up between father and son in the town's Ukrainian church is one of the great moments in contemporary Canadian film — it's the kind of scene that should happen at least once in every family's real life."[220] Rick Groen wrote, "Rubes is an archetype that crosses all boundaries — the cranky patriarch losing his faculties but not his pride, saying less than he feels, and feeling more than he shows. Wodoslawsky plays Wally to match, revealing a man who, for all his acquired affectations, remains his father's son — same reticence, same stubbornness, same courage."[221] The film is, perhaps, overly sentimental, but there is nevertheless a warmth and a sincerity about it that is compelling and leaves one thinking about it long afterwards.

Together, Wodoslawsky and Tom Berry wrote the screenplay, and Berry directed it. Wodoslawsky grew up in Cape Breton, was of Ukrainian descent, and went away for fifteen years, but claimed that the story was not autobiographical.[222] Berry, eighteen years later, still remains thrilled with Rubes's performance, from the initial screen test when he told Berry that he was a retired opera singer — Berry couldn't believe it! — to the film's completion.[223] At their first meeting on the set, Rubes told Berry that he intended to manipulate him and not to be offended. In fact, as the shooting proceeded, Berry could not have been more pleased. The material was good, but Rubes, as always, improved the role with suggestions to director and cast, without subverting it. Jan turned up one day wearing a cap with the inscription, "Old age and treachery will always overcome youth and skill." Fun, yes, but it was also a statement in defence of the aged. The film won the People's Choice Award at the Atlantic Festival Atlantique and was an entry for the 1989 Genie Awards. It was a personal triumph for Jan Rubes.

In the period when Rubes was doing the Glick and Wodoslawsky-Berry movies, he also did eight (!) other films — some movies, some for television, some good, some bad. It brings to mind Laurence Olivier's reply to a critic who asked him why the great actor did commercials and second-class films. He retorted, "Because I am a working actor." So it was with Rubes. For example, one brief TV film of doubtful merit that he did in Hollywood was for an episode of *Fame*, a popular weekly show at the time. He played a theatre director who visits a New York performing arts high school, as much to look up an old flame who he thinks heads it — she doesn't — as to advise the students on their careers. Other films that year featured him in small roles, an inevitable fate for a sixty-seven-year-old actor where leads are usually the province of the young. Jan was earning sizable fees from this work, but he still had a piece of his heart in opera and theatre.

The ambitious Guillermo Silva-Marin, a singer and director of the Toronto Operetta Theatre (TOT), asked Rubes to direct Strauss's *A Night in Venice* at the MacMillan Theatre of the Edward Johnson Building in

October 1987. He couldn't refuse and explained why in the program piece, titled "A Histerical Note":

> I joined the TOT ... for two reasons. I am at the point in my career when I can afford to do "things" I WANT to do, things I think also I will have FUN doing. Secondly "Operetta" (or "musical comedy," as we call it here) played a large part in my musical and acting career, all through my life actually! Some of the melodies you'll hear tonight and will whistle on your way home, my mother and my father used to play as piano-violin pieces when I was a little boy in Czechoslovakia.
>
> Then as a young operatic basso at the Opera House in Prague and Pilsen, I was always enlisted for parts in operettas because, as they said to me: I was handsome and could act as well as sing! And then on this continent I scored "hits," in "hits" such as *South Pacific, Sound of Music, Man of La Mancha,* etc. And, of course, singing and acting in Johann Strauss's *Die Fledermaus* for COC more than 200 times! And directing it for Richard Bonynge and Joan Sutherland in Vancouver.
>
> What should I tell you about *Night in Venice?* Johann Strauss? Vienna of 1883, and the whole world of the "classical operettas fairy tale lands"? Where "His Highness" from an eighteenth century Italian Duchy flirts with a fishermaiden from Venice, while they sing unmistakably Viennese melodies and dance a WALTZ!?
>
> Researching material on Venice, one wrote: "One can think of Venice as a matter of screens and floats and wings ... a series of Istrian limestone platforms, descending like immense steps to canals ... littered with pigeon droppings." Well, I asked for pigeons for our production. I was told that preliminary estimates for a flock of pigeons, their trainer, and union scale for cleaning after the show were prohibitive... So forget it! Really, what we need is your willingness to suspend your

beliefs, stir your imaginations, while keeping your eyes
and ears open. Put on your masks and step into our gon-
dola of dreams … for one night in Venice!

Despite the many films Rubes had on his platter, he took time for this
indulgence and accepted a nominal fee. He wrote some new dialogue and
lyrics with Allen Stewart-Coates, diligently rehearsed the cast, and came
up with a winner. The operetta's original libretto was and is a mess. It
has had a tiresome history of rewrites and revisions since Strauss's death,
without really leaving anyone completely happy with the results. Robert
Everett-Green of the *Globe and Mail* began his review of the performance
by saying, "Lovers of Viennese operetta are like B-movie fans. They love
the form, not in spite of its crudities and absurdities but, to some degree,
because of them."[224] Rubes had fun inventing characters named Padre
Condominio and Ginaloola Brigida. There was also a Fiordiligi and a
Dorabella, "a playful acknowledgment of how the work borrows from
the comic operas of Mozart." The cast was generally first class. Russell Braun played Mario, the romantic army officer. His father, the now
internationally famous Victor Braun, was singing Kurvenal in Wagner's
Tristan und Isolde for the COC at the O'Keefe Centre at the same time.
Young Russell was on the threshold of a career that would emulate his
father's. Raffi Armenian, who knew Viennese music well, conducted the
show with his Kitchener-Waterloo Symphony. He also conducted it in
the Centre in the Square in Kitchener.

At the beginning of 1988, Rubes signed up for villain roles in two
films, *Two Men* and *Blood Relations*. *Two Men*, made for television and written by the same Anna Sandor who did *Charlie Grant's War*, is about Hungarian-Canadian watchmaker Alex Koves (John Vernon), who is tortured
by memories of his parents and brother, who were sent to death camps
during the Second World War. He does not share these haunting memories with his wife and daughter forty years later. Worse, he feels guilty for
having survived. Koves sees by chance a prominent Hungarian-Canadian
businessman, Michael Barna (Rubes), on television. Barna is a pillar of
the community, has a flourishing travel agency, donates money to good
causes, and is a recent winner of a multicultural award. But Koves sees
another Barna, the young assistant in his father's shop in Hungary who

went on to join the infamous Arrow Cross organization and then turned in the Koves family to the Nazis.

Alex is determined to bring Barna to justice but finds that no one really wants to help him, not even Jewish organizations. The feeling is that it happened so long ago that it doesn't matter now. Barna has reformed, so why not leave him alone? Undeterred, Koves goes after Barna, who vehemently denies everything. Eventually they have a confrontation. Koves has a gun and threatens to shoot Barna, but, fortunately, Barna's wife (Patricia Collins) intervenes. Koves backs down. He has had his moment, and the film's final scene shows him spending a moving few minutes in a synagogue for the first time since his childhood. His dying Aunt Rose (Lily Kedrova) had urged him to return to his roots.

Several similar real-life cases had recently been brought to Canada's attention, so the film was timely indeed. John Vernon, who had been working in Hollywood for twenty years, was best known in Canada for his title role in the twenty-two TV installments of *Wojeck*, which ran in 1966. He made public how happy he was to play Alex Koves. Writer Sandor patterned Koves after her stepfather, who, like Koves's father, died in the Holocaust with many of his family. The press generally lauded the film and the cast. Vernon and Rubes were both nominated for

Jan Rubes (Joseph Barna) and John Vernon (Alec Koves) in Two Men, *1988.*

1989 Gemini Awards, for lead and supporting actors respectively. Rubes won his award.

However, there were some uneven moments in *Two Men* that some of its admirers overlooked. Koves's return to practising Judaism to celebrate his change of heart may have pleased many Christians and Jews, but it was artificially contrived and basically irrelevant. What does it have to do with the plot? The Holocaust treated all Jews, practising or not, the same way. Does going to synagogue at the end of the film prove that Koves has had his humanity restored? The aunt, who eggs him on to return to religion, is a superfluous role, well acted as it is. Punishment and revenge are implicit in both the Christian and Jewish religions and are not to be admired. *Two Men* is earnest and well-meaning, but the two main characters, especially Koves, have too many contradictions and simply aren't sufficiently interesting to build a more profound story. You can congratulate the two actors for doing so well with the script, but Sandor should have probed more deeply into Koves's problems and made him appear more intelligent, instead of one-dimensional and simplistic. Barna needed more treatment in terms of what he remembered and what he chose to forget. His background could have been explored more. At the end, one felt that he still disliked Jews. The only time Barna emotes is when he has a gun at his head. There are, by the way, subplots: Barna's son dies in an accident that deeply affects Mrs. Barna, and Koves seems distant with his wife (Martha Gibson) and daughter. It was a good show, but it could have been better.

Blood Relations, Rubes's next film as a villain, was a sleeper. Almost twenty years later it still attracts cult followers of horror movies. The plot, briefly, is about Thomas Wells (Kevin Hicks) and his beautiful fiancée, Marie (Lydie Denier), who are visiting the lavish estate of his estranged father, Andreas Wells — Rubes, with dyed hair, eyebrows, and moustache, and looking younger than his actual years. Andreas is a famous neurosurgeon who handles a scalpel with considerable skill. The body of his late wife, whose brain he has preserved — his hobby is transplanting brains — lies somewhere in the house. Marie, who has a striking resemblance to the dead wife, is impressed by the opulent surroundings and schemes to get in on the huge inheritance being left by Thomas's grandfather, who is close to death. However, there will be only one recipient and no one knows who it is. Andreas tries to seduce Marie. A conflicting relationship is soon revealed between father and son. The situation fits Woody Allen's descriptive "Oedipus Wrecks" scenario.[225] There are many bloody and gruesome moments. Lydie Denier was so affected by the film that she told the director, "I often dreamed that Jan Rubes was trying to kill me. Which is silly, because he is really so sweet."[226] There is a surprise ending if you are still taking the film seriously.

Rubes was originally slated to do the dying grandfather, but his appearance in *Dead of Winter* convinced the producers that he would be better as the mad surgeon.[227] Hollywood actor Robert Stack, who was in the twilight of his career, was also being considered for Andreas.[228] The film was shot in the Parkwood Estate in Oshawa, Ontario. Half of the main building is a museum, so shooting had to be confined to its unused portion, with a museum watchman on duty to make sure that cast and crew didn't abuse the premises. The cinematography was excellent and the cast provided sufficient madness for the purposes of the film.

The 1989 Montreal Film Festival screened *Blood Relations* twice on the same day. The small audience attending the morning screening started to laugh after the first few minutes and continued without let-up for the rest of the film. The afternoon showing played to a full house and the audience waited until halfway through the film before they started laughing. The author of this dubious contribution to film annals, Stephen Saylor, charged the producers less than expected on condition he play a role in the film.[229] As Jack, one of the estate workers, he appeared to be no better an actor than a writer. However, the longevity of *Blood Relations* may well belie any criticism of Saylor's work. Director Graeme Campbell had a good time doing the film, as did Rubes. Campbell echoed what other directors said of Rubes — that he was the consummate professional.

During the 1988 Toronto Film Festival, a group of Jan's friends gave him a testimonial dinner at Le Fave's Restaurant. Peter le Fave's young daughter was at the party all starry-eyed. She had been a Rubes fan since seeing him in *One Magic Christmas* and continued to think of him as Santa Claus.[230] It was revealed at the party that Jan had nine new films coming up. He could well have been the busiest actor in Canada. But just in case some thought his future lay in nasty roles — *Two Men, Blood Relations*

— he would soon be going back to being a bearded grandfather with a heart of gold in a new Heidi film, *Courage Mountain*, to be shot in Austria. Director Christopher Leitch had seen *Witness* on TV in a London hotel room and knew that he had his grandfather.

Heidi (Juliette Caton) is now fourteen. Her beloved grandfather (Rubes) has decided to send a reluctant Heidi to a girls' boarding school in Italy, just over the border from her native Switzerland. Once there, her fellow students mock her rustic ways. She does, however, have a sympathetic headmistress, Miss Hillary (Leslie Caron). The time is 1915, and the Austrians are at war with Italy. The school becomes a military headquarters and the girls are packed off to an orphanage to do forced labour. Escape they must. Heidi leads the girls over challenging mountain passes to Switzerland, with much hardship on the way. They need help, and her old village boyfriend, Peter (Charlie Sheen), comes to the rescue in an overwhelming demonstration of cross-country and downhill skiing. He has a temporary setback hanging on a mountain ledge to avoid sudden death. The audience grips its seats with fear.

According to Teresa Beaupre, a *Toronto Star* reporter who visited the film company, Rubes loved the setting and even passed up one night in his centrally heated hotel room to sleep in the mountain cottage where Heidi and her grandfather live in the film.[231] Jan explained that it helped him to get deeper into the character. This was in November, and it was already cold in the Alps. Jan did only one take of the key scene in which he tells Heidi, as she leaves for school, "The mountain is inside you. It will always be there." A formidable new production company owned by Joel and Michael Douglas, sons of actor Kirk Douglas, produced the movie. One critic said that Rubes plays "a standard issue Swiss grandfather. His character is a cliché, of course, but watching him you're not aware of it. He just feels awfully solid."[232] A family film, it needed more colour and more fun, given the wonderful setting. Joel Douglas called it a "schmaltzy" film, but it could have used even more schmaltz.

CHAPTER 16

1988–1997: Films about sickness and aging;
More tennis championships; Earle Grey Award

Both Jan and Susan Rubes were flourishing. Although they had always had full lives, late middle age brought them still more success and still more kudos. Work has its rewards, and Jan and Susan were workers. On June 17, 1988, YPT and Susan's many friends paid her tribute in a "Gala for Susan Rubes" at the Grand Ballroom of Toronto's Sheraton Hotel. More than 650 people were there, including such stalwart friends as the Hirschfelds from New York and the Velans from Montreal. Toronto Mayor Art Eggleton was there, as were leading showbiz actors, directors, and producers. The printed program's cover duplicated the *Life* magazine cover of February 3, 1947, with young actresses Patricia Neal, Patricia Kirkland, and Susan Douglas tobogganing. Kirkland was playing Ruth Gordon in a play, *Twenty One*, on Broadway at the time, and Neal was on the brink of a Hollywood career. Douglas was playing on Broadway and on radio and was slated to take one of the leads in *Lost Boundaries*. The photo reminded those present that Susan in her early twenties was already a talent to be reckoned with.

Also attending from New York were Eli Wallach and Anne Jackson, who did a skit, "A Night In The Life Of." They spoke humorously about their long friendship with Susan — how Susan had helped Anne when Anne did her first radio show, how their young children had played together in New York, how they had shared babysitters, and how she and Jan had generally enriched the Wallachs' lives. Jan sang "Some Enchanted Evening," accompanied by leading pop musician Hagood Hardy. The three Rubes sons spoke, as did Edward Greenspan, the prominent trial lawyer, who claimed that Susan, as head of CBC Radio, had made him a star when she initiated the popular show *The Scales of Justice*. Susan finally spoke. At first she was uncharacteristically speechless but soon warmed to the task and talked of her current work as president of the Family Channel and its wonderful programs. It was Susan at her best. And, to top off the gala, an announcement was made that the main YPT theatre was now formally designated the Susan Douglas Rubes Theatre.

Towards the end of 1988, First Choice TV produced *No Blame*, its subject HIV/AIDS. The common belief at the time was that it was a male disease and prevalent mainly among homosexuals. Donald Martin's script, however, addressed HIV from the woman's point of view, exploring how women with the disease coped.[233] It is a tale about a pregnant magazine fashion editor, Amy Donaldson (Helen Shaver), who visits her family doctor (Jan Rubes) and asks him for an HIV test. The doctor, who represents the older face of medicine, tells her in a few days that the results are positive.

It is devastating news — she is married and has a five-year-old child — and the world falls in around her. Her husband shows limited sympathy and little concern that their next child might also be infected. Only Amy's women friends give her the support she needs in this distressing time. She goes to a counselling clinic where the young woman counsellor urges her to take another test. At the same time the counsellor reveals inadvertently that she too has HIV. Amy goes to another doctor who tests her again. The results are negative — she does not have the dreaded virus. Amy then gives her counsellor, who is dying from AIDS, much compassion and love over the next few months, and is the better for it.

Donald Martin said that *No Blame* was based on the true story of a woman in California whose life was destroyed when her doctor leaked test information to her employer and husband. Martin therefore created a film that confronts fear and ignorance and tenuous relationships. "I called it *No Blame* because no one is truly to blame and yet everyone is. I want to show people the side of the AIDS crisis that affects them. There are no gay characters, no drug pushers, no prostitutes. She's a Yuppie… her life is perfect."[234]

The film was shown at the World Health Organization's Fifth International Conference on AIDS in Montreal and drew all kinds of plaudits. It was nominated for five Geminis and won the Red Cross film award in Monte Carlo. Of interest was that Donald Martin had to rewrite part of the script before shooting began, because Helen Shaver was actually pregnant — the first script had her asking her family doctor what would happen if she became pregnant. The beautiful actress looked more so as the shooting progressed, and she even reluctantly agreed to do a brief scene at a swimming pool in a bikini. Shaver had a substantial career and later turned to directing.

Then Rubes found himself in another small role in a horror film, *Blind Fear*. Son Tony was also in this one. The action takes place in a hotel in rural New England, although it was actually shot in Canada. The hotel is closing for good, and the last two occupants are the caretaker (Rubes) and a pretty young blind woman (Shelley Hack), who is doing various jobs around the building. Three thieves rob an armoured car in a nearby town, shoot the drivers, and hide at the hotel. Their terrifying leader, played by Kim Coates, is clearly a psychopath. He kills Rubes soon after he and his fellow thieves occupy the house, and then he spends most of the remainder of the film trying to kill the blind woman. There is a surprise ending. Thanks to skillful directing by Tom Berry, the film has its suspenseful moments.

But Berry and Coates hadn't finished with horror. A still more frightening film was *The Amityville Curse*. It takes place in a haunted house to beat all haunted houses in Amityville, Long Island, outside of New York City. A wicked priest (Jan Rubes) is murdered in his confession booth by Frank (Coates), a very disturbed man. The priest's belongings are moved to what will be a haunted house. Fast forward twelve years. People buy the house and the "fun" begins. There are more murders. The young woman of the house finally kills Frank in self-defence, in a most ingenious and gruesome way. Tony Rubes was given special billing — he was one of the visitors to the house.

Jan Rubes (The Grandfather), Josh Garbe (Max), Susan Rubes (The Grandmother), Linda Kash (Mrs. Glick), and Alec Willows (Mr. Glick) in the Max Glick *series.*

Back to more pleasant films. The CBC was so impressed with *The Outside Chance of Maximilian Glick* that it approached its producer, Stephen Foster, and its writer, Phil Savath, to do a TV series based on the same characters. The setting was the same, Beausejour, but one year later, 1964. Most of the characters, including the children, were newly cast. The Rubeses remained as the grandparents. It ran for thirteen weeks and had much popular appeal. However, the CBC lacked either the funds or the initiative to continue it and dropped it as it had dropped *Vanderberg* six years before. The series had lost many viewers when it was shifted from Monday to Friday: the CBC had overlooked the fact that many Jews would be at their Sabbath dinner at that time. *Glick* fans berated the CBC for dropping it. Commenting about Jan to Bob Blakey of the *Calgary Herald* while shooting the series, Susan said, "Jan's really terrific. I don't look at him as Jan. I look at him as the grandfather."[235] She was again the typical Eastern European Jewish mother. This led to her doing the same kind of Jewish mother role in the movie *The Thriller* the next year. However, there she was all caricature — which did little for her or for the film.

How busy could Jan be? The question was becoming more

persistent. After all, he would soon be turning seventy. Yet, this did not stop him from accepting the speaking role of the Majordomo in the prologue to *Ariadne auf Naxos* (the standard version) with Mansouri and the COC in 1988. When asked why he took it on with so much film work about at better fees, he had no explanation — only that he loved the work and had promised Lotfi, "I'll do it." Susan claims that Jan could never say no to the persuasive Mansouri. For this effort, Rubes got a "surprisingly ineffective" from the *Globe and Mail* critic, Robert Everett-Green.[236] Informed listeners differed. It was Mansouri's final season with the COC. He moved on to head the San Francisco Opera in 1989.

There were films and still more films in 1988–89. Most were of little consequence, with small and stereotypical roles, although some had their moments. He made an appearance in *The Beachcomber* series featuring Bruno Gerussi, and in *Cold Front*, a poor movie with Martin Sheen in the leading role. Tony Rubes was also in that cast.

Jan gave up his Czech citizenship in February 1989, which made it easier for him to visit Czechoslovakia. He also applied for a green card to facilitate his taking jobs in the U.S.A. Susan had become a Canadian citizen in 1986. (Getting and keeping Canadian or American citizenship was and continues to be complex and challenging.) Rubes also found that his eyelids were slipping, and this was affecting his vision, no small matter for an actor with remarkably expressive eyes and facial features, and also, incidentally, for a tennis player. Fortunately, a short operation alleviated the problem.

While shooting a scene in San Francisco for the Gene Hackman film *Class Action* in late December 1989, Rubes had a pleasant meeting with Václav Havel, president of the new Czechoslovakia. Havel had for over twenty years resisted Czech communism through his writings and other activities. Jan found him delightful — much too attractive to be a politician. The Berlin Wall had come down that November, and the next month the USSR and four other Warsaw Pact countries jointly condemned the 1968 invasion of Czechoslovakia. Thanks to this peaceful Velvet Revolution, Alexander Dubček led the Czech Federal Assembly into establishing a non-communist multi-party government that marked the beginning of a new life for the country. In 1993, the Slovakians separated from the Czechs to create an independent nation. The renamed

Czech Republic joined NATO in 1999 and in 2004 was admitted to the European Union.

A little-publicized one-hour family TV film, *The Garden*, was shot in Regina in August 1990. Jan welcomed it. He told Patrick Davitt of the Regina *Leader-Post* that "Modern entertainment has created a generation gap. TV, movies, the music today, they are divisive. We used to be able to sit together and enjoy entertainment as a family, but that isn't so easy anymore."[237] The Saskatchewan government, feeling the same way, had sponsored the film. Rubes plays one of his characteristic roles, Jan Karek, a gruff old man who tends his beautiful if somewhat spooky garden in memory of his deceased wife, Elizabeth, who had been devoted to it. "It's her garden and she will always be there," says Karek. Naughty teenagers try to destroy it, but several still younger children, all of whom love Karek, thwart their plans. Karek's young friend Jess leads the younger group. The action moves slowly but the warmth the film exudes is unmistakable. Rubes enjoyed working with the young and inexperienced crew: "Look at them — you can see it in their eyes, the energy, the commitment, the desire." But Jan worried about the children and the extra work they often caused in filmmaking: "You have to get it quickly in one or two takes before they get bored and restless," he said.[238] The film was appropriately telecast on October 30, the night before Halloween.

Happily, Rubes made a number of movies with leading Hollywood actors in the next few years. Most of the films cast him in small but good roles. One was *Deceived*, a thriller of sorts, with an effective Goldie Hawn in the lead; it remains popular in video shops fifteen later. Adrienne (Hawn) is an antiques dealer whose restorer Tomas (Rubes) is killed early in the film, thus signalling that trouble is on the way. In *Class Action* Rubes is Pavel, a retired engineer. He supports the crusading lawyer Jed Ward (Gene Hackman), who is trying to pin guilt on a major manufacturer for making faulty cars. Jed must, however, face his lawyer daughter Maggie (the attractive Mary Elizabeth Mastrantonio), who is working for the opposition. The two, predictably, cross swords.

There were more TV films. Jan played Joseph Kamenska, a custodian of a high school, in one episode of the series *Life Goes On*. Thoughtless students label him a criminal in their underground newspaper because they find that he has a criminal record. Joseph had been convicted on a minor stealing charge twenty years earlier. As a working-class penniless Czech immigrant, he had stolen to feed his family. His going to jail had caused his family great grief, but he had long since paid for his crime. It was another Rubes appearance in a film of minor consequence, but it helped to build his reputation. In fact it was hard to find another actor who appeared on TV more often than Rubes.

In March 1990, Rubes received four film offers on the same day! One never came to pass; the three that did were TV films: *Descending Angel* (1990), *The Witches of Eastwick* (1992), and *By Way of the Stars* (1992). *Descending Angel* is another film that takes place in the present but has its roots in the Second World War. Florian Stroia (George C. Scott) is a leader in the local American-Romanian community. For forty-five years, Stroia has successfully concealed his former membership in the Romanian Iron Cross group and the fact that he, himself, had been responsible for the deaths of more than six hundred Jews in a concentration camp. Michael Rossi (Eric Roberts), who plans to marry Stroia's daughter Irina (Diane Lane), is more than curious about her father's past. Rubes plays Bishop Dancu, the priest of the local Orthodox church, who, when questioned by Rossi about Stroia, shows Rossi an FBI report that clears Stroia of wartime guilt. But Dancu's responses are ambiguous. He views the arrogant Stroia with some suspicion and cautions Rossi in dealing with him. And he avoids the Holocaust issue, leaving one to wonder if he doesn't know all about it. Then Rossi finds conclusive evidence to prove Stroia's guilt. Evil is exposed but an innocent person dies. Stroia's beloved Irina is mistakenly shot by modern-day Nazis who intended the bullet for Rossi. The past has finally caught up with the shattered Florian Stroia.

Six months later, in October 1990 while in Vancouver, health, for the first time, became an issue in Jan's life. Understandably, film companies insist on medical checkups of their casts before commencing shooting. He was found to have an irregular and rapid heartbeat that was diagnosed as atrial fibrillation (AF). If untreated it can lead to a stroke. He was prescribed blood-thinning drugs and told to take periodic blood tests. AF did not, however, inhibit his work or his play, including tennis and golf. He became interested in addressing and fighting AF in Canada and was the national spokesman the following September for the annual AF Awareness Month. (The Dupont Company funded it with an educational grant.) Jan did have a few very minor strokes over the next few years, but all were manageable. He was also found to have a shadow on his lung, but, fortunately, a bronchoscopy followed by a CAT scan revealed nothing serious.

The Academy of Canadian Cinema and Television honoured Rubes with the Earle Grey Award on December 5, 1990, for his services and achievements over the past forty years. The award had been established in 1986. Previous winners were Ed McNamara, Lorne Greene, Kate Reid, and Sean McCann. It was a prize to covet.

Rubes put all work aside to represent Canada in the Crawford Cup tennis tournament in Canberra, the capital of Australia, in March 1991. The tournament, named after the great Australian tennis champion of the 1930s Jack Crawford, was for players in the seventy-plus age group. As expected, Jan made a good showing, coming second in the finals. Then he and Susan took a holiday at the Great Barrier Reef and stayed at Dunk Island. Jan went scuba diving. Susan snorkelled. They found Australians super friendly, even more so than Americans, and much more so than their own sober and restrained Canadian compatriots. Jan's tennis game continued to be first rate. In May 1992, he played in the Crawford Cup competition in the French resort Le Touquet, and, after returning to Canada, he won the Ontario and national competitions during the summer. Not overly competitive in the past, Jan now seemed to relish the challenge, as if he wanted to defy old age.

The French tournament had been a stopover for Rubes on his way to Czechoslovakia to shoot the beginning of a CBC four-part miniseries, *By Way of the Stars*. It is a family film about murder, intrigue, and young friendship in the 1870s and is loosely based on a German novel, *The Long Voyage of Lukas B*. Lukas (Zachary Bennett), a blacksmith's apprentice, witnesses his father being falsely accused of and jailed for theft, and sees the blacksmith he works for arrested for political reasons. He and Ursula (Gema Zamprogna), the snobbish daughter of a countess, leave Prussia together and go to Canada to search for his father, who has fled there, thanks to a peddler, Nathan (Rubes), who had helped him escape from prison. The German Beta Taurus Company, which had suggested the film, paid most of the costs and gave Canadian director Kevin Sullivan creative control.

Susan hugs Jan after he wins the seventy-plus Ontario tennis tournament.

While Jan was in Czechoslovakia, a Czech TV company shot a half-hour documentary on the Rubes brothers. Jan was now seventy-two, Mirek seventy-four. The technically outstanding film showed them walking through the countryside, visiting Mirek's hospital and the theatre in Volyně, drinking beer in an outdoor café, and visiting the Rudolfinum (the arts centre) and the Dvorak Concert Hall in Prague. The deep affection between the brothers shines through in the film. Jan talked about his travels and expressed regret that he had seen so little of Mirek in the more than forty years since he had left Czechoslovakia. On the stage of the impressive Volyně theatre, they reminisced about how, as boys, they had played roles in local plays. Mirek, now retired, talked about his psychiatric work and his years as the youngest director of one of Czechoslovakia's leading mental hospitals. Psychiatry had not been an easy profession to pursue in a communist country. They recalled that their domineering mother had instilled a strong work ethic in both of them, and this led Jan to say, jokingly, that he left Czechoslovakia to escape his mother as much as the communists. Yet they now realized that her mentoring had helped prepare them for the many hurdles they had faced in their long lives.

Speaking as a retiree, Mirek looked back on his life. Jan, on the other hand, looked ahead to the future. He sang a short folk tune and the theme of *Guess What?* and promised to get to know his brother better. Good as the film was, it lacked actual conversation between the two brothers. It could have been the director's doing. Mirek summed up their meeting insightfully: "We both had to find something to live for, and we succeeded."

Stepping back to March 1989, Susan met with Donald Martin to urge him to write a script for Jan as a romantic lover before he got too old.[239] (Susan was never jealous of Jan on screen or on stage.) As Jan put it, "Susan felt that I'm at the age where I will get these little roles playing blubbering immigrants with an accent, and she felt you want to present the older people with some spunk." Martin responded by writing two screenplays. He approached writer Betty Jane Wylie to advise him on aging people, and she ended up collaborating with him on the first script. She said it was the only time she had been offered a job *because* she was post-menopausal! Thus, together, they wrote *Coming of Age: An Ageless Love Story* for TV. It was telecast in December 1993.

The film revolves around two people who rediscover love and the joys of living in the second half of their lives. Jane MacKenzie (Marion Gilsenan) is having trouble adjusting to widowhood. She had been very much her husband's wife, had loved him dearly, and wonders if there is a life left for her. On her reduced income after his death she must take in boarders in lieu of selling her house. Jane rents her own room to an elderly couple, Ruth (Jennifer Phipps) and Arthur (Bernard Behrens).

Sadly, Ruth is struggling with Alzheimer's. The other boarder, Tomas Havel (Rubes), is a happy-go-lucky handyman who does jobs around the house in exchange for reduced rent. He parks his RV in the driveway.

To brighten her outlook towards widowhood, the cheerful Tomas tells Jane Czech proverbs, such as "Squeeze the grapes of sorrow to get the best wine." In a particularly beautiful moment he sings her a Czech folk song. Tomas eventually convinces Jane that she can love again, and that he, a widower, can bring her happiness. They fall in love and Jane spends the night with him in his RV. Jane's daughter, Heather (Jacelyn Holmes), sees her mother leaving the RV in the early morning. At first she feels uncomfortable but soon shares in her mother's happiness. Jane grows personally and rediscovers her body. Life is still there for her. Ruth's condition deteriorates and there is a heartbreaking crisis when Arthur must take her away to a nursing home. Jane and Tomas try to help Arthur, but to no avail. Here writers Martin and Wylie show how caregivers of Alzheimer's victims suffer too. Tomas prepares to leave but hints that he might return to Jane after he completes his tour of the continent in his RV.

The film addresses two concerns of aging people — sex and Alzheimer's. It also confronts some minor problems, such as fast-talking salesmen who try to pressure seniors to buy things they don't need — another incident in the film. But most important, it is about love and hope. Unquestionably, it carries a valuable message for and about a growing segment of the population, enough so that the Seniors' Secretariat of Health and Welfare Canada gave the film a production grant of $500,000. The film was shot by Barrie, Ontario's CKVR, at low cost. Wylie, who had been widowed after two decades of marriage, provided rare insights. Rubes, who acted as associate director-producer, vetoed "Lili Marlene" in a scene with Jane on the roof of his RV, because it was a German song. Instead he substituted "The Beer Barrel Polka." *Coming of Age* was originally done for the Movie Network. The CBC and Global later had a bidding war for it, with Global winning out. Ironically, the CBC wasn't interested in the film when it was first planned and was, according to Martin, chastised by the press for not honouring its mandate as Canada's national public network.

The other Martin movie, *Never Too Late*, also addressed seniors'

Jean Lapointe, Jan Rubes, Olympia Dukakis, and Cloris Leachman (seated)
in Never Too Late, *1997.*

concerns, but from a different slant. It got much more publicity, thanks to having two aging Hollywood stars in the cast, Olympia Dukakis and Cloris Leachman. Rubes described his character as an old sourpuss. "But eventually Rose (Dukakis) turns me around and at the age of 70 we fall in love. Then we go to bed." Woody (Quebec actor Jean Lapointe) and the gleeful wheelchaired lesbian Olive (Leachman) complete the foursome. Led by Olive, all four of them trap the nefarious crooked manager of their seniors' home, who is stealing money from residents. The manager (Matt Craven) is rather unconvincing as the villain, but who cares — the four oldsters have a great time bringing him to justice.

Rubes said that one scene in the script "called for my character to show a post-coital glow, after an encounter with Dukakis. So I had to ask my wife what I looked like in that situation. She told me just to act naturally, tired and old."[240] Susan, who was listening to the interview, brashly added, "He's great in bed. In fact he gets better and better." Donald Martin paid tribute to old people: "We are conditioned to believe that by the age of 65, everything shuts down. I wanted to unlock the characters because I stopped thinking of them as old, but as characters expressing love, passion, intrigue."[241]

As with *Coming of Age*, the movie initially had trouble getting backers. Allegro Films in Montreal finally took on the $3.5-million production. Giles Walker, who had first worked with Rubes in *Harvest* fifteen years before, directed, and Tom Berry was the producer with an assist from Susan as associate producer. There were difficulties in finishing the film because one of the leads insisted on script changes that had to be integrated into the story. *Never Too Late* was the only English-language production done in Quebec that year. It was nominated for a Writers Guild Award as the most original screenplay of 1996.

CHAPTER 17

1993–1996: Order of Canada; Filming in North America and Europe; A leading role on Broadway; Losing a son

Jan Rubes's blossoming career as a film actor coincided with the growing feature film industry in Canada. Hollywood had had a near monopoly of feature productions for movie houses since the 1920s, and, more recently, of films for TV. Canada's first step in helping Canadian feature films was in 1967, when it created the Canadian Film Development Corporation (CFDC) to award annual grants to Canadian film companies and producers.[242] Then, in 1983, CFDC initiated a broadcast development fund to help vitalize Canadian television, since 85 percent of all TV programs played in prime time in Canada came from other countries. The next year the CFDC was renamed Telefilm Canada. Producers from the U.S.A. now eagerly joined their Canadian colleagues in making films in Canada because, in addition to Telefilm grants, the low Canadian dollar was keeping costs down. There were also fine actors and crews available that made Canadian film production even more enticing for Hollywood producers. Canada was soon dubbed Hollywood North.

Be it in Canada or in Hollywood, by 1993 Rubes had become an acknowledged star in character roles and got prominent notice in cast lists. That year he played a small part in a Hollywood film shot mainly on North Carolina's Atlantic coast, *Birds II*, a sequel to the frightening Hitchcock film of three decades earlier. Rick Rosenthal was its director. A killer group of birds attacks the population of a seaside resort with devastating results, a kind of *Jaws* with birds instead of a killer shark. Rubes is the lighthouse keeper who falls prey to the birds about one-third of the way through the film.

Jan and Rick Rosenthal enjoyed playing tennis together. As Rosenthal told it, while playing one day at a local club they took on the two club pros, who, by chance, were both free. The pros were skeptical about whether it was worth their time. Jan and Rosenthal revealed little of their ability in the warm-up, evidently a Rubes tactic, only to trounce the two pros in the two sets that followed. Rubes played cannily, outfoxing his opponents, as usual.[243] Tennis, Jan told Peter Herrndorf in an unguarded moment, had helped his acting career, since so many actors, directors, and producers wanted to play tennis with him.[244] Always a gentleman on the courts, Jan once had to reprimand his friend George Gross, a sportswriter for the *Toronto Sun* and a frequent doubles partner, for cursing loudly after George made a bad shot. The temperate Rubes stopped him and said, "If you must curse do it in Czech or Slovak, so that no one will understand you."[245]

Rubes's earnings were by now substantial, thanks to his growing reputation as a film actor. He certainly deserved the high fees — one need only remember his years of recitals and of touring with the COC and Prologue for little remuneration. And he continued to charge only nominal fees for his work in live theatre and opera. Another film he did in 1994 that paid well but did little for his reputation was *D2: The Mighty Ducks*, about a junior hockey team. It was a sequel to the highly successful 1992 *The Mighty Ducks*. The Walt Disney Company paid Rubes $125,000, his largest fee ever, to play a relatively minor role — the man who supplies skates and wisdom to the hockey team and its manager. The end result was evidently a letdown for those who had seen the first *Ducks* movie. Hockey fan Rubes had fun socializing with the great hockey player Wayne Gretzky, who was involved in the film.

Rubes did some adroit travelling back and forth between Minneapolis for *D2* and Pittsburgh for *Roommates*, with Peter Falk. *Roommates* is

Jan, Susan, and Wayne Gretzky after D2: The Mighty Ducks, *1994.*

about family values, the dignity of old age, working-class ethics, and religion. Falk and Rubes are two old men who age considerably during the film and provide us with some understated jokes about getting old. One bears repeating. Walking together, Jan looks at his friend Peter and says, "We've been good friends for years. What is your name?" Peter reflects for a moment or two and replies, "How soon do you have to know?"

He was not as lucky when it came to fitting in *Mesmer*, a film being shot in Europe. He had to leave *Roommates* before the shooting was concluded, with the result that some of his scenes had to be cut considerably. *Mesmer*, set in 1780s Europe, was shot in Berlin and in and around Vienna. Doubtful direction and a bit of over-the-top acting by Alan Rickman as Dr. Mesmer resulted in confusion. He appears both mysterious and pained — not untypical of Rickman — but perhaps this is what was wanted. Mesmer temporarily cures the beautiful Maria Theresa (Amanda Ooms) of her blindness. The cure, if one wishes to believe it, was probably due to a combination of a blow to her head and his personal magnetism. It was not, as Mesmer claimed, that he had transferred his "universal fluid" to her. Maria Theresa's blindness is actually imaginary, the result of sexual abuse by her father. The German medical establishment had no use for Mesmer and banished him from the country.

The story goes on. Two years later Mesmer is plying his trade in Paris, "mesmerising" rich society matrons who, thanks to his treatment, fall into trances with the occasional one even having an orgasm in the process. Professor Stoerk (Rubes), Mesmer's nemesis, successfully convinces the Parisian medical academy to prevent Mesmer from practising. However, Mesmer's extraordinary powers rise to the surface in the film's penultimate scene, when he warns the incredulous members of the academy that their lives are in danger. The next scene shows the revolutionary mob of 1789 on its way to the academy's palace with murder in their eyes. The film ends before there is a chance to witness mass mayhem. The eighteenth-century settings dress up the film but cannot rescue it. *Mesmer* was premiered at the Montreal Film Festival and has since been all but forgotten. It should have turned out better than it did.

Mesmer provided some bonuses for Rubes. There were four days of shooting in Berlin — just enough time for him to go to the Staatsoper to hear *Cosi*, which he thought feminist-inspired, and *Don Giovanni*, which he found vocally and musically "ordinary." There followed three weeks of shooting in Vienna, where Susan joined him. While there, Jan, a devoted Canadian sports fan, got the news of a historic Canadian baseball event. The Toronto Blue Jays had won the World Series thanks to Joe Carter's ninth-inning home run in the final game — shades of the New York Giants in 1951. Jan took five days off in the middle of the shooting to fly with Susan to Prague to see Mirek, his wife, Jarica, and their son, Honza. They also went to Volyně to visit Jan's parents' graves and to meet with old friends and acquaintances. From there it was back to Vienna for more work on the film.

In early November, a few days after their return to Canada, they set out by car with Chris for their annual trip to Florida. They spent more than a day seeing Washington, including the new Holocaust Museum — a moving experience — and visiting the lavish Canadian Embassy. In the evening, they went to Donizetti's *Anna Bolena* at the Kennedy Center, with the gifted Canadian singer Judith Forst as Jane Seymour. Rubes and Forst had known each other since the summer of 1967, when she had understudied Nancy in Britten's *Albert Herring* at the Stratford Festival.[246] Forst remembers well how kind and welcoming Rubes was. The Stratford engagement had marked the beginning of her career as a leading mezzo at the Met and other top opera houses in North America and elsewhere in the world. She and Rubes had appeared together in Menotti's *The Consul* at the Guelph Spring Festival in 1973. Like other singing actors she lauded Rubes for giving everything he had when performing in an opera and for his positive attitude in helping his colleagues. She thought that Jan always embodied the part. "'Who am I, what am I doing?' would be his question. His approach to performance was, in a word, all encompassing," said Forst. The Kennedy Center was certainly an improvement as an operatic venue for Washington, compared to those in which Jan sang in the 1950s.

Rubes continued to do films for children. One was an episode of *The Adventures of Dudley the Dragon*, a series produced by Breakthrough Films. PBS, a non-profit group, bought it for distribution to its 150 stations. Another was *Lamb Chop and the Haunted Studio*. Its producer, Bernard Rothman, called it a "pocket musical comedy," a Halloween story designed for family audiences (very young children and their parents).[247] Rubes is a "nice" phantom who haunts the studio. Lamb Chop — a cartoon character — is frightened, but once he gets to know the phantom he is won over. Dracula and Frankenstein also appear in this comic one-hour film.

In the previous decade, TV and, to a lesser extent, movies had been filming stories about perpetrators and victims of the Holocaust. Rubes had played both and would continue to do so in films still on the drawing board. But now there was a change of focus — the persecution of homosexuals. There were increasing outcries that homosexuals must be treated fairly and equally by law. Rubes played in one important TV film that addressed this subject, *Serving in Silence: The Margarethe Cammermeyer Story*. (It was one of seven films he did in 1994–95.) Colonel Cammermeyer is a ranking nurse in the U.S. National Guard who, in 1989, applies for the position of chief nurse. She is a divorcee and mother of four children. For her service in Vietnam she had been awarded a Bronze Star; her military record was exemplary, and she loved the army. At the promotion hearing for the prestigious post, she was asked the routine question about her sexuality. Since her personal and military code demanded that she speak the truth, no matter what, she replied that she was a lesbian. (The "don't ask, don't tell" policy was not yet in effect at the time.) Forthwith, the National Guard honorably discharged her on June 11, 1992. Seeking recourse, she sued the army for violating her constitutional rights. Two years later the case was heard by a federal court, which ruled that the army reinstate her. She returned to the National Guard and served, without promotion, until she retired in 1997.[248]

While waiting for the civil case to be heard, Cammermeyer met Barbra Streisand, who asked her if she would like to see her story told in a TV teleplay. At first she demurred, but, after realizing how strongly Streisand and her colleagues felt about the army's arbitrary action, she agreed. Alison Cross did the script. She had also written the teleplay about *Roe vs. Wade*, the Supreme Court decision that legalized abortion in the U.S.A.

The actress Glenn Close jumped at the opportunity to play Cammermeyer. It couldn't have been a better choice. Close not only looked every inch the army officer in the film but also showed in a controlled way the strain Cammermeyer was going through. Jan Rubes plays Far, Margarethe's emotionally cold Norwegian father. Rubes, initially unhappy with his dialogue, rewrote some of it to match his role and personality. Far frowns on his daughter's behaviour, especially when she brings her lesbianism out in the open. Later, after recognizing the principle involved, he supports her, as do her children. Judy Davis plays Diane Divelbess, the California artist whom Margarethe had met in 1988, eight years after her divorce. They are lovers, but are restrained and even humorous in their onscreen relationship. They kiss more as friends than as lovers, except once at the end of the film. This scene angered homophobic church and secular groups, who wanted it censored. NBC aired the film and, to its great credit, refused to change anything, including the kiss. In Margarethe Cammermeyer's closing argument at the 1994 trial she said:

> You've heard expert witnesses testify that there are few if any differences between homosexuals and hetero- sexuals in terms of mental health or sexual conduct, including promiscuity. You've heard the experts testify that gays are not security risks, that their sexual orienta- tion does not affect their job performance nor their abil- ity to lead, that gays do not try to convert heterosexuals — that those are stereotypes based on fear not fact.... The case before you involves one of our country's old- est and most cherished traditions. A tradition that we have been willing to go to war for, to let members of the armed services fight and die for — and that's a tradition and heritage of personal freedom. The Pledge of Alle- giance ends "With liberty and justice for all." It doesn't say "except for homosexuals."

Jan Rubes had more than a professional interest in *Serving in Silence.* The Rubeses' son Chris was homosexual, although he wasn't penalized professionally as Cammermeyer was. He had first excelled in surgery but was more interested in emergency work. He'd had a significant career as an emergency room physician at Toronto General Hospital before going to Toronto's Sunnybrook Hospital. Believing that emergency pre- hospital treatment was far more important than generally considered, he developed a training program for paramedics, who until then had been considered only ambulance drivers. The program took hold nationally with Chris at the helm. He also did considerable work as a volunteer, including being chair of the Emergency Medical Technology Conjoint Committee. And he was a member of the Conjoint Accreditation Ser- vices, which assesses medical education programs.

A professional commitment brought Jan and Susan to New York for a five-month stay in the spring and summer of 1995. James Lapine, a leading American playwright and director, had asked Jan to do a major role in the revival of his play *Twelve Dreams*, scheduled to open at the three-hundred-seat Mitzi Newhouse Theater at Lincoln Center on June 8. It had first been staged by New York's Music-Theater Group in 1978 as a work in progress and then fully presented by the New York Shakespeare Festival four years later. The Newhouse, the smaller of two drama theatres at Lincoln Center, is a leading New York venue.

Rubes missed the stage and looked forward to this assignment. He prepared for the role by reading the script through with a Toronto friend, Dianne Elder, a former member of the YPT board. She described how, at their second meeting, he already knew all of his lines, such was his industry and memory.[249] *Twelve Dreams* is based on one of psychiatrist Carl Jung's case studies outlined in his *Man and His Symbols*. Jung's theory of the collective unconscious is corroborated in the play by the dreams and death of a young girl. It is Christmas 1936 in a New England college town. Emma, a motherless ten-year-old girl (Mischa Barton), gives her psychiatrist father, Charles (Harry Groener), a book of drawings illustrating twelve of her strange dreams. Some of them depict animals and violence. (The dreams are briefly described in the program.) Charles discusses the dreams with his mentor, the "professor" (Rubes), who is visiting him. The professor — clearly Jung, although never identified as such — believes that the dreams are about not animals but destruction, and that "they seem to foretell the death of the dreamer." It is soon evident that Emma's fate in the play is inexorably sealed.

The dreams are bizarre. In one, a number of small animals grow tremendously and then swallow her. In another, she goes to heaven where weird and disgusting dances are being performed. She then flees to Red Hell and sees angels. And in yet another dream, she touches a big round lighted ball. Vapors come out of it, and then a man appears and kills her.

There are several other issues in the play, one being how Charles copes with a rich and flirtatious patient, Dorothy (Donna Murphy). Another is about Charles's insecure student-colleague, Sanford (Matthew Ross), who is infatuated with Charles's assistant, an erotic ballet teacher, Miss Banton (Meg Howrey). One reviewer wrote that Lapine "does an adroit job of interweaving day-event and night-revelation. The dream

Right: Jan Rubes (The Professor), Harry Groener (Charles Hatrick), Mischa Barton (Emma), and Donna Murphy (Dorothy Trowbridge) in Twelve Dreams, *Lincoln Center, 1995. Below: Jan (The Professor) in* Twelve Dreams, *1995.*

sequences are spookily compelling and splendidly differentiated. The play has the true fierceness of dream logic — the sense that you are watching events unfold that are both unpredictable and ineluctable. Five musicians pilot us from one realm to the other, artfully building toward songs that never emerge."[250] *Twelve Dreams* is about neurotic people, which, some might say, makes for good theatre. Coincidentally, a book by Richard Noll that attacks Jung's competence and veracity had been published prior to the play's opening, adding grist to the mill.

Some critics praised *Twelve Dreams* while others panned it. Most of them took the middle ground and said that it was both good and bad. Arguably, few critics understood it, and yet their first impressions would influence the play's theatrical future — how long its run will be. Happily, nearly all of the critics praised the staging, the sets, the lighting, the music composed by Allan Shawn, and the dancing staged by Lar Lubovitch. How did Jan's "professor" role fare with the influential New York press? He was described by one as "a stock Teutonic academic of Hollywood's nineteen thirties with adorable wandering hands and a tediously personable lecture manner."[251] Another critic likened him to film and stage actor Paul Lukas, which could only be a compliment.[252]

James Lapine had no doubts in his choice of Rubes to do the professor. He remembered Jan "exuding a great deal of integrity and intelligence which seemed perfect for the role.... He carried himself with grace and dignity and spoke with such care and import that he never failed in serving the play.... I think he approached his role with sensitivity and was always gracious to both me and his fellow actors."[253]

It was hard to take John Simon of *New York Magazine* seriously. Remarkably outspoken, contentious if not downright insulting, he called Jung a "phoney" and a "liar," and Lapine "no less a faker than Jung." Simon maintained that the production was not as good as the earlier one and that Jan was "especially poor." He disliked his "thick accent, ponderous delivery, and oleaginous demeanor."[254] There was a staging effect in the play that went wrong on opening night. According to the *New York Times*, two doves were released at the end of the first act "to swoop out over the audience as part of a dream." One ill-starred dove didn't find his way back to his cage and "sat on the lighting grid overhead, cooing lustily from time to time through Act II. Mr. Lapine could not have upstaged his play more effectively had he stepped in front of the audience and shot himself in the foot."[255]

The opening night of *Twelve Dreams* was quite an occasion for two very special reasons. Not only was Jan in a starring role in a New York production, but also it was his seventy-fifth birthday. Cast, family, and friends helped him celebrate at a New York restaurant after the performance. Jan diligently kept the many cards and notes written to him. Those from his colleagues, not unexpectedly, show how much they valued him and how much his professionalism was influencing the cast. The gifted young Mischa wrote on her card, "You make the birds sing sweetly." Donna Murphy, who had won a Tony the year before and did a powerful performance in *Twelve Dreams*, wrote Jan, "Your presence in this piece is an unusual, invaluable gift to us all. Thank you for your generous support." She also wrote that, in honour of the occasion, a contribution had been made in his name to the Starlight Foundation, which grants the wishes of critically, chronically, and terminally ill children.

While in New York, Jan and Susan stayed in an apartment on West Fifty-seventh Street, a five-minute walk from Lincoln Center. They were able to renew their acquaintance with the city in which they had lived for almost ten years. They also spent much time with old friends. *Twelve Dreams* ran for 101 performances, eight shows a week, no small challenge for a septuagenarian. The play closed on August 6, and Jan and Susan headed back to Toronto the next day.

Films again. First he had to learn the role of an Alzheimer's patient, Hans Kellner, in the episode "Time Enough to Say Goodbye," in the CBC hospital series *Side Effects*. It was bad luck that *Side Effects* was competing with another hospital series, *ER*, being produced in the U.S.A. Rubes would soon do a role on that series too. In December Jan got a surprise Christmas present when he learned that he was to be appointed to the Order of Canada, as Susan had been two decades before.

But it was an incredibly sad year, nonetheless, for both of them. Chris was dying. They spent most of the winter in Toronto to be close to him in his final months. He died of pneumonia on February 25, 1996. He was only forty-three. His partner of ten years had died in 1993. Sadly, Chris had been plagued with illnesses since then. Although his death was expected, Susan could not come to grips with it easily, and nursed him until his final breath. His memorial service was held at the Anglican Church of St. Clement in Toronto (Chris had wanted to be buried as an Anglican). More than 450 people attended, including many doctors and paramedics, such was his esteem. As one of his colleagues wrote, "Chris was one of the true pioneers and visionaries in pre-hospital care. His commitment to high standards of patient care and his professionalism were evident at all times."[256] Several of Chris's co-workers have testified how he successfully collaborated with colleagues, how he sought out opinions from staff and encouraged them to be creative, how he was a team player, and how he exerted his leadership without being overbearing.[257]

The Paramedic Award of Excellence was subsequently established in his name. Five years later the Christopher J. Rubes Centre for Emergency Medical Services Studies opened in Toronto to carry on his work. Its director, Alan Craig, thanked Susan and Jan for attending the centre's dedication and wrote, "Chris's portrait — and his spirit — grace the entrance to the Centre, and remind us daily of his sense of purpose, integrity, and vision."[258]

Chris had always been close to his parents and to his two younger brothers. He had played tennis well and, according to his co-worker

Jan, Susan, Jonathan, and Tony at the opening of the Christopher J. Rubes Centre for Emergency Medical Services Studies, 2001.

Terri Burton, had always dressed impeccably, even though he took off his shoes and hid them under the table at meetings. He had appreciated the arts, taken great pride in his parents' work, and loved to hear his father sing. Chris had also sung, but Jan said jokingly that he had a serviceable voice, nothing more.[259]

There were no working engagements that spring and summer, which may have been for the best for the grieving parents. Jan was invested into the Order of Canada on May 8. They sold their ski chalet at Blue Mountain and, in September, went to Czechoslovakia to visit with family. There Jan had a thirty-minute TV interview, played in a documentary about Karel Ancerl at the Prague Opera, and attended conductor Rafael Kubelik's funeral, which brought back memories of meeting him in Montreal almost fifty years before while shooting *Forbidden Journey*. Kubelik had stayed in touch with Jan and Susan in the ensuing years, always contacting them when he conducted in Toronto.

The first work in some time came up at the end of October 1996, when Rubes was offered roles in two episodes, "Tunguska" and "Terma," of the popular *X-Files* series. He immediately took Russian lessons to prepare for the role of Vassily Peskow, a former Cold War KGB agent engaged by a group of Russian and American power seekers to do some dirty work. Peskow is up to the task. He first strangles a doctor who knows all about the viruses that the bad guys want to use, and then, in a hospital, he administers a lethal injection into one of the supporters of law and order. As the film draws to its conclusion Peskow accepts congratulations from his Russian boss. It is an unbelievable tale — who cares anyway? The principals are two FBI agents. The male agent is prone to punching people in the stomach, and the female agent has a facial expression that never varies through thick and thin as she works for the common good. There is extraordinary photography, including an immense fire in which mysterious gases from Mars are burned up. The series, with its incredible tales, attracted in force those TV watchers who love science fiction. Rubes's episodes were shot in Vancouver, which gave Jan and Susan the chance to see Otto Lowy, their old Czech friend, who had worked with Jan in *Play Gypsies* in 1982.

CHAPTER 18

1996–2007: More films; Remembering Terezin; Failing Health; *Our Fathers, Appassionata*

Jan Rubes had little work in 1995–96. This might have been a self-imposed break because of Chris's illness and death. Not so, however, the next year, when, happily, he was flooded with offers that continued through the turn of the century. Jan loved to act, and everyone, including Susan, marvelled at his natural talent. If he missed singing, he didn't say so. There was also a bonus as he approached his ninth decade — he no longer had to work because he needed money. He and Susan, between them, had accumulated a reasonable nest egg for the days when they both would stop working. Although Jan didn't slow down, he had the comfort of knowing that if he didn't get a role it no longer mattered, at least not financially.

In June 1997 the University of Toronto awarded Susan Rubes an honorary doctorate. She said in her acceptance speech, "Life is a magical train that can make your life an adventure beyond compare. I say this with real passion, because, for me, that is how it has been… I wouldn't have wanted it any other way." She was seventy-three and Jan seventy-eight, and together they were involved in a total of seven films that year. The following spring, Jan was awarded his second honorary doctorate, this one from the University of Windsor. Their achievements were being rewarded.

Unquestionably, their lives are success stories. As artists they have done what they wanted and thought best for themselves, and, even more significantly, best for others. Canadian opera and theatre owes much to both of them. They have also reaped benefits from their lasting love, which has given them the stability and underpinning to cope with in-evitable setbacks — personal and professional. They were lucky, too, to have come to Canada when it was moving towards artistic maturity, and they were sufficiently alert to rise to the occasion and seize the opportu-nities offered. Simply put, getting old for these two holds few perils.

Films provided the Rubeses with a variety of roles. Jan and Susan played Mr. and Mrs. Duček in one episode of the popular hospital TV series *ER*, titled "The Long Way Around." The show was set in a Chi-cago hospital and the shooting was done in mid-winter, when Chicago's temperature and wind chill are usually at their worst. So it was then, and the two of them shivered. Mr. Duček is shot — it is, after all, Chi-cago — and taken to the ER. His wife visits him in his recovery room. Little did they know that Susan's only scene would be cut before the show was aired.

On balance it was work they could have done without. They couldn't wait to get back to the comfort of Florida, where they now owned a con-dominium at Pelican Cove, Sarasota. Pelican Cove is a richly landscaped gated community with many unusual trees. The Rubes place is on Sara-sota Bay and is blessed with beautiful sunsets. There are tennis courts, swimming pools, a library, and a community centre where concerts are given. Jan and Susan spend half a year annually in this upper-middle-class setting. Sarasota also has an opera company that has a two-month season in a pleasant opera house in the heart of the city. Jan helped the company linguistically when it did — in Czech — *Hubicka* (*The Kiss*) and *The Bartered Bride*.

CBC Radio continued to value Rubes's expressive speaking voice, and engaged him to host a five-part documentary series, "Vienna, Schu-bert, and Brahms," on *Ideas*, the network's leading intellectual-cultural program. It ran for five consecutive evenings in April 1997 to commem-orate the two hundredth anniversary of the birth of Schubert in Vienna in 1797, and the one hundredth anniversary of the death of Brahms, also in Vienna, in 1897. And still involved with music, however peripherally, Rubes played a small role in a film, *Sarabande*. It is the fourth of six one-hour films in a series titled *Yo-Yo Ma: Inspired by Bach*. Each film features one of Bach's unaccompanied suites for cello. The music is the starting point for a story that tenuously relates to it. *Sarabande*, written and directed by Atom Egoyan, deals with four principal characters and how Bach's music helps them to cope with their illnesses, real and imaginary. All four are stiff and unconvincing. Rubes has a small role as one of the doctors consulted. The film was produced by Rhombus Media, which has done many outstanding documentaries and docudramas on music. This one was a letdown; perhaps the other five in the series were better. Of course, Ma's playing, as expected, was magnificent.

Jan's next film, *Flood: A River's Rampage*, was about an actual continental disaster — the Mississippi flood in the summer on 1993. Huge portions of Minnesota, Iowa, Illinois, and Missouri were affected by it. The soil's moisture levels in the river valleys were unusually high because of excessive rainfall the previous autumn, and a snowy and rainy winter had exacerbated conditions. Drenching thunderstorms took over in June and continued without let-up, forcing the river to overflow its banks. By the end of the summer some communities had had over thirty inches of rain, and crest levels were nineteen feet above normal.

In 1997, the Family Channel shot the film just north of Toronto and along Lake Ontario. The movie's fictionalized drama shows how a small town along the Mississippi was saved from the flood by concerted community action. The hero of the film was a farmer, Herb (Richard Thomas). He and Pat (Kate Vernon), a handsome U.S. army engineer, develop an unusual plan to divert the flood waters, and this saves the town from complete ruin. Rubes plays Jacob, Herb's father. Jacob is warned that when the flood comes it could well engulf his house. Stubborn, he refuses to evacuate. He is told, "Buildings can be rebuilt, not people," but this does not affect his decision. Only when the river engulfs his house and reaches its very rooftop does he see the folly of his ways. His two grandchildren come to warn him, only to be trapped in the flooded house with him. Jacob is forced to hang, literally, from the roof of his house to escape the mounting water. After many hours he is rescued by a helicopter. The children swim for it, find a tree to hold on to, and are rescued the next day. Although the outcomes are predictable, both rescues are breathtaking. A contrite Jacob later apologizes to his family for endangering the lives of his grandchildren.

One of the terms of Rubes's contract for this film was that Tony assist him during the shooting of such challenging moments as the rooftop incident. Tony had the time to do it, since his acting career was increasingly on hold. Call it what you will — a result of his gentle temperament or not being in the right place at the right time — there were few new engagements going his way. Since his graduation from York University, he had played in stage shows and films but hadn't moved ahead to his satisfaction. After spending some time in Los Angeles, in 1993 he returned to Toronto, where he acted occasionally and coached children for TV roles. He also did a few stints as an assistant director. Rejection was hard to take.

At last, Tony found his niche as a golf professional. In 2002, he married Brenda Risom, a marketing consultant at Peak FM, a radio station in Collingwood.[260] Their son, Jasan Christopher — truly a family name — was born in 2003. They live in Collingwood at the Rubes house, sharing it with Jan and Susan during the summer months. It is a cheerful three-generation home where preschool toys abound, both

Jan tries out the roof before shooting Flood: A River's Rampage, *1997.*

inside and out. The original Collingwood cottage, located on a private road, has been enlarged steadily over the forty years since Jan and Susan purchased it. An in-ground swimming pool was recently added. Of interest is that the house was once only a stone's throw from Georgian Bay, but the water has receded so much that it is now about one hundred metres from the shore. Jonathan and Judith, with their two grown sons, Morgan and Colin, own a country place nearby. The Rubeses are a close-knit family.

Jan was in a number of other films in the same busy 1997. Most of them gave him little artistic satisfaction. However, a film's shooting location can be partial compensation for a poor production. Such was the case for *Nightmare Man*, shot in Fiji in August. The schedule wasn't too strenuous, so Jan and Susan had a fine Pacific holiday, including snorkelling and the like. Then, imagine flying to Warsaw for a one-day shoot! Jan did this for a movie, *White Raven*, with Ron Silver, a film that seems to have vanished. It is an incredible tale about a massive diamond (the White Raven) used to ransom a girl from a concentration camp during the Second World War. The Warsaw trip enabled Jan to spend a few days in Prague with relatives. And then there was *Due South*, one of the most popular series on television. Begun in 1994, it ran until 1999. In its third season the show's writers created the role of Dr. Mort Gustavson, with Jan Rubes specifically in mind.[261] Why Rubes? Because he would play the opera-loving coroner who sings arias while he dissects dead bodies.

A special event that Jan underlined in his diary was a cantata, *For the Children: Poems by the Children of Terezin*, premiered at Temple Sinai in Toronto on November 16, 1997. The work called for an adult narrator (Rubes) and a child narrator between the ages of ten and fourteen. They are supported by a children's treble chorus and a small chamber group — string quartet, clarinet, and percussion. The Toronto Children's Chorus, with conductor Jean Ashworth Bartle, had commissioned Robert Evans, a secondary school music teacher, to compose this heart-rending music to complement the poems that children in the Terezin concentration camp had written before dying in the Holocaust.[262]

Evans found the tragedy of the Holocaust overwhelming. He told William Littler that he had prepared for the task by visiting Terezin in

January 1996: "I have never felt such penetrating cold. I didn't weep as a lot of people do when they visit Terezin, but it crawled deeper and deeper into my gut and consciousness. It became a crusade. I wanted my cantata to mean something." Evans believed that the Terezin children "had a conscience about our world that many adults would marvel at." He wanted Canadian children to know what happened at Terezin.[263] Evans's close friend, conductor and CBC music producer Robert Cooper, said in his eulogy at Evans's funeral in 2005 that Evans made journeys to Poland and the Czech Republic, and to the hells of Auschwitz, Birkenau, and Terezin, before he could even begin composing, He visited Holocaust museums and held interviews with survivors. He immersed himself in the intimate horror each child must have felt. The result was "a tender, ironic, whimsical, and bitter-sweet cantata on the wondrous spirit of the children of the Holocaust."[264]

There are eighteen short sections, nearly all of them based on poems by Terezin children. Rubes movingly recited four poems. Two are included here. At the composer's request, he recited the last two lines of "Home" in the original Czech, as well as in English.

"You Gray Steel Clouds" by Hanus Hachenburg

You gray steel clouds, driven by the wind
Carrying within you ash-gray smoke
Carrying within you the blood-red phantom of strife
Like the eternal pilgrim waiting for his death.
I want one day, like you, to cover distances
Far into the future, never to return.
Forever our hope and our symbol
You, whose tempest can veil the sun
You, driven by time, but followed by day!

"Home" by Franta Bass

I gaze and gaze
Into the wide distant world,

Toward the southeast;
I look towards my home,
Towards the town where I was born,
My town, my native town,
How gladly I would return to you.

There were also four poems recited by the outstanding child narrator, Laura Cameron. Here is one of them.

"To Olga" by Alena Synkova

Listen!
The boat whistle has sounded now
And we must sail
Out toward an unknown port.
Listen!
Now it's time.

We'll sail a long long way
And dreams will turn to truth.
Oh, how sweet the name Morocco!
Listen!
Now it's time.

The wind sings songs of far away,
Just look up to heaven
And think about the violets.
Listen!
Now it's time.

Evans wrote the final verse, "Remember." It alternates between "Pie Jesu, Donna Eis Requiem" and the Hebrew prayer for the dead, "Yiskor Elohim," which, freely translated, means "Remember God." However ecumenical "Remember" is in its spirit and scope, some people questioned the appropriateness of including even a small part of a Christian prayer when all the Terezin children were Jewish.

The work triggered Rubes's memories of his days in Prague during the war, when Jews, forced to wear the Star of David, were deported to Terezin, and Czechs like himself, because of ignorance or fear of death, did nothing. Despite the many films Jan had done as a victim or a villain of the Holocaust, this work got to him like no other. The chorus, which has an international reputation, sang with impeccable intonation and diction. The program was broadcast on the CBC and produced by Matt Baird and Robert Cooper. According to Ben Steinberg, music director at Temple Sinai, the audience of eight hundred applauded generously at its conclusion. Cooper conducted a second performance of the work in Toronto, eight years later.[265]

A film based on a popular and sensitive novel by David Guterson, *Snow Falling on Cedars*, was planned for 1998. Set in 1954, it is about another brand of prejudice and racism involving Japanese-Americans on a fictional island, San Piedro, off the coast of Washington near Seattle. Jan was given a small role as a farmer, Ole Jurgenson, while Max von Sydow played the far more prominent role of the defence lawyer. Jan flew to Vancouver where some of the film was being shot and later made a second trip to Seattle for a wrap-up. Jan loved the novel and was impressed with the film. It had a grand opening at Roy Thomson Hall in Toronto, preceded by a dinner at which Jan was congratulated for being in the movie. After the showing, people asked, "Where was Jan?" His two scenes had hit the cutting room floor because the director thought the film was too long. It was as much a surprise to Jan as it was to everyone else. Even the producer, who was present, didn't know about the cuts.

As Jan's work slowed down, he and Susan had more time to be with their family. The pain of Chris's death was easing by the summer of 1998, so they travelled with Jonathan and his family to the Czech Republic. The Canadian Rubeses first spent time in Prague. Their hotel was opposite the former communist secret police headquarters, which brought back memories. Then they visited some tourist attractions, including Archduke Ferdinand's hunting lodge (his assassination in Sarajevo in 1914 was one of the provocations that brought on the Great War) and a run-down thirteenth-century castle near Volyně. The fun-loving Honza had greeted them on their first day in the Czech Republic. Now forty-three, he was working for Czech TV as a producer and acquisitions director.

Susan's half-brother, Mirek Burstein, whom we remember from Limelight days, had returned to Czechoslovakia and been given rightful ownership of his father Alfred's horse farm after the communist government had been deposed. Mirek's horses were so well trained in dressage — the art of guiding a horse without reins through various manoeuvres using imperceptible signals such as leg pressure — that he had even contemplated touring them in North America. He had also built up a prosperous pet food business in the Czech Republic. Czechs had traditionally fed their pets with table leftovers, but times had changed and Western ways were taking over. Jan's brother, Mirek, now eighty, was in declining health. He died in 2003. The Rubeses concluded their trip by visiting John Hirschfeld and his wife on the Greek island of Paros. They rented a house while there and enjoyed the Aegean sunsets before finally heading home.

Another role in a concentration camp film was offered to Rubes at the end of 1998. It is about a villainous camp director still on the loose half a century later and a victim's descendant determined to bring him to justice. The new twist is that this TV show, "Tribunal," is an episode in a science fiction series, *The Outer Limits*. We are in a concentration camp. Leon, a Jewish inmate, is forced to stand by and watch the ruthless German Lieutenant Rademacher shoot down his wife and send his daughter to the gas chamber. A mysterious onlooker, Nicholas, grabs an SS jacket, then pulls out his antique — and magic — watch and vanishes into a glowing circle.

Leon survives. He remarries after the war and has a son, Aaron (Saul Rubinek). Aaron, a lawyer, tracks down Rademacher, who is now Robert Greene (Rubes). As with other films about war criminals still at large, Aaron has a hard time convincing the powers that be that Greene is Rademacher and should be prosecuted. After some time travelling led by the mysterious Nicholas, Greene ends up back in a 1944 concentration camp dressed as an inmate. Rademacher shoots him in cold blood, even after Greene pleads with him on hands and knees, trying to explain that he really is Rademacher and thus should be spared. The heartless killing of Leon's wife and daughter has been avenged. Rubes outdoes himself in this gory scene. The film is a powerful example of cruelty that knows no bounds, but whether it helped audiences understand the Holocaust better is doubtful.

Jan couldn't resist offers to work in films, even as he approached his eightieth birthday at the turn of the millennium. Most of the films were mediocre, but a few have left their mark, not so much for Jan's acting, which was always good, but for their content. In *Music from Another Land*, a family film of little consequence, he plays a baker who, with his wife, helps the young handsome lead (Jude Law) find happiness. In contrast, *Anthrax* was more significant. Made for TV by the Movie Network, it is about a minor outbreak of anthrax among cattle on an Alberta ranch. The community blames the outbreak on a local anthrax research institute sponsored by the government. Egged on by Adam (David Keith), a visitor with a questionable background and a dubious agenda, about twenty local citizens, including some children, stage a sit-in at the institute. Rancher Arthur Kowalski (Rubes), who claims to have lost fifteen cattle to anthrax, is one of them. He is a troublesome old man who smokes incessantly. Arthur and Adam illegally enter the institute's laboratories, and Arthur's smoking sets off an alarm. In the confusion, an anthrax vial is broken. Arthur inhales the resultant fumes and is dead within an hour. Not so Adam, who pockets a vial of anthrax fluid and slips out the institute's back door.

The local RCMP officer (Cameron Daddo) quarantines the entire sit-in group, which includes his wife, his mother in-law, and his son. All of the protesters are subsequently put into a detoxification building until authorities are assured that none of them is carrying the disease. In the meantime, Adam is seeking a ransom for the stolen anthrax. If he doesn't get it, he threatens to explode the vial in a densely populated area and infect thousands of people. He chooses the university, where a rock and roll concert is going on in its atrium. After an exciting chase, Adam, who has also managed to kidnap the RCMP officer's son, is finally done away with and the anthrax vial is placed in safe hands. Nevertheless, the government decides to close the institute. The film quite innocently anticipated the brief anthrax scare that followed on the heels of 9/11 in the U.S.A. Because of the scare, the film was shelved. Too bad.

Then came a change of pace. In 1999 Rubes took a leading role in the Robert Tinnell "ghost" movie *Believe*. Although it was shot in Quebec with a provincial grant and Telefilm money, the action is supposed to take place in Maine. Ghosts and their activities fascinate an impressionable and bright teenager, Thad Stiles (Christopher Heyerdahl). After being expelled from his school for promoting ghost scares, Thad is sent to his grandfather's palatial home, where he actually finds a real-life ghost! Jason Stiles (Rubes) is the cranky and rich grandfather who can't get along with his son and grandson and loves no one. The ghost problem is solved with the help of Thad's teenage girlfriend, Katherine (Jayne Heitmeyer), who lives nearby. The ghost (Andrea Martin), who turns out to be a good Samaritan, comes to life just long enough to clear up the mystery behind the misunderstanding between grandfather Stiles and Katherine's Uncle Ellicott (Ben Gazzara). The solution is a bit too pat and devalues the suspense that leads up to it. Stiles changes for the better and showers love in all directions. His altered behaviour in the final scenes is effective indeed in this attractive family film.

Another family film, *A Christmas Secret* — this one for TV — was also shot in 1999 and released the next year. It is a delightful tale about Jerry, a university zoology professor (Richard Thomas) who is convinced that he saw a flying reindeer when he was a child. One of his graduate students gives him book about a flying reindeer, which is so compelling that he drops everything to find the reindeer. Jerry winds up in a beautiful playland somewhere in the Far North, where he meets Nick (Beau Bridges), a.k.a. St. Nicholas. Nick is many hundreds of years old, although of course he doesn't look it. Rubes is a resident Norwegian scientist in the playland — he is only 150 years old! — who explains the origins of the Christmas phenomena to Jerry. In the meantime, Jerry has become a missing person in the world he left behind. At Christmas, St. Nicholas guides his team of reindeer through the sky laden with gifts for children everywhere. He takes Jerry with him and returns him to his relieved wife and daughter. The miraculous world that Jerry visited remains a secret, in this lovely make-believe story that enchants young and old.

In the science fiction TV series *Mentors*, a teenage boy is given the power to call up historical figures from the past. Rubes appears in one show as the sheep herder Moses, of biblical fame. He moves into the present and helps a family find happiness in the Passover season. Another movie with a Jewish connection, *The Burial Society*, was shot in 2002. It concerns a Jewish accountant (Rob LaBelle) fleeing mobsters who believe he stole $2 million from them. He hides out with the Chevrah Kadisha, a Jewish society that prepares the dead for burial according to Jewish rites. Rubes is the leader of the three-member group. One can't be sure if the film is a thoughtful exploration of Jewish traditions or just a slow-moving suspense drama. It attracted attention among some film buffs and was nominated for awards at film festivals and competitions. Other more critical watchers simply found the film stilted and forced, and best forgotten.

The Burial Society was shot in Vancouver. Rubes then flew back to Sarasota to join Susan for the drive north to Collingwood. In the middle of the night Susan heard a thump from Jan's side of the bed. He had fallen to the floor and was in great distress. An ambulance came quickly and Jan was rushed to hospital. He'd had a severe heart attack that left him with but 20 percent of his heart operational. It meant that, although not an invalid, he would tire more easily and would have to limit his physical activity. After a period of recuperation, he found that he could play golf again — nine holes only and using a golf cart to get around — but tennis was a thing of the past. Two smaller strokes followed, and he

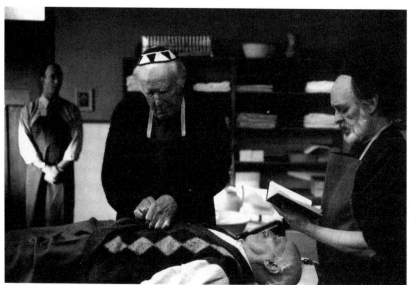

Rob LaBelle (Sheldon Kasner), Jan Rubes (Marvin Telakunsky), and Bill Meilin (Harry Epstein) in The Burial Society, *2002.*

found he was having some difficulty remembering lines. This was hard to take for an actor who prided himself on just this ability, no matter how complex and detailed the lines might be.

Nevertheless, now in his mid-eighties, Jan Rubes appeared in two more TV films. The first one, *Our Fathers*, is a true story that focuses on sex abuse by Catholic priests with preadolescent and adolescent boys in the Metropolitan Boston area. In 2002 the *Boston Globe* had published several articles that attacked the pederast priests and, more significantly, Cardinal Bernard Law, archbishop of Boston's large Catholic diocese, for having tolerated their abominable crimes. David France, an investigative reporter for *Newsweek* magazine, wrote a story about the scandal and followed it with a 650-page bestselling book, *Our Fathers: The Secret Life of the Catholic Church in an Age of Scandal.* The screenplay is based on this book. There are a few close-ups of boys wincing as groping priests touch them, but most of the film focuses on the victims as adults and how they recall their suffering. Many of the actual victims agreed to have their real names used in the film, such was their anger and their wish to see justice done. The abuse they suffered at the hands of these errant priests had seriously affected, if not ruined, their adult lives.

The film takes Cardinal Law (Christopher Plummer) especially to task since he was guilty of engineering cover-ups. Law must finally confess under oath in a court hearing that he and some of his deputies knew of the abuses and had dealt with them by moving the guilty priests to other parishes, rather than exposing them for their criminal acts. Sensing the storm building around him, Law goes to the Pope (Jan Rubes), who is in denial, much as is the Cardinal. He provides Law with the same evasive language that the Cardinal has dished out to others in the past. Rather than asking Law to resign, the Pope says, "Holy mother the church does not make sacrifices at the altar of public opinion." He tells the weeping Cardinal, "Go home, and work to solve the problem. And know that you have my support and my prayers."

A maverick priest, Dominic Spagnolia (Brian Dennehy), attacks Law only to be attacked, himself, for his homosexual relations with another man. His defence is that his offence was in the past at a time when he had temporarily left the priesthood. Eventually lawyer Mitchell Garabedian (Ted Danson) helps depose Cardinal Law and wins a multi-million-dollar class action suit for the nearly one hundred abused plaintiffs. Of interest was that while the scandal was unfolding Cardinal Law's counsel advised him to resign without delay, since Rome might give him another post, probably in Rome. It happened just that way — he was appointed Archpriest of St. Mary Major at the Vatican, a leading seat of Christendom.

The film's release in 2005 was delayed because of Pope John Paul II's death. Some reviewers pointed out that the Boston scandal was not mentioned in the eulogies that flooded the media. His depiction in the film, however brief, made him appear to be more a political leader than someone interested in addressing the Church's problems. However, the charges brought against the depraved priests attracted sufficient attention to lead to charges against other priests across the U.S.A. and Canada. Both Plummer and Dennehy — Dennehy was raised a Roman Catholic — were eager to do the film because of its subject matter. *Our Fathers* was shot in Toronto, not Boston, because Showtime, the TV company that did the film, kept running into obstacles from Boston's city fathers. The shooting, they said, would overlap the tourist season. They also cited security concerns — the latter concern, it was suggested, emanated from Washington. Or was it the Catholic Church?

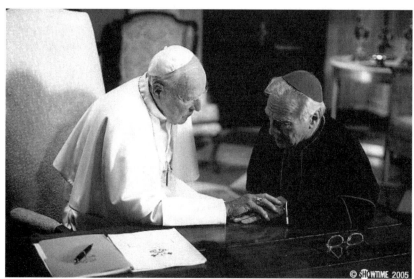

Jan Rubes (The Pope) counsels Christopher Plummer (Cardinal Law) in Our Fathers, *2005.*

It was the last time, one suspects, that Plummer and Rubes will appear in the same film. As for Plummer and Dennehy, they played together on Broadway in 2007 in the Jerome Lawrence and William Edwin Lee classic, *Inherit the Wind*. It is a dramatization of the Scopes evolution trial in Tennessee in 1925, with William Jennings Bryan (Dennehy) and Clarence Darrow (Plummer) as courtroom adversaries. The show was especially timely, given the rise of religious fundamentalism in the U.S.A. and Canada. Plummer was nominated for a Tony for his performance.

Jan Rubes's most recent film is a 2005 CBC-TV docudrama called *Appassionata: The Extraordinary Life and Music of Sonia Eckhardt-Gramatté*. Eckhardt-Gramatté was born out of wedlock in Moscow in 1899. Her Russian mother had been a music and French teacher at Leo Tolstoy's estate, and rumours persist, thanks to Sonia's husband, Ferdinand Eckhardt, that Tolstoy was her father. A child prodigy on both piano and violin, she received most of her musical education in Paris. Sonia moved to Berlin in 1914, with her mother and sister. Penniless, Sonia supported the family for a time by playing in cafés. Although there were soon solo engagements to be had she turned increasingly to composition. She married the German expressionist painter Walter Gramatté in 1920. The astute Leopold Stokowski, who was then conducting the Philadelphia Orchestra, engaged her to perform her own works for piano and violin with his orchestra. She did the same with the Chicago Symphony. Gramatté died in 1929, and five years later Sonia married the Austrian art historian Ferdinand Eckhardt, an admirer of Gramatté's paintings. Sonia continued to mourn her beloved Walter but found love of a different kind with Ferdinand. He promoted Sonia's and Gramatté's art throughout his lifetime.

Sonia and Ferdinand moved to Vienna in 1938, where, at Stokowski's suggestion, she studied composition for three years with Max Trapp. She would say that before Trapp she had been a poet, and after Trapp she was a knowledgeable composer. She struggled constantly to be treated as an equal to male composers. To help her cause, she wore men's clothing. The Nazi period and the war prevented Sonia's reputation from spreading. It was not until after the war that Vienna, if reluctantly, looked on her as an important composer. Her music had gone through two stages, post-Romantic and neoclassical. The third stage, which she said was intervallic, was beginning to gestate in the late 1940s.

In 1953 Ferdinand Eckhardt was appointed director of the Winnipeg Art Gallery. Winnipeg was not an easy change of locale for Sonia to accept after Berlin and Vienna, but, nevertheless, she taught and composed there until her death in 1976. She resisted being known as Mrs. Eckhardt, the wife of the gallery director. Rather, she was known as the composer S.C. Eckhardt-Gramatté. Her solo music for violin and piano, her chamber music, her triple concerto, and her other compositions may be recognized more in the future. A committee helped Eckhardt set up an annual competition for Canadian composers in her name after her death. Eckhardt died in 1995.

Rubes, as Eckhardt, to whom he bears a considerable resemblance, is the "anchor man" for the film, narrating and commenting on Sonia's past, sometimes in conversation with a frequent and sympathetic woman visitor. There are flashback scenes, a mix of old photographs and re-enactments, all overlaid with commentary by other leading musicians who had known and worked with Sonia. In the film Eckhardt conveys his respect for Sonia and her first husband with much warmth. Rubes's speaking voice seems even more mellifluous and seductive in his old age, and his facial expressions are as communicative as ever. In fact, Rubes *is* Eckhardt. He captures the very essence of the cultivated scholar who deeply loved his gifted wife.[266] Jan could relate to a musician like Sonia, and his central European roots helped him to relate equally to Eckhardt.

Paula Kelly, who wrote and directed this docudrama, said that Jan had no trouble remembering his lines, even though in personal dealings with family and friends he increasingly was forgetting details of past events. And Kelly echoed what singers, actors, and directors have said about Rubes: "He takes his colleagues' measure, he shows his life experience in his acting, he connects his presence and personality with others beyond the superficial, and he demonstrates how a true professional does his job." *Appassionata*, an admirable film about rich personalities, was shot in Winnipeg and Europe. Unfortunately, the CBC did little to publicize it, so few have seen it so far.

It may have been Jan Rubes's last film. In the winter of 2007 he moves more slowly than in the past and sleeps a good deal during the day. His hearing is poor and he is a reluctant user of hearing aids. But his charm remains, as does his friendly demeanour. Susan is as alert as ever and remembers most of the important events she and Jan have shared since they met fifty-seven years ago. Jan misses acting. Recently he had to turn down a film role since it would involve learning too many lines.

Jan has said that he worked to live, to support his family, but in truth he has lived to work and has been one of those lucky people who enjoyed it. If he had retired after his singing and operatic career came to an end he would have missed the many interesting and demanding roles he did in stage plays, on radio, and, of course, in films. For, in effect, he has had not one life but two — singing and acting — and a lot in between. Susan and Jan love one another as they always have. Their two sons, their two daughters-in-law, and their three grandsons enrich their lives, as do their relatives and friends in North America and the Czech Republic. They travel little. They have a rewarding old age. Both have left their mark on the performing arts in Canada.

ENDNOTES

Chapter 1

1   *Encyclopaedia Britannica*, Toronto, 1958, v. 6, p. 963.

Chapter 2

2   Walter Ducloux, letter to Jan Rubes, Sept. 29, 1948.
3   *Opera News*, Feb. 14, 1949, pp.7–10.
4   Eva Rubes Weinberger, letter to author, Jan. 15, 2007.
5   Rubes fonds.

Chapter 3

6   For accounts of the early days of the opera school see Ezra Schabas and Carl Morey, *Opera Viva: A History of the Canadian Opera Company*, Toronto, 2000, and Ezra Schabas, *There's Music in These Walls: A History of the Royal Conservatory of Music*, Toronto, 2005.
7   Margaret Aitken, *Toronto Telegram*, Jan. 12, 1948.

8   Chester Duncan, "Critically Speaking," CBC TransCanada Network, June 12, 1949.

9   George Crum and Patricia Snell, interview with author, April 27, 2006.

10   Ibid.

11   Martin Friedland, interview with author, Jan. 18, 2006.

12   The author, coincidentally, attended the same school, graduating in 1940.

13   George Freeley, *Morning Telegraph*, March 22, 1946.

14   Lewis Nichols, *The New York Times*, March 21, 1946.

15   Pat McDougall, *The Senior Times*, Feb. 10, 1994.

16   Ibid.

Chapter 4

17   There were a number of amateur films shot by company members.

18   Typed translated copy, Rubes fonds, n.d.

19   Lynda Mason Green and Tedde Moore, eds., *Standing Naked in the Wings: Anecdotes from Canadian Actors* (Toronto: Oxford University Press, 1997).

20   *Saturday Night*, Sept. 19, 1950.

21   *New York World-Telegram*, Dec. 2, 1950.

22   Rubes fonds, n.d.

23   Unidentified clipping, Rubes fonds.

24   Trent Frayne, *The Globe and Mail*, June 14, 1988.

25   There are reviews from four Chicago newspapers in Rubes's scrapbook, all laudatory.

26   Paul Hume, *The Washington Post*, Aug. 16, 1952, and *Times-Herald*, Aug. 16, 1952.

27   Press clipping, Rubes scrapbook.

28   Rubes fonds, April 19, 1953.

29   Ross Parmenter, *The New York Times*, Oct. 18, 1953.

Chapter 5

30   John Kraglund, *The Globe and Mail*, Aug. 9, 1955.
31   *CBC Times*, May 15, 1957.
32   *Flashback*, CBC-TV, June 12, 1966.

Chapter 6

33   Paul McIntyre, interview with author, Sept. 21, 2006.
34   Nelly Walter, letter to Jan Rubes, May 9, 1957.
35   Jan Rubes, letter to Nelly Walter, May 12, 1957.
36   Steven Henrikson, interview with author, Sept. 29, 2006.
37   John Kraglund, *The Globe and Mail*, Aug. 7, 1955.
38   *Gustav Kobbé's Complete Opera Book* (London: Putnam, 1976), p. 1141.
39   John Kraglund, *The Globe and Mail*, July 9, 1956.
40   John Kraglund, *The Globe and Mail*, Oct. 27, 1955.
41   Howard Taubman, *The New York Times*, June 24, 1956.
42   Unidentified Greenville newspaper, n.d., Rubes fonds.
43   Thea Dispeker, letter to Jan Rubes, July 26, 1957.
44   John Kraglund, *The Globe and Mail*, Feb. 28, 1955.
45   George Kidd, *Evening Telegram*, Feb. 28, 1955.
46   *Winnipeg Free Press*, Aug. 15, 1961.
47   Ibid.
48   Ezra Schabas and Carl Morey, *Opera Viva: A History of the Canadian Opera Company* (Toronto: Dundurn Press, 2000).
49   John Kraglund, *The Globe and Mail*, Oct. 16, 1959.
50   Rubes wrote two pieces about this tour. They have been slightly edited. Copies are in the Rubes fonds.
51   William Lord, interview with author, Feb. 3, 1999.
52   *Maclean's*, Jan. 2, 1960, pp. 1, 36–37.
53   W.J. Pitcher, *Kitchener-Waterloo Record*, 1959.
54   Herbert Whittaker, *The Globe and Mail*, July 23, 1959.
55   George Falle, *The Canadian Music Journal*, vol. 4, no. 1 (1959), pp. 5–6.

Chapter 7

56   See Gwenlyn Setterfield, *Niki Goldschmidt: A Life in Canadian Music* (Toronto: University of Toronto Press, 2003), for a thorough account of the Vancouver International Festival.

57   John Beckwith, *The Canadian Music Journal*, vol. 3, no. 1 (1958), pp. 34–36.

58   Setterfield, p. 90. Sutherland claimed it was Glyndebourne alone, while Goldschmidt claimed it was an audition. Probably both occurred.

59   Joan Sutherland, *The Autobiography of Joan Sutherland: A Prima Donna's Progress* (London, 1997), pp. 66–67.

60   Ibid.

61   Irving Kolodin, *Saturday Review*, August 3, 1958.

62   These items are from the Rubes fonds. Dates and names of journals are partially or wholly unidentified.

63   *Gustav Kobbé's Complete Opera Book*, pp. 1503–14.

64   Kenneth Winters, *The Canadian Music Journal*, vol. 6, no. 2 (1961), pp. 26–27.

65   Alfred Frankenstein, *San Francisco Chronicle*, Aug. 4, 1961.

66   Henrikson, interview.

67   Paul Hume, *The Washington Post and Times Herald*, Nov. 8, 1957.

68   John Briggs, *The New York Times*, Dec. 22, 1959.

69   Day Thorpe, *Washington Evening Star*, Dec. 23, 1959.

70   Paul Hume, *The Washington Post and Times Herald*, Jan. 29, 1959.

71   Howard Taubman, *The New York Times*, Jan. 6, 1959.

72   Howard Taubman, *The New York Times*, March 22, 1960.

73   Thomas Archer, *Montreal Gazette*, April 28, 1958.

74   Eric McLean, *Montreal Star*, Aug. 16, 1960.

75   Claude Gingras, *La Presse*, Aug. 17, 1960.

76   George Bloomfield, interview with author, Nov. 22, 2006.

77   William Littler, *Toronto Star*, Jan.12, 2003.

Chapter 8

78   John Gray, *Maclean's*, Jan. 2, 1960, pp. 32–40.

79 Ibid.

80 Annette Snowdon, "Reminiscing," unidentified periodical, c.1978, pp. 57–58. Rubes fonds.

81 *Opera Canada*, vol. IV, no. 1, Feb. 1963, p. 15.

82 John Kraglund, *The Globe and Mail*, Oct. 25, 1962.

83 D'Arcy Rickard, *Lethbridge Herald*, Nov. 15, 1966.

84 Barbara Franklin, interview with author, Feb. 25, 2006.

85 Ann Henry, *Winnipeg Tribune*, Aug. 17, 1961.

86 Rickard, *Lethbridge Herald*, Nov. 15, 1966.

87 Weinberger, letter to author.

88 Ibid.

89 *Winnipeg Free Press*, June 14, 1960.

90 Rexton S. Bunnett, et al, *Collins Guide to Musicals* (Glasgow: HarperCollins, 1997), pp. 198–99.

91 Frank Morris, *Winnipeg Tribune*, July 4, 1969.

Chapter 9

92 Thelma Dickman, "Everybody's Opera," *Imperial Oil Review*, 1963, pp. 9–14.

93 George Zukerman, interview with author, Feb. 11, 2006.

94 *Opera Canada*, vol. VII, no. 2, May 1966, p. 14.

95 George Jonas, interview with author, Aug. 5, 2006.

96 Ibid.

97 John Kraglund, *The Globe and Mail*, March 5, 1966.

98 Ibid.

99 Rubes report to Canada Council following Jasan tour, n.d.

100 John Kraglund, *The Globe and Mail*, Sept. 16, 1964.

101 Michael Schulman, "Jan Rubes in 2,000 Beds," *Performing Arts in Canada*, Fall 1973, p. 30–31.

102 Kenneth Winters, *Toronto Telegram*, Sept. 16, 1969.

103 Riki Turofsky, interview with author, Nov. 20, 2006.

104 Ibid.

105 Kenneth Winters, *Toronto Telegram*, July 9, 1966.

106 Lorne Betts, *Hamilton Spectator*, July 9, 1966.

107 John Kraglund, *The Globe and Mail*, Sept. 16, 1966.

108   Michael Schulman, *Canadian Composer*, May 1979, no. 141, pp. 10, 12, 14, 16.

109   Carrol Anne Curry, interview with author, March 23, 2006.

110   Kenneth Winters, *Toronto Telegram*, July 8, 1967.

111   Ruby Mercer, "Opera among the Glaciers," *Opera Canada*, May 1967, vol. 8, no. 2, p. 31.

112   See issues of *Opera Canada* for lists of places where the COC toured from 1958 to the late 1970s.

113   Schulman, *Canadian Composer*, May 1979.

114   Raffi Armenian, interview with author, July 29, 2006.

115   Weinberger, letter to author.

116   *Toronto Star*, Oct. 31, 2006.

117   Eva and Clem Weinberger, interview with author, Oct. 30, 2006.

118   Sutherland, *Autobiography*, p. 216.

Chapter 10

119   *The New York Times*, Nov. 21, 1963.

120   Sid Adilman, *Toronto Star*, Dec. 29, 1976.

121   Clyde Gilmour, *Toronto Star*, Nov. 24, 1975.

122   Adilman, *Toronto Star*, Dec. 29, 1976.

123   Herbert Whittaker, *The Globe and Mail*, Oct. 17, 1966.

124   *Opera Canada*, vol. VIII, no. 2, May 1967, p. 33.

125   Margaret Zeidman and Giulio Kukurugya, interview with author, July 26, 2006.

126   Mary Carr, interview with author, March 15, 2006; Michael Schulman, *Performing Arts in Canada*, Spring 1973.

127   Anne Linden, interview with author, April 24, 2006.

128   Herbert Whittaker, *The Globe and Mail*, Nov. 8, 1971.

129   John Kraglund, *The Globe and Mail*, March 11, 1969.

130   Jerry Rogers, *Hamilton Spectator*, April 5, 1969.

131   Ibid.

132   John Beckwith, *Toronto Star*, June 1, 1964.

133   Jamie Portman, *Calgary Herald*, Oct. 25, 1966.

134   Lorne Betts, *Hamilton Spectator*, April 15, 1971.

135   Zeidman and Kukurugya, interview.

Chapter 11

136   See Walter Pitman, *Louis Applebaum: A Passion for Culture* (Toronto: Dundurn Press, 2002), for a detailed study of Group Four.
137   This and other quotes are from the Rubes fonds, from program information prepared by OECA, and from talks with Rubes.
138   Blaik Kirby, *The Globe and Mail*, n.d.
139   Sutherland, *Autobiography*, pp. 235–36.
140   Mary Deanne Shears, *Toronto Star*, Sept. 22, 1972.
141   See *Opera Viva*, pp. 95–128, for an account of this period.
142   Joyce Singer, *Toronto Sun*, April 18, 1987.
143   William Littler, *Toronto Star*, April 30, 1974.
144   Blaik Kirby, *The Globe and Mail*, March 21, 1973.
145   Victor Feldbrill, interview with author, April 14, 2006.
146   John Kraglund, *The Globe and Mail*, Jan. 25, 1975.
147   Henry Barney Ingram, interview with author, March 3, 2006.
148   Zeidman and Kukurugya, interview.
149   Monica Simon Hofmann, interview with author, April 18, 2006.
150   Curry, interview.
151   William Littler, *Toronto Star*, Jan. 28, 1975.
152   Herman Geiger-Torel, letter to Jan Rubes, Aug. 12, 1975.
153   Eric McLean, *Montreal Star*, May 1, 1975.
154   Maureen Peterson, *Ottawa Journal*, May 1, 1975.
155   *The Mirror*, May 30, 1973.

Chapter 12

156   Urjo Kareda, *Toronto Star*, July 18, 1975.
157   Bryan Johnson, *The Globe and Mail*, Dec. 23, 1977.
158   Gina Mallet, *Toronto Star*, Dec. 17, 1977.
159   Peter White, *The Globe and Mail*, Dec. 28, 1976.
160   Gina Mallet, *Toronto Star*, Dec. 28, 1976.
161   Herbert Whittaker, *The Globe and Mail*, Dec. 17, 1977. There is a

photo of the four men (Radock only his legs) accompanying this article.

162 Schulman, *Canadian Composer*, May 1979.

163 Frank Rizzo, from Rubes fonds, no newspaper identification, n.d.

164 Bryan Johnson, *The Globe and Mail*, March 8, 1978.

165 Bryan Johnson, *The Globe and Mail*, Feb. 20, 1978.

166 Ray Chatelin, *Vancouver Province*, Oct. 23, 1976.

167 Susan Mertens, *Vancouver Sun*, March 11, 1977.

168 John Kraglund, *The Globe and Mail*, Jan. 17, 1977.

169 Blaik Kirby, *The Globe and Mail*, Feb. 22, 1978.

170 Jo Anne Claus, *Saint John Telegraph-Journal*, Oct. 12, 1978.

171 Ibid.

172 Carolyn Turney, *Fredericton Gleaner*, Oct. 16, 1978.

173 Schulman, *Canadian Composer*, May 1979.

174 Zeidman and Kukurugya, interview.

175 Ray Conlogue, *The Globe and Mail*, May 28, 1979.

176 Myron Galloway, Rubes fonds, n.d. no source.

177 Gina Mallet, *Toronto Star*, Oct. 25, 1979.

178 Schulman, *Canadian Composer*, May 1979.

179 MacKenzie Porter, *Toronto Sun*, May 5, 1980.

180 Bob Pennington, *Toronto Star*, Dec. 16, 1980.

181 MacKenzie Porter, *Toronto Sun*, Dec. 19, 1980.

Chapter 13

182 Anonymous clipping, Rubes fonds.

183 James Nelson, Canadian Press, Ottawa dateline, reprinted in part in the *Winnipeg Free Press*. March 7, 1980.

184 Bill Musselwhite, *Calgary Herald*, March 8, 1980.

185 Ron Base, *Toronto Star*, March 9, 1980.

186 Giles Walker, interview with author, Oct. 17, 2006.

187 Jack Fraser, *Saskatoon Star-Phoenix*, Jan. 10, 1980.

188 Sid Adilman, *Toronto Star*, June 24, 1980.

189 Gordon Greene, letter to author, Sept. 18, 2006.

190 Sylvia Train, *Toronto Sun*, June 14, 1982.

191   James Coles, interview with author, April 15, 2006.

192   David Barber, *Kingston Whig-Standard*, May 13, 1982.

193   Bill Hutchison, *Kingston Whig-Standard*, May 8, 1982.

194   Jan Rubes, letter to Neil Sutherland, Dec. 31, 1981.

195   Michael Durland, *Canadian Cinema*, Feb. 1984.

196   Lorraine LaPage, *Montreal Standard*, Nov. 11, 1983.

197   Peter Herrndorf, interview with author, Nov. 25, 2006.

198   Gina Mallet, *Toronto Star*, June 8, 1983.

199   Donald Martin, *Broadcast Week*, Jan. 26–Feb. 1, 1985.

Chapter 14

200   Peter Weir, letter to author, Feb. 17, 2007.

201   Harrison Ford, interview with author, Feb. 15, 2007.

202   Sylvia Train, *Toronto Sun*, July 11, 1984.

203   Kelly McGillis, interview with author, March 27, 2007.

204   Ruth M. Kelly, *Primetime*, Showcase, Nov.17, 1985, p. 5.

205   Bob Pennington, *Toronto Star*, Feb. 5, 1985.

206   Joan Irwin, *Toronto Star*, n.d.

207   Craig McInnes, *Toronto Star*, Jan. 10, 1986.

208   Janet Maslin, *The New York Times*, Nov. 22, 1985.

209   McInnes, *Toronto Star*, Jan. 10, 1986.

210   Stuart Hamilton, interview with author, March 27, 2007.

211   John Kraglund, *The Globe and Mail*, March 24, 1986.

212   Tom McMahon, probably *The Los Angeles Times*, n.d.

213   Jim Slotek, unidentified periodical, datelined Hollywood.

214   Henry Mietkiewicz, *Toronto Star*, June 26, 1986.

215   Bob Pennington, *Toronto Sun*, June 27, 1986.

216   Fiona Reid, interview with author, Nov. 1, 2006.

217   Jim Slotek, *The Globe and Mail*, Jan.25, 1985.

218   Stephen Nichols, *The Globe and Mail*, Aug. 12, 1988.

Chapter 15

219   Lindsay Brown, *The Daily News*, Oct. 18, 1988.

220   John Griffin, *Montreal Gazette*, Sept. 12, 1988.

221   Rick Groen, *The Globe and Mail*, Sept. 13, 1988.

222   Ken McLeod, *Cape Breton Post*, Oct. 14, 1988.

223   Tom Berry, interview with author, Nov. 17, 2006.

224   Robert Everett-Green, *The Globe and Mail*, Oct. 9, 1987.

225   Rita Zekas, *Toronto Star*, Jan. 19, 1990.

226   Unidentified journal, n.d., in Rubes fonds.

227   *Hollywood Canada*, February–March 1989.

228   Graeme Campbell, interview with author, Oct. 16, 2006.

229   Ibid.

230   Sylvia Train, *Toronto Sun*, n.d.

231   Theresa Beaupre, *Toronto Star*, Nov. 26, 1988.

232   *Washington Times*, Feb. 16, 1990.

Chapter 16

233   Donald Martin, interview with author, Oct. 25, 2006.

234   Rita Zekas, *Toronto Star*, June 14,1988.

235   Bob Blakey, *Calgary Herald*, Oct. 18, 1991.

236   Robert Everett-Green, *The Globe and Mail*, April 11, 1988.

237   Patrick Davitt, *Regina Leader-Post*, Aug. 16, 1990.

238   Ibid.

239   Martin, interview.

240   Bill Brownstein, *Montreal Gazette*, Nov. 16, 1995.

241   Rita Zekas, *Toronto Star*, April 18, 1997.

Chapter 17

242   "Milestones in Telefilm Canada's History" (Canada, 2007), Telefilm Canada, legal notes.

243   Rick Rosenthal, interview with author, May 9, 2006.

244   Herrndorf, interview.

245   George Gross, interview with author, Feb. 15, 2006.

246   Judith Forst, interview with author, March 6, 2007.

247   Bernard Rothman, letter to Rubes, July 15, 1994.

248   "Margarethe Cammermeyer," *Wikipedia, The Free Encyclopedia*, http://en.wikipedia.org/wiki/Margarethe_Cammermeyer.

249   Dianne Elder, interview with author, March 1, 2007.

250   Brad Leithauser, *Time*, July 10, 1995.

251   Jan Stuart, *New York Newsday*, June 9, 1995.

252   Donald Lyons, *The Wall Street Journal*, June 13, 1995.

253   James Lapine, communication with author, Nov. 26, 2006.

254   John Simon, *New York Magazine*, June 19, 1995, p. 77.

255   Vincent Canby, *The New York Times*, June 9, 1995.

256   Margaret Dukes, letter to Susan and Jan Rubes, March 4, 1996;
       interview with author, Nov. 8, 2006.

257   Alan Craig, letter to Susan and Jan Rubes, June 5, 2001.

258   Ibid.

259   Terri Burton, interview with author, Nov. 9, 2006.

Chapter 18

260   Anthony Rubes, interview with author, Aug. 31, 2006.

261   Rita Zekas, *Toronto Star*, Oct. 12, 1997.

262   Robert Cooper, interview with author, Nov. 20, 2006. Mr. Coo-
       per also loaned me a full score of the work.

263   William Littler, *Toronto Star*, Nov. 13, 1997.

264   Robert Cooper's eulogy for Robert Evans, March 15, 2005.

265   Ben Steinberg, interview with author, Dec. 4, 2006.

266   Paula Kelly, interview with author, Feb. 19, 2006.

PHOTO CREDITS

Except where otherwise noted, photos are from Rubes Files.

133 (top and bottom)	Peter Smith photo; Stratford Festival Archives
136 (top)	Douglas Spillane photo; Stratford Festival Archives
136 (bottom)	Alex Gray photo; Canadian Opera Company Archives
146	Harold Whyte photo; CBC Still Photos Collection
165	Robert C. Ragsdale photo; Stratford Festival Archives
172	Young People's Theatre; Guelph University Archives
181	Young People's Theatre; Rubes Files
183	Robert C. Ragsdale photo; Canadian Opera Company Archives
188	CBC Still Photos Collection
203	CBC Still Photos Collection
208	Courtesy of Paramount Pictures
215	Courtesy of MGM Studios
222	Rubes Files; Courtesy of TVA Films
226	George Kraychyk photo; CBC Still Photos Collection
234	George Kraychyk photo; CBC Still Photos Collection
242	Rubes Files; Courtesy of TVA Films
253 (top and bottom)	Joan Marcus photo
270	Big Little Picture Ltd.; Rubes Files
272	Courtesy of Ken Worroner, Showtime

INDEX

(Page numbers in bold refer to photo captions.)